Charles Kingsley, Frances Eliza Grenfell Kingsley

Letters & Memories

Charles Kingsley, Frances Eliza Grenfell Kingsley

Letters & Memories

ISBN/EAN: 9783744687775

Printed in Europe, USA, Canada, Australia, Japan

Cover: Foto ©Thomas Meinert / pixelio.de

More available books at **www.hansebooks.com**

 THE BIDEFORD EDITION

NOVELS, POEMS & LETTERS
OF CHARLES KINGSLEY

LETTERS & MEMORIES

VOLUME II

EDITED BY HIS WIFE

ILLUSTRATED

NEW YORK AND LONDON
THE CO-OPERATIVE
PUBLICATION SOCIETY

Copyright, 1899
BY J F. TAYLOR & COMPANY

Letters and Memories.
Volume II.

LETTERS AND MEMORIES OF
CHARLES KINGSLEY

Vol. II—1

CONTENTS
VOLUME II

CHAPTER XIV
1856. AGED 37

Winter at Farley Court — Letters to Mr. Bullar — Letter from a Sailor at Hong-Kong — Trades-Union Strikes — Preface to Tauler's Life — Fishing Poems and Fishing Flies — To F. Maurice — Invitation to Snowdonia — Visit to North Wales — American Visitors . . . 1

CHAPTER XV

The Father in his Home — An Atmosphere of Joy — The Out-door Nursery — Life on the Mount — Happy Sundays — Fear and Falsehood — The Training of Love — Favorites and Friends in the House, in the Stable, and on the Lawn 36

CHAPTER XVI
1857. AGED 38

Winter at Home — Bright Summer Days — The Crowded Church — Charlotte Brontë — Speculation and Practice — Work beyond the Grave — To an Independent — Tom Brown — Recreation — "Go Hark" — Love beyond the Grave — "Two Years Ago" — Indian Mutiny — "Christ Reigns" — Humor divine — Temporary Failure of Associations 50

CHAPTER XVII

1858. AGED 39

Eversley Work — Diphtheria — Lectures and Sermons at Aldershot — Blessing the Colors of the 22nd Regiment — Staff College — Advanced Thinkers — Letter from Colonel Strange — Esau and Jacob — Poems and Santa Maura — Birth of his Son Grenville — Second Visit to Yorkshire — Correspondence with Mr. Hullah on Songs — In Yorkshire — Grounds of Faith — Letters on Miracles to Sir William Cope — A Happy Christmas . 77

CHAPTER XVIII

1859. AGED 40

Sanitary Work — First Sermon at Buckingham Palace — Queen's Chaplaincy — First Visit to Windsor — Letter to an Atheist — To Artists — Charles Bennett, Frederick Shields — Ladies' Sanitary Association — Exhausted Brain — Pollution of Rivers — The Eternity of Marriage 98

CHAPTER XIX

1860-1862. AGED 41-43

Professorship of Modern History — Death of his Father and of Mrs. Anthony Froude — Planting the Churchyard — Visit to Ireland — First Salmon Killed — Wet Summer — Sermon on Weather — On Prayer — Letter from Sir Charles Lyell — Residence in Cambridge — Inaugural Lecture in the Senate House — Reminiscences of an Undergraduate — Lectures to the Prince of Wales — Essays and Reviews — Children's Employment Commission — Death of the Prince Consort — "The Water Babies" — Installation Ode at Cambridge — Visit to Scotland — British Association — Lord Dundreary — Degradation Theory — American Lectures — The Professor and the Boats — Cotton Famine in Lancashire . 120

Contents   vii

CHAPTER XX

1863. AGED 44

Fellow of the Geological Society — Geology of Palestine and the Bible — Work at Cambridge — Wellington College Museum — Lecture at Wellington — Letter from Dr. Benson — Wonders of Science — Man and the Ape — Mocking Butterflies — A Chain of Special Providences — Toads in Rocks — Prince of Wales's Wedding — D.C.L. Degree at Oxford — Bishop Colenso - Sermons on the Pentateuch 158

CHAPTER XXI

1864-1865. AGED 45-46

Illness — Controversy with Dr. Newman — Apologia — Journey to the South of France — Biarritz — Pau — Narbonne — The Schoolboy's Sea — Béziers — Pont du Gard — Nismes — Avignon — University Sermons at Cambridge — Letter on the Trinity — On Subscription — Savonarola — The Literary World — Wesley and Oxford — Bewick's Autobiography — Visit of Queen Emma of the Sandwich Islands to Eversley and Wellington College — Death of King Leopold — Lines written at Windsor Castle 184

CHAPTER XXII

1866-1867. AGED 47-48

Cambridge — Death of Dr. Whewell — The American Professorship — Monotonous Life of the Country Laboring Class — Penny Readings — London Sermons — Strange Correspondents — Letters to Max Müller — The Jews in Cornwall — Prussian War — The Meteor Shower — Society and Equality — The House of Lords — "Fraser's Magazine" — Darwinism — St. Andrews and British Association — Stammering 211

Contents

CHAPTER XXIII

1868. AGED 49

Attacks of the Press — Lectures on Sixteenth Century — Letters on Emigration — Newman's Dream of St. Gerontius — Military Education — Sandhurst — Comtism — On Crime and its Punishment — Parting with his Son — Letter from Rev. William Harrison — Theological Views — The Book Lover — Kingsley's Tolerance . 235

CHAPTER XXIV

1869-1870. AGED 50-51

Work of the Year — Resignation of Professorship — Women's Suffrage Question — Letters to Mr. Maurice and John Stuart Mill — Canonry of Chester — Social Science Meeting at Bristol — West Indian Voyage — Tropic Scenes — Return Home — Eversley a Changed Place — Flying Columns — Heath Fires -- First Residence at Chester — Botanical Class — Field Lectures — Human Soot — Medical Education of Women — Franco-Prussian War — Wallace on Natural Selection 252

CHAPTER XXV

1871. AGED 52

Lecture at Sion College — Correspondence — Ideal Feudalism — Scientific Agriculture — Words of Condolence — Expeditions of the Chester Natural Science Society — Lectures on Town Geology — A Lump of Coal — The Race Week at Chester — Letters on Betting — Camp at Bramshill — Prince of Wales's Illness — Sermon on Loyalty and Sanitary Science — Lectures at Bideford, Woolwich, and Winchester 289

Contents

CHAPTER XXVI

1872. AGED 53

Opening of Chester Cathedral Nave — Deaths of Mr. Maurice and Norman McLeod — Cathedral Stalls and Learned Leisure — Bishop Patteson — Notes on Modern Hymnology — Lecture at Birmingham and its Results — Lectures at Chester — Correspondence on the Athanasian Creed — On Disestablishment — A Poem . . . 322

CHAPTER XXVII

1873-1874. AGED 54-55

Harrow-on-the-Hill — Canonry of Westminster — Congratulations — Parting from Chester — Sermons in Westminster Abbey and at King's College — Voyage to America — Eastern Cities and Western Plains — Letter from John G. Whittier — Niagara — Salt Lake City — Yosemite Valley and Big Trees — San Francisco — Illness — Rocky Mountains and Colorado Springs — Last Poem — Return Home 341

CHAPTER XXVIII

1874-1875. AGED 55

Return from America — Work at Eversley — Illness at Westminster — New Anxiety — Last Sermons in the Abbey — Leaves the Cloisters for ever — Last Return to Eversley — The Valley of the Shadow of Death — Last Illness and Departure — Answered Prayer — His Burial — Funeral Sermons — Letters of Sympathy — The True and Perfect Knight — At the Grave — The Victory of Life over Death and Time 375

CHARLES KINGSLEY

CHAPTER XIV

1856

AGED 37

WINTER AT FARLEY COURT—LETTERS TO MR. BULLAR—
LETTER FROM A SAILOR AT HONG KONG — TRADES UNION
STRIKES — PREFACE TO TAULER'S LIFE — FISHING POEMS
AND FISHING FLIES—TO F. MAURICE— INVITATION TO
SNOWDONIA — VISIT TO NORTH WALES— AMERICAN
VISITORS.

"I am very sorry for what you say about my not writing anything *startling;* because it shows that . . . you are beginning to
judge me in part upon the reports of others. There are some
people whom I must *startle*, if I am to do any good. . . . But to
startle the majority of good and sensible men, or to startle, so as
to disgust at once a majority of any sort, are things which I most
earnestly should wish to avoid. At the same time, I do strongly
object on principle to the use of that glozing, unnatural, and silly
language (for so it is in us now), which men use one after another
till it becomes as worn as one of the old shillings."

DR. ARNOLD.

THE winter of 1856, spent at Farley Court, a
lovely spot in Swallowfield parish, adjoin-
ing to and overlooking Eversley, was a bright and
happy one. The long rest in Devonshire had told
on him, and now living on high ground, and in a
dry house, acted as a tonic to him as well as to
his family, and infused fresh life into his preaching and his parish work. The old incubus of the
Crimean War, after two years' pressure, was removed, and the new one of the Indian Mutiny,
which weighed even more heavily upon him from

the thought of the sufferings of women and children, was as yet in the future, and his heart rebounded again. The formation of the camp at Aldershot created fresh interests for him at this time and during his remaining years, by bringing a new element into his congregation at Eversley, and giving him the friendship of many military men. In July he was at Aldershot on the memorable occasion of the Queen's first inspection of the remnant of her Crimean army, and saw the march-past of the different regiments before her Majesty, a sight never to be forgotten. In his night-schools, which were well attended, he gave lectures on mines, shells, and other subjects connected with Natural History, illustrated with large drawings of his own. His sermons were most powerful — among them one on Ghosts, the appearance of a ghost in the neighborhood (which he stalked down and found, as he expected, to be a white deer escaped from Calverly Park), having greatly alarmed his parishioners.[1] He gave various

[1] Another ghostly visitor puzzled him this winter. On the occasion of a public dinner given to an officer of The Guards on his return from the Crimean War, Mr. Kingsley allowed his son to be present to hear the first of the speeches and then ride back in the dusk to Farley Court on his pony alone. Halfway between the park gate and the house, "*Something*" passed over his head which thoroughly frightened the boy, who galloped to the stables shouting that he had seen a ghost, and bringing the coachman and others rushing out. To all, even to his father, next day, he told the same story: that a great, white, waving sheet had skimmed over his head and that the pony had also seen it and shied. Every one was incredulous, except the father, who, knowing that the boy was not afraid of ghosts and was a quick observer, would not be likely to exaggerate; consequently he bided his time; which came a few weeks later, when on coming back from a cottage lecture at Eversley one evening, he burst into the house radiant — " Boy, I 've seen your ghost! — you were all right! — I watched for him and saw him a week ago but

lectures in the diocese. He wrote a preface to Tauler's Sermons; two articles on Art and Puritanism, and on Mystics and Mysticism,[1] and began his new romance. His spare hours were devoted to the study and classification of the Phryganæ, carried on by the side of trout streams during a holiday in North Wales and in an occasional day's fishing at Wotton and Wild Moor. His private correspondence this year shows the life and vigor and versatility[2] of his own mind, and his power of approaching other minds from different sides.

TO T. HUGHES, ESQ.

"I wish you would make a vow and keep it strong; for F. says, that if you will, I may — to go with me to

could n't make him out, so I did n't tell you: but to-night your sheet flew close over my head, and what do you suppose he was? A flock of white swans flying probably from Bramshill pond to the Loddon at Swallowfield. We are in a direct line between the two." Following this up, Mr. Kingsley found that at certain seasons of the year the swans at Bramshill regularly left the pond after dark to feed in the river at Swallowfield. (M. K.)

[1] Since published in the Miscellanies.
[2] His versatility often puzzled those who knew him and his writings only partially. A reminiscence of this was given by a reviewer: "'What an unintelligible mystic Kingsley is!' said a guest at some festivity, of which perhaps few partakers are now living; 'I wonder if he himself understands his own writings.' His hearer did not see the appropriateness of the description, and the conversation took a line on which the speaker had more to say, — a subject connected with science. 'There is an admirable article on that subject,' he continued, 'in such and such a Review; it throws more light upon it, and gives more practical suggestions concerning it, than anything I have read for years.' 'It was written by Kingsley,' said the other — and the good man took refuge in his dinner. It was a startling transformation to find his religious mystic an authority on the practical applications of science! Here, we think, lies the secret of a large part of Kingsley's power."

Snowdon next summer for a parson's week, *i. e.* twelve days. For why? I have long promised my children a book to be called 'Letters from Snowdon,' and I want to rub up old memories, and to get new ones in parts which I have not seen. An ordnance map, a compass, fishing-tackle, socks, and slippers are all you want. Moreover, I do know where to fish, and one of the crackest fishers of the part has promised to give me as many flies of his own making as I like, while another can lend us boat or coracle, if we want to fish Gwynant Dinas. We could kill an amount of fish perfectly frightful, and *all the big ones*, by the simple expedient of sleeping by day, walking evening and morning, and fishing during the short hot nights. Wales is a cheap place, if you avoid show inns; and, save a night at Capel Curig, we need never enter a show inn. We may stay two or three days at Pen-y-Gwyrrryynnwwdddelld —— there — I can't spell it, but it sounds Pennygoorood, which is the divinest pig-sty beneath the canopy, and at Bedgelert old Jones the clerk, and king of fishermen, will take us in — and do for us — if we let him. The parson of Bedgelert is a friend of mine also, but we must depend on our own legs, and on stomachs which can face braxy mutton, young taters, Welsh porter, which is the identical drainings of Noah's flood turned sour, and brandy of more strength than legality. Bread horrid, Fleas MCCCC *ad infinitum*. Bugs a sprinkling. For baths, the mountain brook; for towel, a wisp of any endogen save Scirpus triqueter, or Juncus squarrosus; and for cure of all ills, and supplement of all defects, baccy. Do come — you have no notion of the grandeur of the scenery, small as it is compared with the Alps."

His brother-in-law, Mr. Froude, who was to go too, proposed Ireland instead of Wales, which led to his writing these lines:

At Farley Court

Oh, Mr. Froude, how wise and good,
    To point us out this way to glory —
They're no great shakes, those Snowdon lakes,
    And all their pounders myth and story.
Blow Snowdon! What's Lake Gwynant to Killarney,
Or spluttering Welsh to tender blarney, blarney, blarney?

So, Thomas Hughes, sir, if you choose,
    I'll tell you where we think of going,
To 'swate and far o'er cliff and scar,
    Hear horns of Elfland faintly blowing;
Blow Snowdon! There's a hundred lakes to try in,
And fresh caught salmon daily, frying, frying, frying.

Geology and botany
    A hundred wonders shall diskiver,
We'll flog and troll in strid and hole,
    And skim the cream of lake and river.
Blow Snowdon! give me Ireland for my pennies
Hurrah! for salmon, grilse, and Dennis, Dennis, Dennis!

To ———, Esq. — *February* 27. — " . . . With regard to * * * I fear neither you nor any man can give him a fresh *back to his head:* enlarge that deficient driving wheel in the cerebellum, so as to keep the thinking and feeling part of the brain at work. It is sad to see how much faults of character *seem* to depend on physiognomic defects; but do they really depend upon it? Is a man's spirit weak because he has a poor jaw, and a small back to his head; or is his jaw poor, and his cerebellum small, because his spirit is weak? I would fain believe the latter; fain believe that the body is the expression of the soul, and is moulded by it, and not, as Combe would have it, the soul by the body: my reason points to that belief; but I shrink from my own reason, because it seems to throw such tremendous moral responsibility on man, to forbid one's saying 'Poor fellow, it is not his fault, it is a constitutional defect;' for if one says that a man is not responsible for the form of his own soul —

where does all virtue and vice go to? And this brings one straight to the question of madness, on which I fully agree with you. I said so in print, long ago, in a sermon on Ahab at Ramoth Gilead, which you will find in my first set of National Sermons. And I have seen cases myself which I could attribute to nothing else. I cannot but believe that a peculiar kind of epilepsy of which I have had two cases among the poor of my parish, and some of the horrible phenomena of puerperal mania, are 'the unclean spirit' of the New Testament. I am perfectly certain that the accesses of mingled pride, rage, suspicion, and hatred of everybody and everything, accompanied by the most unspeakable sense of loneliness and '*darkness*' (St. John's metaphor, for it is the only one), which were common to me in youth, and are now, by God's grace, very rare (though I am just as capable of them as ever, when I am at *unawares* and give place to the devil by harsh judgments or bitter words) were and are nothing less than temporary possession by a devil. I am sure that the way in which those fits pass off in a few minutes, as soon as I get ashamed of myself, is not to be explained by '*habit*,' either physical or moral (though '*moral* habits' I don't believe in), but by the actual intervention of an unseen personage, I believe our Lord Jesus Christ Himself, driving away that devil. I had once a temporary madman here among our cottagers, who in his first fit tore off his clothes and ran away into the woods naked. (I suspect that desire of nakedness to be the blind effort to be merely himself, and to escape from the sense of oppression caused by some thing or being, over and above self, *i.e.* from possession.) In that fit I did not see him, it was before I came here. In his second he turned melancholy mad, walked up and down in silence, and when he spoke, declared that the devil had hold of him, and would not let him sleep. The doctor luckily believed in demoniacal possession, and came to me, saying, 'I can't cure this man's mind by making his liver act. You must make his liver act by curing his mind.' I went to the patient and agreed with him fully, that the devil *was* in him; and I said, 'I will tell you why he is in you; because, my dear man, you have been a thief, and a cheat, and a liar' (as all the world knew), 'and have sold yourself to the father of lies. But if you will pray to God to forgive you (and then I set forth those precious promises in Christ, which the *Record* thinks I don't believe), 'and will lead a new and honest life, you may snap your fingers at the devil.' And after awhile the man got well, and has had no return for seven years. I did that in the face of the troublesome fact, that his son (and a great rogue too) was subject to melancholy madness also, and that his sister was evidently cracked — her madness being causeless jealousy. That looked like a 'constitutional' defect in the family blood; but I thought the man must know his own business best, and took him at his word, and on the same plan I had very fair success with his son also. But enough."

TO JOHN BULLAR, ESQ.

March 12, 1856. — "Your letters are very pleasant; but they weigh me down with the thought of how little one knows — and after all how little man knows. I have craved after knowledge — I have not found it. I have with Solomon given my heart to know madness and folly, yet acquainting myself with wisdom, and can only say with 'the Faust of the Old World,' 'Cast thy bread on the waters and thou shalt find it after many days. Give a portion to seven and also to eight, for thou knowest not what evil shall be on the earth. Hear the conclusion of the whole matter. Fear God and keep his commandments, for this *is the whole duty of man*. As for wisdom, it is vanity, and much study is a weariness to the flesh, and of making many books there is no end.' Knowing? 'Knowest thou how the bones grow in the womb of her that is with child?' or why the little Diatomaceæ split into separate cells when their time is come? Everywhere, skin deep below our boasted science, we are brought up short by mystery impalpable, and by the adamantine gates of transcendental forces and incomprehensible laws — gates of which the Lord, who is both God and Man, alone holds the key, and alone can break the seal: and if He has not broken them for Himself, He has not broken them for us. I, too, have tormented my soul with metaphysics and thought about thinking, and I know no more than at first, and from Locke to Kant and Hegel, I believe nobody knows. What are we each of us but — 'an infant crying in the night, and with no language but a cry'?

"Is it likely to be less so, then, with theologies and ecclesiastical systems? It was not so with St. Paul, certainly, even granting him to have been (what he never asserted himself to be) infallible. He has no ecclesiastical system. The *facts* of church arrangement in his time, as far as he mentions them, are utterly different from anything which has been seen in Christendom for more than a thousand years. 'God hath set some in the church, first apostles, prophets, evangelists, workers of miracles, helps, &c.' What does all that mean? Nobody knows, but each tries to squeeze out of it a word or two, which will fit their little theory, Popish or Protestant. Those prophesyings, unknown tongues, interpretations, all that mysterious machinery, which he speaks of in 1 Cor. xiv. as an integral part of assembled worship and as a peculiar proof of God's presence, and the influence of His spirit — what have we like that? What even was it? Nobody knows. In one place he seems to look down on it, almost as a form of hysteria

— in another to exalt it as the very power of God. I can't understand it, and I know nobody who does.

"While as for doctrine — he says himself that he only knows in part, and prophesies in part — sees through a glass darkly — that his knowledge is but as that of a child, speaking and understanding as a child, and that all the knowledge he has shall vanish away, just as the tongues will fail and the prophecies cease, and that all which will endure will be charity, real, active love; that the intellectual element, and its outward manifestations, of system and worship and perhaps dogma, are temporary, and the moral-spiritual one the only permanent eternal thing of which he has hold. And yet I am asked to build up out of St. Paul's writings a complete system of theology and anthropology '*tout rond*' without a flaw, or a point for doubt — And when I turn to St. James I find him contradicting St. Paul so flatly in words, as to exercise all the ingenuity of commentators to make the two agree (*as no doubt they do*) in fundamental doctrine. And when I turn to St. John, I find an entirely new aspect of the truth; and in his first chapter an assertion that it was 'to those *who believed on Him* that He gave power to become the children of God' in the face of St. Paul's appeal to the very heathen poets that *all men* are the offspring of God. And in Galatians iv. that the difference between the heathen and the Christian, or perhaps between the human race before and after Christ, is that the one is God's child under tutors and governors, and the other God's full-grown and conscious son who has received the υἱοθεσία, which is *not* adoption υἱοποίησις, but the mere putting on the toga virilis. How am I to reconcile them? I know not. And now perhaps you have been thinking me little better than a skeptic, yet I am not. Some things I see clearly, and hold with *desperate* clutch. A Father in Heaven for all, a Son of God incarnate for all — (That incarnation is the *one* fact which is to me worth all, because it makes all others possible and rational, and without it I should go mad), and a Spirit of the Father *and the Son* — (I attach infinite importance to that double procession — the Holy Spirit of the Greek Church is to me nothing and no-sense), who works to will and to do of His own good pleasure — in whom? In every human being in whom there is one spark of active good, the least desire to do right, or to be of use — the fountain of all good on earth. Beyond that I see little, save that Right is divine and all conquering — Wrong utterly infernal, and yet weak, foolish, a mere bullying phantom, which would flee at each brave blow, had we courage to strike at it in God's name.

"But, as for speculations as to what man's soul or unseen element is, and what happens to it when he dies, theories of Elysium and Tartarus, and of the future of this planet and its inhabitants, I leave them to those who see no miracles in every blade of grass, no unfathomable mysteries in every animalcule, and to whom Scripture is an easy book, of which they have mastered every word, by the convenient process of ignoring three-fourths of it. . . . Yes, Mr. Bullar, you complain that the Church of England is fallen to a low ebb. She is no lower (I think her a great deal higher) than any other Christian denomination. She will be higher as long as she keeps her Articles, which bind men to *none* of the popular superstitions, but are so cautious, wide, and liberal, that I could almost believe them to have come down from heaven. But as soon as a generation of Bishops arises (either High or Low) who persist in demanding of candidates for ordination the popular creed, making those Articles mean that creed, and nothing else, then God help us; for the day of the Lord will be at hand, and will be revealed in flaming fire, not merely to give new light and a day-spring from on high to those who sit in darkness and the shadow of death, but to burn up out of sight, and off the universe, the chaff, hay, and stubble, which men have built on the One Living foundation Christ, in that unquenchable fire, of which it is written that DEATH and HELL shall one day be cast into it also; to share the fate of all other unnatural and abominable things; and God's universe be — (what it must be some day, unless it be a failure, the imperfect work of an imperfect workman, and God is to be eternally baffled by evil —) very good. How that will happen, I know not, neither care. But I know how it will *not* happen; not by God having, as some fancy, to destroy this planet as a failure and a blot, nor by the larger part of the human race passing endless time in irremediable torments. One such case ought to be enough to destroy the happiness of all the saved (unless they are grown suddenly cruel), and keep all heaven one everlasting agony of compassion. To believe that God should determine to torments endless one whom He could reform, is an insult to His love and justice, which I will die rather than utter. And it is an equal insult to His wisdom, to say that He is too — (what words shall I use without blasphemy?) to be unable to reform, convince, persuade, and soften the worst and stupidest heart, I mean even merely externally by actual argument, by reformatory discipline, however severe, which should prove to the man by sharp pangs that he was a fool, and that evildoing would not pay; and by that winning love, returning good for evil, which, as we all know, is the most powerful of all to soften and convert. But much more by the most powerful influence of all, the direct transcendental working of God's spirit, or the man's spirit, which, I suppose, we are to believe in, unless we are Arminians. . . ."

Charles Kingsley

"Till mankind have come to their senses on this point, I see but little hope for Christianity, and between me and the hearts of all good men, whom I long to embrace, that horrible dream yawns as a great gulf fixed. I cannot look them in the face without an effort, because I know that they hold a notion which is to me an immoral superstition, borrowed from the old heathens and rabbis (though our Tartarus is ten times as cruel and immoral as Virgil's), and of which no apostle seems to know anything whatever; and worse, because I know they would regard me with horror, if they knew that I disbelieved it.

"Therefore, my dear Mr. Bullar (as you are one to whom I have been strangely drawn), if you, like the rest, believe in Tartarus, and hold that our Lord came to promulgate that doctrine, and not (as His plain words seem to me to do) to correct those very notions in the rabbis which have descended to us from them, then let us not try to hold any more counsel together concerning the deep things of God. It will be honest on neither side, if both our theology and our anthropology differ by one enormous and all-important postulate. Let us talk of sanitary and social reform, and of birds and flowers, of he little pleasures of the sunshine and the spring, which are still allowed to the human race before it descends into endless flame, agony, and despair, while a few (and, perhaps, I among them) ascend to a 'heaven,' where I should be ashamed to be happy for one moment. Meanwhile, I shall cherish in secret the hope that the night is nigh past, that if not I, yet at least my children, will see a second European reformation, Tartarus follow its more foolish, but far less immoral and infernal child Purgatory, and the whole of Christendom leap up as men freed suddenly from the weight of a hideous nightmare to give thanks and glory to Him who descended into hell, and 'har-

From a Sailor

rowed it' as the glorious old words, now long forgotten, say, when He died for us, and all mankind."

Among the anonymous letters of this year, he was deeply touched by one from a naval officer, dated "H.M.S. 'St. George,' off Hong Kong," thanking him for his "noble sermon" of "Westward Ho!"

"Some months ago I read it for the first time, then sailed on a long cruise, and now on returning have read it again with prayer that has been answered, for God's blessing has gone with it. I feel as I never felt before, that Protestantism is the religion of this life especially, and that I have been heeding the future to the neglect of the living present. Many a day of late, thinking of you, I have gone on deck to my duty and seen God, where theoretically only I have been in the habit of looking for Him, on the sea, in the clouds, and in the faces of men; and the Holy Spirit descending, has stirred my pulses with the sense of universal love prevailing, above, around, and beneath. . . . I am able to speak of God and of religion with less of the humiliating hesitation that I am accustomed to, and trust that He will give me that manliness that will enable me so to talk of His workings, which, alas! we are in the habit of practically ignoring."

The writer some years afterwards made himself known to him as Captain Alston; and a strong personal attachment grew up between two men who had so much in common; he consulted Mr. Kingsley on all points connected with his noble work on board 'the Reformatory Training Ships on the Thames and the Clyde, at a later period, and, in reply to a letter about Workmen's Libraries, Mr. Kingsley writes to him:

"The best periodical for them is certainly Norman McLeod's 'Good Words,' which is quite admirable, and has now a very large circulation — 70,000, I believe. I do not think that I would give them Carlyle yet. If I did, it would be 'Past and Present.' And yet, things have so mended since it was written that that would be unfair. The 'French Revolution' is the book, if they would only understand it.

"I am truly thankful to hear that I have helped to make a churchman of you. The longer I live, the more I find the Church of England the most rational, liberal, and practical form which Christianity has yet assumed; and dread as much seeing it assimilated to dissent, as to Popery. Strange to say, Thomas Carlyle now says that the Church of England is the most rational thing he sees now going, and that it is the duty of every wise man to support it to the uttermost."

To J. NICHOLS, ESQ., of Manchester. — *March* 28, 1856 — "I admire your boldness in lifting up your voice to expose the tyranny of 'Union' Strikes. From my own experience of demagogues, I can well believe every word you say as to the 'humbug' connected with the inner working of them. As for the prospects of 'Association,' my experience goes with yours as to associations for *production*. The failure in those which I have seen fail, has always been their democratic constitution and anarchy. The secret of success, in those which I have seen succeed, has been the presence of some one master-mind; and even he has had hard work, unless backed by benevolent capitalists, who have been able to say to refractory members, 'Well, *we* hold the supplies, and if you kick, we withhold.' Association will be the next form of industrial development, I doubt not, for

Trades Union Strikes

production; but it will require two generations of previous training, both in morality and in *drill*, to make the workmen capable of it. Association for distribution is what I look to with far higher hope. I am sure, for example, that if the method of the 'People's Stores and Mills (flour)' at Rochdale, were generally carried out, the saving to wages, to public honesty, and (considering the present adulteration of goods) to public health, would be immense...."

To ——, Esq., of Sheffield. — 1856. — "No one more heartily wishes that such matters as you write to me on could be altered. But, after years of experience, trial, and disappointment, I am convinced that they cannot. The thing must be left alone; and the only advice I can give is, Emigrate, but never *strike*. I look forward to a time in which such things will be righted by a general labor-news and wages-arbitration; but I have no means of starting either; and I don't think the world will have for many a year to come. I am very sad about all these matters; but all I can recommend is, *peace*, and making the best use, and most prudent use, of wages when they are to be got. If one half the hundreds of thousands which have been spent by trades' unions in interfering with the natural accidents of trade, had been spent in insuring (by association for relieving overstocked labor markets) against those accidents, all might have been well; but now I see little before the English workman but to abide as he is, and endure.

. . . .

"If these trade unions," he writes in 1862, "are to be allowed to exist they can only exist on the ground of being not only organs for combination, but for keeping the combination men within the law. If they will not disprove that such outrages have been committed by union men; if they will not, in honor to their own class, be the first to drag such hounds to justice; if they will do nothing to free themselves from the old stigma that from 1820-48 they have themselves notoriously engaged in such outrages and murders — then let them be put down by law as incapable morally as politico-economically. With you I have defended the right of combination among the workmen, in hope that they would become wiser than of yore. But if they continue to murder, I see nothing for them but the just judgment of public opinion which will sweep them away, and I fear inaugurate a reign of tyranny and of capital. I and others have been seeing with dread the growing inclination of the governing classes to put down these trade unions, &c., by strong measures. What am I to say when I see the working men themselves, in the face of this danger, justifying the measures of those who wish to be hard on them? I have seen enough of trade unions to suspect that the biggest rogues and the loudest charlatans are the men who lead or mislead the honest working men; but if the honest working men themselves make no move towards detecting and exposing the authors of such outrages, they must suffer with their blind and base leaders. If they fancy they are too strong for the classes above them, that they can defy the laws of England and the instincts of humanity, then they will find themselves mistaken, even if they have to be taught their folly by a second Bristol riots or a second Peterloo."

His Preface to "The Life and Sermons of Tauler" written at this time came out of the depths of his heart. It concludes with these striking words:

"With Tauler, whether he be right or wrong in any given detail, practical righteousness of the divinest kind and loftiest kind is at once the object, and the means, and the test, of all upward steps. God is the Supreme

Preface to Tauler's Life 17

Good which man is intended to behold; but only by being inspired by Him, owing all to Him, and copying Him, can he behold Him, and in that sight find his highest reward, and heaven itself. . . . There are those who, opprest by doubts and fears and sorrows, may find in Tauler's genial and sunny pages a light which will stand them in good stead in many an hour of darkness. There are those, heaped beyond desert with every earthly bliss, who have had to ask themselves, in awful earnest, the question which all would so gladly put away — ' Were I stripped to-morrow of all these things, to stand alone and helpless as I see thousands stand, what should I then have left?' . . . Tremblingly they have turned to religion for comfort, under the glaring eye of the dark spectre of bereavement, but have felt about all commonplaces, however true, as Job felt of old: Miserable comforters are ye all! Oh! that I knew where I might find HIM. . . . To such Tauler can tell something of that still waste, where a man, losing all things else, shall find himself face to face with God, and hear from Him that which no man can utter again in words even to the wife of his bosom. . . . And for 'darker struggles and deeper problems,' and 'the abyss of boundless doubt,' — he can tell how he came to find an eternal light shining for ever in that utter darkness, which the darkness could not comprehend; an eternal ground in the midst of that abyss, which belonged not to the abyss, nor to the outward world which had vanished for the moment, nor to space, nor time, nor any category of human thought, or mortal existence; and that its substance was the everlasting personal good, whose love is righteousness. Tauler can point out the path by which he came to see that Light, to find that Rock of Ages; — the simple path of honest self-knowledge, self-renunciation, self-restraint, in which every outward step towards right exposes some fresh depth of inward sinfulness, till the once proud man, crushed down like Job and Paul, by the sense of his own infinite meanness, becomes like them, a little child once more, and casts himself simply upon the generosity of Him who made him. And then there may come to him the vision, dim, perhaps, and fitting ill into clumsy words, but clearer, surer, nearer to him than the ground on which he treads, or than the foot which treads it, — the vision of an everlasting spiritual substance, most human and yet most divine, Who can endure ; and Who, standing beneath all things, can make their spiritual substance endure likewise, though all worlds and stars, birth, and growth, and death, matter, space, and time, should melt in very deed,

> 'And like the baseless fabric of a vision,
> Leave not a rack behind.'"

With spring his thoughts turned to fishing; and one April morning when the southwest wind wafted certain well-known sounds from the Camp at Aldershot, the South-Western Railway, and Heckfield Place, to the little Rectory, these lines were written and put into his wife's hand:

> Oh blessed drums of Aldershot!
> Oh blessed southwest train!
> Oh blessed, blessed Speaker's clock,
> All prophesying rain!
>
> Oh blessed yaffil, laughing loud!
> Oh blessed falling glass!
> Oh blessed fan of cold gray cloud!
> Oh blessed smelling grass!
>
> Oh bless'd southwind that toots his horn
> Through every hole and crack!
> I'm off at eight to-morrow morn,
> To bring *such* fishes back!
>
> *April* 1, 1856.

Fishing Poems and Flies

To H. STAINTON, ESQ. — "As to caddises, I see three years' work at least before getting them at all in order, if (as you say) the thing has not been done; for my belief is, that the species are either very local, or very variable, depending on differences of soil and river-bed, and that they will give a great deal of trouble. My fishing-tackle maker sickened me the other day by — 'you talk of yellow sallies, sir, I've seen twenty different sorts — a different sort for every stream;' and if this is the case with one fly, local, not common and strongly marked, what must be the case with the herd? I will do what I can this year to arrange the typical species of our Hampshire, Surrey, and Berkshire streams (chalk, or iron gravel), and may get a few Snowdon species in August. My belief is that the generality of Snowdon species are quite distinct from ours, *e.g.*, the all-killing gray Gwynant (Phyancæ), which was to me new when I went to Snowdonia. If you will do me the favor of hints as to what to do, and how to do it, I should enjoy, amid the intervals of country parish labor, to apply myself to them. I have great advantages, being surrounded by rivers and ponds, and finding my sole amusement in fly-fishing, — once a week, but no more. And only a fly-fisher can do the work, for he only watches, and is forced to watch, the works and ways of the family *in situ*. . . ."

". . . I have put into the new edition of 'Glaucus' a hint for a few fly-fishers in various parts to form themselves into a 'Naiad club' to investigate these water-flies. It might do much to science, and still more to the men. I know the value of a little science, as an angler. In Snowdon, three years ago, when no one could catch anything, I found, for the first time in my life, Chloroperla viridis (yellow Sally) running on the burning boulders of a stream; luckily had a good imitation (which I had never used), recognized the natural fly by my scrap of science, and had good sport on it, while no one else caught anything, never having seen such a fly, though it was swarming under their feet! So much for unscientific observation. And men who had been using the artificial Gwynant (Hydropsyche), had never seen the natural fly till I caught it, and showed them the reality of what they had shown me as fur and feathers. I think if one could stir up sportsmen to think and watch these things one might make them happier men. I have now close to me a splendid angler and deerstalker, and I have made him set up an aquarium of caddises, and so forth, for his wife this winter, and am sure that it has given him a new interest in life. . . ."

To LORD ——. ". . . But as to 'What is the Good?' I suppose the only answer is 'God himself is the Good.'

"But of Him we can form no intellectual conception; and it is this, in addition to a thousand things, which makes me feel the absolute certainty of a resurrection, and a conviction that this, our present life . . . is merely some sort of chrysalis state.

"What does God require of thee but to do justly, to love mercy, and to walk humbly with Him? —is nearly all I know —Sin, ἁμαρτία, is literally, as it signifies, the missing of a mark, the falling short of an ideal, and not the transgression of an arbitrary decree; and that each miss brings a penalty, or rather is itself the penalty (for I do not believe in arbitrary rewards and punishments), is to me the best of news, and gives me hope for myself, and every human being, past, present, and future, for it makes me look on them all as children under a paternal education, who are being taught to become aware of, and use their own powers in God's house, the universe, and for God's work in it; and in proportion as they learn and do that, they attain salvation, σωτηρία, literally *health* and *wholeness* of spirit, 'soul,' which is, like health of body, its own reward — one great part of that reward being *not to know* that they have a soul — as health of body makes one unconscious of one's body."

To REV. F. MAURICE. — ". . . My dear master, though the solution of this and many another problem which you have started, remains for our descendants, yet you must not grow sad, or think that you have not done, and are not still doing, a mighty work, in pointing out the laws by which alone they can be solved. You are like a man surveying a tropic forest, which he can only do by hewing his path yard by yard, unable to see a rood before him; other men will follow him, till, and plant, and build, while he dies in faith, not having received the promises. And you will look down from heaven upon this nation working on under the new spiritual impulse which you have given it, and which will assuredly conquer, just as Captain Sturt will look down on that glorious Australian empire to-be, which he rescued out of the realm of Hades and the blank useless unknown, at the expense of his health, his eyesight, and his life. As Charles Mansfield, perhaps, may look down on that Paraguay which will surely realize some day his highest dreams of its capabilities; for his book (light though it seem) will not be forgotten, and other men will carry out the conception, which he, perhaps, *could not* have done from over-conscientiousness, and worship of too lofty an ideal. I can see, too, more and more, why, as you seem to lament, you are shut out so strangely from sympathy with flowers and beetles that you might have sympathy with men. And are they not of more value than many beetles? Of the evangelical phraseology one word is true, that 'an immortal soul' (if people only knew what an immortal soul meant!) is of more value than all the material universe. And I can understand why there should be men like you, to whom it is said, 'Thou shalt not be tempted to waste thy time over the visible world, because thy calling is to work out that spiritual moral world, of which man can learn *just nothing* from the visible world — which he can only learn from his own soul, and the souls of other men.'

"My dear master, I have long ago found out how little I can discover about God's absolute love, or absolute righteousness, from a universe in which everything is eternally *eating* everything else. Infinite cunning and shift (in the good sense). Infinite creative fancy it does reveal; but nothing else, unless interpreted by moral laws which are in oneself already, and in which one has often to trust against all appearances, and cry out of the lowest deep (as I have had to do) — Thou art not Siva the destroyer. Thou art not even Ahriman and Ormuzd in one. And yet, if Thou art not, why does Thy universe seem to say that Thou art? Art Thou a '*Deus quidam Deceptor*,' after all? — No. There is something in me — which not my nature, but Thou must have taught me — which cries and will cry: Though Thou slay me, as Thou hast slain world on world already — though I and all this glorious race of men go down to Hades with the ichthyosaurs and the mammoths, yet will I trust in Thee. Though St. Peter's words be fulfilled (as they may to-morrow by the simplest physical laws) and the elements melt with fervent heat, and the earth and all the works therein be burned up — yet I know that my Redeemer, He who will justify me, and make me right, and deliver me out of the grasp of nature, and proclaim my dominion over nature, liveth, and will stand at the latter day upon the earth, and in some flesh or other I shall see God, see Him for myself as a one and accountable moral being for ever. But beetles and zoophytes never whispered *that* to me. . . . The study of Nature can teach no *moral theology*. It may unteach it,

Invitation to Snowdonia

if the roots of moral theology be not already healthy and deep in the mind. I hinted that in 'Glaucus': but I would do no more, because many readers mean by 'moral' and 'theology' something quite different from what you and I do, and would have interpreted it into a mere iteration of the old lie that science is dangerous to orthodoxy. But I won't talk of myself, save to say that I sometimes envy you, who are not distracted from work at the really *human* truths, by the number of joints in a grub's legs. I ought to have written to you, but had nothing to say. My life runs on here in a very simple, easy way, what with the parish and Mrs. Kingsley, and the children, and a little literary work, in which I am trying to express in a new form the ideas which I have got from you, and which I have been trying to translate into all languages, from 'The Saint's Tragedy' to 'Glaucus.' I have no other work on earth, and want none.

"Do not talk of your time being short, for you have much to do yet — all the more, perhaps, because you do not know what it is. The cloud is always thickest when and where the wind is about to shift, and roll it all away out of the blue sky."

To TOM HUGHES, ESQ. — "My dear old lad, are you willing to go to Snowdon? Killarney is very tempting; only, as I get old, somehow, I don't like new places; I like to thumb over the same book, and trot over the same bog, and feel 'homey' wherever I be. . . . My plan would be this —

There is no inn in Snowdon which is not awful dear,
Excepting Pen-y-gwrydd (you can't pronounce it, dear),
Which standeth in the meeting of noble valleys three.
One is the vale of Gwynant, so well beloved by me,
One goes to Capel-Curig, and I can't mind its name,
And one it is Llanberris Pass, which all men knows the same.
Between which radiations vast mountains does arise,
As full of tarns as sieves of holes, in which big fish will rise,

That is, just one day in the year, if you be there, my boy,
About ten o'clock at night, and then I wish you joy.
Now to this Pen-y-gwrydd inn I purposeth to write,
(Axing the post town out of Froude, for I can't mind it quite),
And to engage a room or two, for let us say a week,
For fear of gents, and Manichees, and reading parties meek,
And there to live like fighting-cocks at almost a bob a day,
And arterwards toward the sea make tracks and cut away,
All for to catch the salmon bold in Aberglaslyn pool,
And work the flats in Traeth Mawr, and will, or I'm a fool.
And that's my game, which, if you like, respond to me by post;
But I fear it will not last, my son, a thirteen days at most.
Flies is no object; I can tell some three or four will do,
And John Jones, Clerk, he knows the rest, and ties and sells 'em too.
Besides of which I have no more to say, leastwise just now,
And so, goes to my children's school and umbly makes my bow.

C. K.

. . . .

" Of all men on earth I should like to have Tom Taylor for a third. Entreat him to make it possible, and come and be a salvidge man with us; and tell him I can show him views of the big stone work which no mortal cockney knows, because, though the whole earth is given to the children of men, none but we jolly fishers get the plums and raisins of it, by the rivers which run among the hills, and the lakes which sit a-top thereof. Tell him I'll show him such a view from Craig-y-Rhaidyr of Snowdon from the sole of his foot to the crown of his head, as tourist never saw, nor will see, 'case why, he can't find it; and I will show him the original mouth of the pit which is Llyn Dulyn, and the lightning lake, where the white syenite is blasted into shivers, which make you shiver, if you be sentimental — but *I* only think of the trouts — which the last I saw killed in Llyn Melch was 3½ pounds, and we'll kill his wife and family; and crowberry and desolate Alpine plants grow thereby, aud we will sleep among them, like love among the roses,

Invitation to Snowdonia

Thomas. And oh, what won't we do, except break our necks? and I'll make Tom Taylor come down over Craig-y-Rhaidyr, which is 700 feet of syenite, the most glorious climb I know. We can go from Reading, and the Holyhead mail will drop us at Bangor at 5 in the morning. There we can either go on by coach to Pen-y-Wynod, or walk in the cool of the morning, fishing as we go, and send our traps by coach, to be dropped for us. Pray bring a couple of dozen lake-sized hooks, to tie flies on. You'll be pleased to hear that I got a fishing at Lady Mildmay's famous Warnborough preserve last night — the day was B. B. B., burning, baking, and boiling, and as still as glass, so I did not tackle-to till 5.30 — and between that and nine I grassed twenty fish, weighing twenty-two pounds, besides losing a brace more whoppers. Biggest brace killed, three pounds and two pounds — a dead bright calm, and a clear stream — in fifteen minutes I had three fish, two of three pounds and one of two pounds, but lost one of them after a long fight. Not so shady, Tom, for all on *shorm-fly and caperer.* Mind and don't get these flies too small. I don't mind small hooks, if a big fly be tied thereon — see what a difference a wise man and a fool may make. (Here was a sketch of two flies —'wise man's fly,' and 'cockney maiden's fly.') Let's have lots for our money, say I, in flies, as in all things. Why do fish take your caperer, spite of his ugliness, but because he looks the fattest one they ever saw yet? Think over these things."

At last the happy day in August was fixed, and the following invitation sent before the three friends started for Snowdonia:

> Come away with me, Tom,
> Term and talk is done;
> My poor lads are reaping,
> Busy every one.

Curates mind the parish,
Sweepers mind the Court,
We'll away to Snowdon
For our ten days' sport,
Fish the August evening
Till the eve is past,
Whoop like boys at pounders
Fairly played and grassed.
When they cease to dimple,
Lunge and swerve, and leap,
Then up over Siabod,
Choose our nest and sleep.
Up a thousand feet, Tom,
Round the lion's head,
Find soft stones to leeward
And make up our bed.
Eat our bread and bacon,
Smoke the pipe of peace,
And, ere we be drowsy,
Give our boots a grease.
Homer's heroes did so,
Why not such as we?
What are sheets and servants?
Superfluity.
Pray for wives and children
Safe in slumber curled,
Then to chat till midnight
O'er this babbling world,
Of the workmen's college,
Of the price of grain,
Of the tree of knowledge,
Of the chance of rain;
If Sir A. goes Romeward,
If Miss B. sings true,
If the fleet comes homeward,
If the mare will do,—
Anything and everything—
Up there in the sky
Angels understand us
And no "saints" are by.
Down, and bathe at day-dawn,
Tramp from lake to lake,

Washing brain and heart clean
Every step we take.
Leave to Robert Browning
Beggars, fleas, and vines;
Leave to squeamish Ruskin
Popish Apennines,
Dirty Stones of Venice
And his Gas-lamps Seven;
We've the stones of Snowdon
And the lamps of heaven.
Where's the mighty credit
In admiring Alps?
Any goose sees "glory"
In their "snowy scalps."
Leave such signs and wonders
For the dullard brain,
As æsthetic brandy,
Opium and cayenne;
Give me Bramshill common
(St. John's harriers by),
Or the vale of Windsor,
England's golden eye.
Show me life and progress,
Beauty, health, and man;
Houses fair, trim gardens,
Turn where'er I can.
Or, if bored with "High Art,"
And such popish stuff,
One's poor ear need airing,
Snowdon's high enough.
While we find God's signet
Fresh on English ground,
Why go gallivanting
With the nations round?
Though we try no ventures
Desperate or strange;
Feed on common-places
In a narrow range;
Never sought for Franklin
Round the frozen Capes:
Even, with Macdougall,

[1] Bishop of Labuan.

Bagged our brace of apes;
Never had our chance, Tom,
In that Black redan;
Can't avenge poor Brereton
Out in Sakarran;
Tho' we earn our bread, Tom,
By the dirty pen,
What we can we will be,
Honest Englishmen.
Do the work that's nearest,
Though it's dull at whiles,
Helping, when we meet them,
Lame dogs over stiles;
See in every hedgerow
Marks of angels' feet,
Epics in each pebble
Underneath our feet ;
Once a year, like school-boys,
Robin-Hooding go,
Leaving fops and fogies
A thousand feet below.

To HIS WIFE. — *August* 11. In the train. "A glorious day. Snowdonia magnificent. The sensation of going through the tubular bridge very awful and instructive. The sound of it, the finest bass note I have ever heard. Anglesey, an ugly wild flat place, like Torridge Moors, with great dunes of blown sand along the coast, fit for those weird old Druids. . . ."

CAPEL CURIG, *August* 12.— "We are sleeping here, being too tired to get an inch further. We never slept forty winks last night in the train; started from Bangor at 5, and were on our legs till 5 P.M. We went up Nant Francon, then up to Idwal. Fish would not rise; but the rivers are flooded, and, therefore, we shall have noble sport. But the glory was what I never saw before, all those grand mountains, 'silver-veined with rills,' cataracts of *snow-white cotton threads*, if you will, zigzagging

Visit to North Wales 29

down every rock-face — sometimes 1000 feet — and the whole air alive with the roar of waters. The greenness and richness of the mountains after our dusty burnt-up plains, is most refreshing. All day we had steaming gleams; but the clouds on Glydyr Vawr only broke to form again, and we had twenty showers, shrouding the cliffs with long gray veils of lace. I wish I could tell you what color the mountains are. Not pink, not purple, not brown, but a sort of pale pink madder, with vast downs of bright green grass interspersed. And oh, as we walked past Colonel Pennant's cyclopean walls at Bangor, and saw that great gap high up in the air ten miles off, and knew that we should be in it ere noon, it was like a dream; and all the more dreamy for the sleeplessness of the past night. We found a noble fountain, which Colonel Pennant has built by the roadside, and there washed ourselves into our senses, and went on. At Bethesda we tried for breakfast, at six A. M., and were refused by all the few houses which were open, till we found a nice little woman, who gave us infinite broiled ham, tea, and porter, to carry up the hills. We tried Ogwen River for salmon peel, amid those exquisite parks and woods; but it was too much flooded. By night I had picked my first Saxifraga stellaris, and knew that I was in the *former world*. The parsley fern is growing between every stone, and the beech fern too, but the latter very poor. I have dried for the children the water-lobelia, and Sparganium natans, to do which I walked up to my knees in Idwal. Snowdon is now looking like a great gray ghost with seven heads, and as soon as one head is cut off a fresh one grows; but more are cut off than grow, and the clouds which stream up from the S.W. fall lower and lower, and have now canopied the whole head of Moel Siabod, who is looking in at our window 2000 feet down, the impudent fellow, though I am 1000 feet high. Wherefore we shall have more rain. . . . To-morrow up at six; walk to Pen-y-gwryd, and then up to Edno!"

PEN-Y-GWRYD. — "I have had, as far as scenery is concerned, the finest day I ever had. We started for Edno at 10, but did not find it till 2, because we mistook the directions, and walked from 10 till 1.30 over a Steinerer Maar, a sea of syenite and metamorphic slate which baffles all description, 2000 feet above Gywnant, ribs and peaks and walls of rock leaping up and rushing down, average 50 to 100 feet, covered with fir, club moss, crowberry and bearberry, and ling, of course. Over these we had to scramble up and down, beating for Edno lake as you would beat for a partridge, but in vain. All we found was one old cock-grouse, who went off holloaing ' Cock-cock-what-a-shame-cock-cock' till we were fairly beat. In despair we made, not a dash, but a crawl, at Moel Meirch ('Margaret's Peak,' some pathetic story, I suppose), which rises about 100 feet above the stony sea, a smooth pyramid of sandy-pink syenite. Hughes got up first, by a crack, for the walls are like china, and gave a who-whoop; there was Edno half a mile beyond, and only a valley to cross, beside a few climbs of 50 feet. So there we got, and ate our hardboiled eggs and drank our beer, and then set to, and caught just nothing. The fish, always sulky and capricious, would not stir. But the delight of being there again, 2200 feet up, out of the sound of aught but the rush of wind and water and the whistle of the sheep (which is just like a penny whistle ill-blown), and finding oneself *at home* there! Every rock, even the steps of slate and footholds of grass which * * * and I used to use, just the same. Unchanged for ever. It is an awful thought. Soon we found out why the fish would n't rise. The cloud which had been hanging on Snowdon, lowered. Hebog and Cnicht caught it. It began to roll up from

Visit to North Wales 31

the sea in great cabbage-headed masses, and grew as dark as twilight. The wind rolled the lake into foam; we staggered back to an old cave, where we shall sleep, please God, ere we come home, and then the cloud lowered, the lake racing along in fantastic flakes and heaps of white steam, hiding everything 50 yards off one minute, then leaving all clear and sharp-cut pink and green. While out of it came a rain of marbles and Minnié bullets — a rain which searches, and drenches, and drills. Luckily I had on a flannel shirt. We waited as long as we dared, and then steered home by compass, for we could not see 50 yards, except great rows of giants in the fog, sitting humped up side by side, like the ghosts of the sons of Anak staring into the bogs. So home we went, floundering through morass, and scrambling up and down the giants, which were crags 50 to 100 feet high, for we dared not pick our road for fear of losing our bearings by compass. And we were wet — oh, were we not wet? but, as a make-weight, we found the 'Grass of Parnassus' in plenty, and as we coasted the vale of Gwynant, 1500 feet up, the sight of Snowdon, sometimes through great gaps of cloud, sometimes altogether hidden, the lights upon that glorious vista of Gwynant and Dinas, right down to Hebog — the flakes of cloud rushing up the vale of Gwynant far below us — no tongue can describe it. I could see Froude's fir-wood, and home-close, quite plain from Moel Meirch. It looked as if you could have sent a stone into it, but it was four miles off. I have got for you grass of Parnassus; Alpine club-moss; ladies' mantle; ivy-leaved campanula; beech fern; A. Oreopteris (sweet fern). The great butterwort is out of flower (as is the globe flower), but it stars every bog with its shiny yellow-green stars of leaves. Goodbye. I am up at half-past three for Gwynant, which is full of salmon. I have just got your dear letter. Tell Rose that I am drying all the plants I can for her. . . .

Tell Maurice I saw a grouse and a water-ouzel — lots of these last. . . ."

When the short holiday came to an end, the three friends were asked by the landlord of the inn, at Pen-y-gwryd, to write their names in his visitors' book. They wrote as follows:

TOM TAYLOR.

I came to Pen-y-gwryd with colors armed and pencils,
But found no use whatever for any such utensils;
So in default of them I took to using knives and forks,
And made successful drawings — of Mrs. Owen's corks.

CHARLES KINGSLEY.

I came to Pen-y-gwryd in frantic hopes of slaying
Grilse, Salmon, 3 lb. red-fleshed Trout, and what else there's no saying;
But bitter cold and lashing rain, and black nor'eastern skies, sir,
Drove me from fish to botany, a sadder man and wiser.

TOM HUGHES.

I came to Pen-y-gwryd a larking with my betters,
A mad wag and a mad poet, both of them men of letters;
Which two ungrateful parties, after all the care I've took
Of them, make me write verses in Henry Owen's book.

T. T.

We've been mist-soak'd on Snowdon, mist-soaked on Glyder Vawr,
We've been wet through on an average every day three times an hour;
We've walk'd the upper leathers from the soles of our balmorals;
And as sketchers and as fishers with the weather have had our quarrels.

Visit to North Wales

C. K.

But think just of the plants which stuff'd our box, (old Yarrel's gift,)
And of those which might have stuff'd it if the clouds had given a lift;
Of tramping bogs, and climbing cliffs, and shoving down stone fences
For Spiderwort, Saussurea, and Woodsia ilvensis.

T. H.

Oh my dear namesake's breeches, you never see the like,
He burst them all so shameful a crossing of a dyke.
But Mrs. Owen patch'd them as careful as a mother,
With flannel of three colors — she had n't got no other.

T. T.

But can we say enough of those legs of mountain muttons,
And that onion sauce lies on our souls, for it made of us three gluttons,
And the Dublin stout is genuine, and so 's the Burton beer;
And the apple tarts they 've won our hearts, and think of soufflets here!

C. K.

Resembling that old woman that never could be quiet,
Though victuals (says the child's song) and drink formed all their diet:
My love for plants and scrambling shared empire with my dinner,
And who says it was n't good must be a most fastidious sinner.

T. H.

Now all I 've got to say is, you can't be better treated;
Order pancakes and you 'll find they 're the best you ever eated.
If you scramble o'er the mountains you should bring an ordnance map.
I endorse all as previous gents have said about the tap.

Charles Kingsley

T. T.

Pen-y-gwryd, when wet and worn has kept a warm fireside for us,
Socks, boots, and never mention-ems, Mrs. Owen still has dried for us.
With host and hostess, fare and bill so pleased we are that going,
We feel for all their kindness, 't is we not they are Owen !

T. H.   T. T.   C. K.

Nos tres in uno juncti hos fecimus versiculos ;
Tomas piscator pisces qui non cepi sed pisciculos,
Tomas sciagraphus, sketches qui non feci nisi ridiculos,
Herbarius Carolus montes qui lustravi perpendiculos.

T. H.

There's big trout I hear in Edno, likewise in Gwynant lake,
And the governor and black alder are the flies that they will take,
Also the cockabundy, but I can only say,
If you think to catch big fishes I only Hope you may.

T. T.

I have come in for more of mountain gloom than mountain glory,
But I've seen old Snowdon rear his head with storm-tossed mist wreaths hoary;
I stood in the fight of mountain winds upon Bwlch-Cwm-y-Llan,
And I go back an unsketching but a better minded man.

C. K.

And I too have another debt to pay another way,
For kindness shown by these good souls to one who's far away,
Even to this old collie dog who tracked the mountains o'er,
For one who seeks strange birds and flowers on far Australia's shore.

American Visitors

In the course of the autumn several American friends, including Mrs. Beecher Stowe, made pilgrimages to Eversley; among them one from the Southern States thus recalls the Rectory life in 1856:

". . . It is your own fault if Eversley does no more seem to me a name. When I think of Mrs. Kingsley and of you I seem to myself to be sitting with you still in those quaint old rooms. Still Maurice comes by with an insect or a flower, or just a general wonder and life in his eyes — still I hear the merry laugh of the little Princess, and see Dandy lying lazy, smiling and winking in the sun; and I fill my olive-wood pipe, and saunter in and out of the aromatic old study, and lounge, a new man and a happier one, on the sloping green lawn, under the good old fir-trees. And so I talk on as if I were with friends long known, and known long to be cherished much. All of which is wholly your fault and Mrs. Kingsley's. . . . If you are not too busy, I am sure you will write and tell me how the novel advances (Two Years Ago!), and how Eversley in all its regions is. . . ."

CHAPTER XV

THE FATHER IN HIS HOME — AN ATMOSPHERE OF JOY — THE OUTDOOR NURSERY — LIFE ON THE MOUNT — HAPPY SUNDAYS — FEAR AND FALSEHOOD — THE TRAINING OF LOVE — FAVORITES AND FRIENDS IN THE HOUSE, IN THE STABLE, AND ON THE LAWN.

"Come to me, O ye children!
For I hear you at your play,
And the questions which have vexed me
Have vanished quite away.

. . . . . .

In your hearts are the birds and the sunshine,
In your thoughts the brooklets flow;
But in mine is the wind of autumn,
And the first fall of the snow.

. . . . . .

Come to me, O ye children!
And whisper in my ear,
What the birds and the wind are singing
In your sunny atmosphere.

For what are all our contrivings,
And the wisdom of our books,
When compared with your caresses,
And the gladness of your looks?

Ye are better than all the ballads
That ever were sung or said;
For ye are living poems,
And all the rest are dead!"

LONGFELLOW.

WE must pause a moment in the midst of work and letters; we have seen the rector in his church and parish, and now must see

The Outdoor Nursery 37

the father in his home. "Cheerfulness or joyousness," said Jean Paul Richter, "is the atmosphere under which all things thrive — especially the young" — and with this atmosphere the parents tried to surround the children at the Rectory — not only as a means of present enjoyment, but as a tonic to brace the young creatures to meet the inevitable trials of life. They had the best of everything; the sunniest and largest rooms indoors; and because the house was on low ground, — the grass sloping down from the churchyard, their father built them on the "Mount," — the highest and loveliest point of moorland in the glebe, a real bit of primeval forest — as an outdoor nursery, a hut, where they kept books, toys, and tea-things, and spent long happy days; and there he would join them when his parish work was done, bringing them some fresh treasure picked up in his walk, a choice wild flower or fern, or rare beetle, sometimes a lizard or a fieldmouse; ever waking up their sense of wonder, calling out their powers of observation, and teaching them lessons out of God's great green book, without their knowing how much they were learning.

And then the Sundays, the hardest day of the week to him, were bright to the children, who began the day with decking the graves in the dear churchyard, an example which the poor people learnt to follow, so that before morning service it looked like a flower garden; and when his day's work was done, however weary he might be, there was always the Sunday walk, a stroll on the moor, and some fresh object of natural beauty pointed out at every step. Indoors, the Sunday picture books were brought out. Each child had its own, and chose its subject for the father to draw, either some Bible story, or bird, or beast, or flower mentioned in Scripture. Happy Sundays! never associated with gloom or restrictions, but with God's works as well as His word, and with sermons that never wearied.

Punishment was a thing little known in his house. Corporal punishment was never allowed. His own childish experience of the sense of degradation and unhealthy fear it produced, of the antagonism it called out between a child and its parents, a pupil and his teachers, gave him a horror of it. It had other evils, too, he considered, besides degrading both parties concerned. "More than half the lying of children," he said, "is, I believe, the result of fear, and the fear of punishment." On these grounds he made it a rule (from which he never departed) not to take a child suspected of a fault, at unawares, by sudden question or hasty accusation, the stronger thus taking an unfair advantage of the weaker and defenceless creature, who, in the mere confusion of the moment, might be tempted to deny or equivocate. "Do we not," he asked, "pray daily, 'Lord, confound me not,' and shall we dare to confound our own children by sudden accusation, or angry suspicion, making them give evidence against themselves, when we don't allow a criminal to do that in a court of law? The finer the nature the more easily is it confounded, whether it be of child, dog, or horse. Suspicion destroys confidence between parent and child." "Do not train a child," he once said to a friend, "as men train a horse, by letting anger and punishment be the *first* announcement of his having sinned.

Fear and Falsehood

If you do, you induce two bad habits: first, the boy regards his parent with a kind of blind dread, as a being who may be offended by actions which to *him* are innocent, and whose wrath he expects to fall upon him any moment in his most pure and unselfish happiness. Alas! for such a childhood! Εἰδὼς λέγω! Next, and worse still, the boy learns not to fear sin, but the *punishment* of it, and thus he learns to lie. At every first fault, and offence too, teach him the principle which makes it sinful — illustrate it by a familiar parable — and then, if he sins again it will be with his eyes open!"

He was careful, too, not to confuse or "confound" his children by a multiplicity of small rules. Certain broad, distinct laws of conduct were laid down. "It is difficult enough to keep the Ten Commandments," he would say "without making an eleventh in every direction." This, combined with his equable rule, gave them a sense of utter confidence and perfect freedom with him. They knew what they were about and where to find him, for he had no "moods" with them, while with theirs he could yet sympathize and be patient. "Where others so often fail" — as a friend remarked of him, "in the family, there he shone." To see him at his best and highest was to see him in his home — to see "the tender, adoring husband, so gentle and so strong" — the father "who treated his daughters like princesses," his sons as trusted companions, his servants as friends, those faithful servants who thought no labor heavy to give him ease and comfort, and who, when they followed their beloved master to the grave, had lived half a lifetime in his service. It was truly said of him, that in "that inner circle all men knew that he was to his children and servants a yet 'finer gentleman,' to use the grand old English word he loved to use, than he was in the finest circles." "Pitiful and courteous" — he carried out this apostolic precept in his home; and however difficult life might be to himself, his daily care was to make it easy to those around him. Like a brave man as he was, he kept his feelings of depression, and those dark hours of wrestling with doubt and disappointment and anxiety, which must come to every thinking, feeling human being, within the sanctuary of his own heart, unveiled only to one on earth, and to his Father in Heaven. And when he came out of his study in the morning, and met his children and guests at breakfast, he would greet them with bright courtesy and that cheerful disengaged temper acquired by strict self-discipline, which enabled him to enter into all their interests, and the joy and playfulness of the moment. The family gatherings were the brightest hours in the day, lit up as they were with his marvellous humor. Bright — not only because of the joy his great heart took in his nearest and dearest — but bright on the Bible principle — that "a merry heart is a continual feast," and sunshine necessary to the development and actual health and growth of all things, especially the young. "I wonder," he would say, "if there is so much laughing in any other home in England as in ours." He became a light-hearted boy once more in the presence of his children, and still more remarkably so in that of his aged mother, when he saw her face clouded with depression during her later years, which were spent under his roof. He brought sunshine

The Training of Love 41

into her room whenever he entered it, as well as the strong spiritual consolation which she needed, and received in his daily ministrations by her bedside morning and evening.

The griefs of children were to him most piteous. "A child over a broken toy is a sight I cannot bear;" and when nursery griefs and broken toys were taken to the study, he was never too busy to mend the toy and dry the tears. He held with Jean Paul Richter again, that children have their "days and hours of rain," days when "the child's quicksilver" falls rapidly before the storms and cold weather of circumstances, and "parents should not consider or take much notice, either for anxiety or sermons,"[1] but lightly pass over these variations of temperature, except where they are symptoms of coming illness. And here his knowledge of physiology and that delicate organization of brain, which had given him many a sad experience in his own childhood, made him keen to watch and detect such symptoms. Weariness at lessons, and sudden fits of temper, he would say, often spring from purely physical causes, and must not be treated hastily as moral, far less spiritual delinquencies, being, possibly, mere phases of depression, which disappear with change of occupation, air and scene, and the temporary cessation of all brain work.

Justice and mercy, and that rigid self-control, which kept him from speaking a hasty word or harboring a mean suspicion, combined with a divine tenderness, were his governing principles in all his home relationships. "This tenderness," as once was said of a great man, "was

[1] "Levana," chap. 8.

never so marked as when he was looking at or talking with little children. At such times the expression which came over his face was wonderfully beautiful and touching. Towards these little creatures he had an eager way of stretching out his hands, as if to touch them, but with a hesitation arising from the evident dread of handling them too roughly. The same sort of feeling, too, he manifested in a minor degree, towards small animals, little dogs, kittens and birds."[1]

It has been observed with truth that there was an "element of fierceness," about him, which would flash out in the presence of wrong and oppression, of meanness and untruth, and betray itself by abrupt and fierce rejoinder. But in the home which he had made the very atmosphere of truth and love, of confidence and freedom of opinion, he was never abrupt, but tender, courteous and self-forgetful, yielding to every will and temper but his own. And he *respected* as well as loved his children, from the early days when Heaven lay about them in their infancy, and he hung with reverent and yet passionate wonder over the baby in its cradle, to grown-up years when he looked upon them as friends and equals. Home was to them so real a thing that it seemed in a way as if it must be eternal. And when his eldest son, in America, heard of the father's death, and of another which then seemed imminent, and foresaw the break-up of the home, he stood as one astonished, only to say, in the bitterness of his soul:

"I feel as if a huge ship had broken up piece by piece, plank by plank, and we children were left cling-

[1] Life of Sir W. Napier.

The Training of Love 43

ing to one strong spar alone — God ! . . . Ah, how many shoals and quicksands of life he piloted me through, by his wonderful love, knowledge, and endurance — that great father of ours, the dust of whose shoes we are not worthy to kiss. . . ."

Since that bitter day, this beloved son has added his memories to the many in this book of memories:

"'Perfect love casteth out all fear,' was the motto on which my father based his theory of bringing up his children; and this theory he put in practice from their babyhood till when he left them as men and women. From this, and from the interest he took in all their pursuits, their pleasures, trials, and even the petty details of their every-day life, there sprang up a 'friendship' between father and children that increased in intensity and depth with years. To speak for myself, and yet I know full well I speak for all, he was the best friend — the only true friend I ever had. At once he was the most fatherly and the most unfatherly of fathers — fatherly in that he was our intimate friend, and our self-constituted adviser; unfatherly in that our feeling for him lacked that fear and restraint that make boys call their father 'the governor.'

"I remember him as essentially the same to all of us always: utterly unchanged and unchanging since the time that he used to draw Sunday pictures for us to the time when he treated us as men and women of the world. Ours was the only household I ever saw in which there was no favoritism. It seemed as if in each of our different characters he took an equal pride, while he fully recognized their different traits of good or evil; for, instead of having one code of social, moral, and physical laws laid down for one and all of us, each child became a separate study for him; and its little

Charles Kingsley

'diseases *au moral*,' as he called them, were treated differently according to each different temperament.

"The time above all others in which he opened out his heart to us, I think, was walking over on Sunday evenings to the services held in the little school-room at Bramshill. I can *see* him now, on one of those many summer evenings, as he strode out of the back garden gate with a sorrowful 'No! go home, Sweep!' to the retriever that had followed us stealthily down the walk, and who now stood with an ear cocked, and one paw up, hoping against hope, that he might be allowed to come on. I can *feel* him striding by me in the narrow path, while from the bright sky and the look of the country he drank in nature, till his eye lit up, his chest expanded, his step grew elastic, and he was a boy again with me. I can *hear* him tell me, at the bottom of the field, of a heavy fall out hunting over the fence into the meadow, and his ringing laugh at the recollection of his own mishap. His cheery 'Good afternoon' to the cottager at the corner; the 'Well-done, boy,' and grim smile of approval, with which he greeted a jump over the gate at the top of the hill, on which he sits a moment to take in the long sweeps of purple heather running down to the yellow corn land — the brown roof of the Rectory bursting up among its trees — the long flats of the little valley, with its greens and cricketers. 'For cricket,' he used to say, 'is better than beer, and the poor lads don't get a chance to play on week-day: but remember *you* do.' And then the walk on over the moor, chatting gaily of the fox's earth hard by, the green tiger beetle that whirred from under our feet, the night-jar (goat-sucker) that fluttered up from a sandy place in the path, and swooped madly away among the fir-trees, while ever and anon some thought would strike a deeper chord, and a few words put something that mayhap had been an old stumbling-block, into an en-

Favorites and Friends 45

tirely new and true light. All his deepest teaching, his strongest influence was, in a way, of the negative kind inasmuch as there were no long lectures, no pithy arguments; but in his own life he showed, spoke, and lived his doctrines, so that his utter unselfishness, his genial tenderness towards their mother and themselves, gave the children an example that could not be passed by unnoticed, however unworthily followed. The only thing that he really required of us was reverence and respect for people older than ourselves, which was also one of the most strongly marked traits in his own character, and one which made him entirely ignore himself and his own superiority, in most cases, in speaking to men older than he was. This required reverence, however, on our part, never created any feeling of restraint when with him; too true a friendship existed between us. Perhaps the brightest picture of the past that I look back to now — that we can all look back to — is, not the eager look of delight with which he used to hail any of our little successes — not any special case of approval, but it is the drawing-room at Eversley in the evenings when we were all at home and by ourselves. There he sat, with one hand in mother's, forgetting his own hard work and worry in leading our fun and frolic, with a kindly smile on his lips, and a loving light in that bright gray eye which made us feel that, in the broadest sense of the word, he was our father."

But to speak of his home without mentioning his love of animals would be to leave the picture incomplete. His dog and his horse were his friends, and they knew it, and understood his voice and eye. He was a perfect horseman, and never lost his temper with his horse, talking to and reasoning with it if it shied or bolted, as if it had been a rational being, knowing that, from the fine organization of the animal, a horse, like a child, will get confused by panic fear, which is only increased by punishment. His dog Dandy, a fine Scotch terrier, was his companion in all his parish walks, attended at the cottage lectures and school lessons, and was his and the children's friend for thirteen years. He lies buried under the great fir-trees on the Rectory lawn, with this inscription on his gravestone, "Fideli Fideles," and close by "Sweep," a magnificent black retriever, and "Victor," given to him by the Queen, a favorite Teckel, with which he sat up during the two last suffering nights of the little creature's life. Cats, too, were a continual delight to him; the stable had always its white cat, and the house its black or tabby, whose graceful movements he never tired of watching. His love of animals was deepened by his belief in their future state — a belief which he held in common with John Wesley, Agassiz, Bishop Butler, and many other remarkable men. On the lawn dwelt a family of natter jacks (running toads), who lived on from year to year in the same hole in the green bank, which the scythe was never allowed to approach. He had two little friends in a pair of sand wasps, who lived in a crack of the window in his dressing-room, one of which he had saved from drowning in a hand-basin, taking it tenderly out into the sunshine to dry; and every spring he would look out eagerly for them or their children who came out of, or returned to the same crack. The little fly-catcher, who built its nest every year under his bedroom window, was a constant joy to him. He had also a favorite slow-worm in the churchyard which his parishioners were warned not to kill, from the mistaken idea prevalent in Eversley that slow-worms were poisonous. All these tastes he encouraged in his children, teaching them to love and handle gently, without disgust, all living things, toads, frogs, beetles, as works and wonders from the hand of a Living God. His guests were surprised one morning at breakfast when his little girl ran up to the open window of the dining-room holding a long repulsive-looking worm in her hand. "Oh! daddy, look at this *delightful* worm." He had but one aversion which he could never conquer — and it was of himself he spoke in 'Glaucus,' after saying, that every one seems to have his antipathic animal: "I know one bred from his childhood to zoölogy by land and sea, and bold in asserting, and honest in feeling that all without exception is beautiful, who yet cannot, after handling, and petting, and examining all day long every uncouth and venomous beast, avoid a paroxysm of horror at the sight of the common housespider."[1]

But, of all God's creations, birds were to him the most wonderful, he would say. He knew their every note, and was never tired of watching their character and habits. He looked for the arrival of the birds of passage every spring with a strange longing, and seemed less restless after the swallow had appeared at Eversley. His eyes would fill with tears at each fresh arrival, and again each autumn as he grieved over their departure.

[1] This horror, curiously enough, became hereditary in one of his sons, who, however, never knew of the father's dislike to this class of spider till he was a grown man. (M. K.)

"Your bird-books are delightful," he writes, while Professor of Modern History, to a friend; "gladly would I throw up history, to think of nothing but dicky-birds — but it must not be yet. Some day, ere I grow too old to think, I trust to be able to throw away all pursuits save natural history, and die with my mind full of God's facts, instead of men's lies. . . ."

. . . .
. . . .

"Many, now scattered far and wide," says one who knew and loved the Rector in his home, and has an especial right to speak, "must remember how picturesque the Rectory itself was. Even a stranger passing by would have stopped to look at the pleasant ivy-grown house, with its long, sloping, dark roofs, its gables, its bow-windows open to sun and air, and its quaint mixture of buildings, old and new. And who among his friends will ever cease to remember the lawn, and glebe-land sweeping upward toward the half-cultivated, half-wild copse; through which the hidden path, henceforth sacred ground to those who loved him, leads up and out to Hartford Bridge Flats? Marked features in the scene to them, and now widely known, were the grand Scotch firs on the lawn, under which on summer evenings I have seen many sweet pictures, and heard many noble words, and the branches of which now wave solemnly above his last resting-place.

"Here — in this beautiful home-scene, and truly ideal English Rectory — was the fountain-head — as I certainly think, and as he often said — of all his strength and greatness. Indeed, great as I knew him to be in his books, I found him greater at his own fireside. Home was to him the sweetest, the fairest, the most romantic thing in life; and there all that was best and brightest in him shone with steady and purest lustre.

"I should not venture to speak of this, unless permis-

Favorites and Friends 49

sion had been granted me to do so, feeling that it is the most difficult of tasks, to lift the veil from any family life without lowering its sacredness; and that it is wholly beyond my power to preserve in words the living 'sweetness and light' which pervaded his household. That household was indeed a revelation to me, as I know it was to others; — so nobly planned and ordered, so earnest in its central depths, so bright upon its surface.

"Of the wonderful love of his home-life I must not, cannot speak. Such things are not for the world. And yet, for all who wish to know what Mr. Kingsley really was, what the fashion of his life, and the aims for which he worked, not to know that love for those nearest and dearest to him was the very lever of his life, the very soul of all his joy, would be to know him all amiss, and lose the very key-note of his being. He has told it all himself to those who have ears to hear in every book he wrote, and to those who knew him well, his every look and every action told the fact yet more emphatically. Some men take pains to conceal their love. It seemed his pride to declare it. How often has he said to me — and I venture to record it, because I *know* he would wish it to be recorded — that whatever he had done or achieved was due to the love that had come to him at a great crisis to guide and to strengthen and to glorify his life."

CHAPTER XVI

1857

AGED 38

WINTER AT HOME — BRIGHT SUMMER DAYS — THE CROWDED CHURCH — CHARLOTTE BRONTÉ — SPECULATION AND PRACTICE — WORK BEYOND THE GRAVE — TO AN INDEPENDENT — TOM BROWN — RECREATION — "GO HARK!" — LOVE BEYOND THE GRAVE — "TWO YEARS AGO" — INDIAN MUTINY — "CHRIST REIGNS"— HUMOR DIVINE — TEMPORARY FAILURE OF ASSOCIATIONS.

"There is a mean curiosity, as of a child opening a forbidden door, or a servant prying into his master's business;—and a noble curiosity, questioning in the front of danger, the source of the great river beyond the sand, — the place of the great continents beyond the sea; a nobler curiosity still, which questions of the source of the River of Life, and of the space of the Continent of Heaven, things which the Angels desire to look into."

RUSKIN.

"I have boundless faith in 'time and light.' I shall see what is the truth some day, and if I do not *some one else will*, which is far more important. . . ."
C. K.

THE year 1857 opened brightly on Charles Kingsley, for it found him, for the first winter for three years, in his own home at Eversley, with his wife and his three children, and in the fullest vigor of his manhood.

"I am writing nothing now; but taking breath, and working in the parish — never better than I am at present; with many blessings, and, awful confession for

Winter at Home

mortal man, no sorrows! I sometimes think there must be terrible arrears of sorrow to be paid off by me — that I may be as other men are! God help me in that day! . . ."

He had finished his "Two Years Ago." The year was rich in letters and lectures and friends; and he writes to Mr. Peter Wood, then rector of Devizes, where he was to give a lecture on the study of natural history:

"I look forward to seeing you with great delight, as a renewing of the days of my youth, at least of the better element of them, for I trust you will find me a better and calmer, if not a wiser man than you knew me in old times, though just as great a boy as ever. . . . Of the local geology of Devizes I know nought. I am not a man of chalk (save in reference to trouts), but a man of clays, and gravels, and sands, who wanders these moorlands till I have all but exhausted their flora, fauna, and geological features, though I hope to stumble on fresh wonders some day, by the aid of the microscope."

". . . I am better off now than I have been for years!" he writes to Mr. Hughes. "God be thanked, and God grant, too, that I may not require to be taken down by some terrible trouble. I often fancy I shall be. If I am, I shall deserve it, as much as any man who ever lived. I say so now — justifying God beforehand, lest I should not have faith and patience enough to justify Him when the punishment comes. . . . Many thanks for your wholesome letter — the rightest letter I have had for many a day. It has taught me a great deal, dear old man; and you are nearer to God than I am, I see well. . . ."

The "terrible trouble" came,—but not in the shape of personal grief or domestic affliction; and, till the awful news from India burst upon England, all went well. He was made this year a Fellow of the Linnean Society, which had been one of the ambitions of his life. He preached in his own church as distinctly as he did in his "Two Years Ago" (to those who could read between the lines) those views on the Intermediate State and the Future Life, which he held sacred to the last, basing his interpretation of Scripture on quotations from the Fathers. He lectured at Bristol and in the diocese, on "Great Cities: their Influence for Good and Evil,"[1] Thoughts in a Gravel Pit, and on Chaucer, and worked hard at sanitary and educational subjects. He wrote "The Winter Garden," the most perfect of all his Prose Idylls, this year. A strange medley of visitors proposed themselves, and were made welcome, at the Rectory. One day a Unitarian minister, clergymen of the Church of England, Dissenters, Americans — all came on missions of their own, and opened their hearts to him as they could to no other man. Visits from many dear friends, Max Müller, Anthony Froude, Cowley Powles, and Tom Hughes, refreshed his spirit. And on the lawn, under the old fir-trees on bright summer days, he and his guests discussed all things in heaven and earth — theology, natural science, poetry, and art, each in turn. And as by day he would revel in the sights of Nature, so on still summer nights he would interpret her sounds. He loved to gather his friends and children round him on the grass under his favorite

[1] Published in the Miscellanies.

Bright Days

acacia-tree; and while intently listening himself to the well-beloved sounds wafted across the glebe, he would teach them to distinguish what, but for his acute senses, might have escaped notice — the strange note of the night-hawk — the croaking of frogs in the far-off ponds on the common — the nightingale in the mount answering those in the garden — the call of the pheasant in Coombes's Wood — the distant bark of a fox — and close at hand the clicking and cracking of the ripe fir cones. In his presence life was at its full — all nature spoke — the silence was full of sound — the darkness full of light — the air, of fragrance. And "there has passed away a glory" from that little spot of "earth" which can never return — though rays of it still linger in the memories of those who knew it in his time.

Sunday after Sunday he had the keen delight of seeing Crimean officers from Aldershot and Sandhurst in his congregation. Among others, one who had been dangerously wounded in the Redan, at Sevastopol, and who, when lying between life and death at Scutari, had read "Yeast," and determined, if he ever came back alive, "to go and hear the clergyman preach who could give such a picture of a hunting scene as the one in the opening chapter." One Sunday he came — while still on crutches — a stranger to Mr. Kingsley, but soon to become a friend, a constant attendant at church, and always a welcome guest at the Rectory early Sunday dinner.

To Rev. F. Maurice. — "I find that the Aldershot and Sandhurst mustachios come to hear these discourses of mine every Sunday — and my heart goes out to them in great yearnings. Dear fellows — when I see them in the pews, and the smock frocks in the open seats, I feel as if I was not quite useless in the world, and that I was beginning to fulfil the one idea of my life, to tell Esau that he has a birthright as well as Jacob. I do feel very deeply the truth which John Mill has set forth in a one-sided way in his new book on Liberty — (pp. 88–90, I think), about the past morality of Christendom having taken a somewhat abject tone, and requiring, as a complement, the old Pagan virtues, which our forefathers learnt from Plutarch's Lives, and of which the memory still lingers in our classical education. I do not believe, of course, that the want really exists: but that it was created, principally by the celibate misanthropy of the patristic and mediæval church. But I have to preach the divineness of the whole manhood, and am content to be called a Muscular Christian, or any other impertinent name, by men who little dream of the weakness of character, sickness of body, and misery of mind, by which I have bought what little I know of the human heart."

Besides the military men who came, the little church was often full of strangers; and one Sunday, when twelve carriages were standing in and outside the stable-yard, the sexton was heard to say, he could not think why there was "such flitting to and fro to our church on Sundays." Having heard the same preaching for fifteen years himself, he could not tell what the wonder of it was. To the Rector this increasing notoriety was painful: "I cannot bear having my place turned into a fair on Sundays, and all this talking after church." And to avoid the greetings of acquaintances and the observation of strangers in the churchyard, he had a little back gate made

The Crowded Church 55

into his garden, to which he escaped after service through the vestry door. His whole soul and energy were thrown so intensely into the services of his church, that when they were over he found quiet essential to help him to calm down from the excitement.

Having no curate this year, he seldom left home; and when pressed to come up to London and hear a new setting of one of his own songs finely sung there, he refused, adding, "I love home and green fields more and more, and never lust either after Babylon or the Continent. . . ." In the autumn, after the first news of the mutiny, some friends, knowing how hard-worked and sad he was, invited him to go with them to the Manchester Exhibition, then open, with all its glorious pictures: but when the day came he could not make up his mind to leave a poor sick man, who he felt would miss his daily visits. With his keen love of art, it cost him a pang to give up the sight of such a collection of pictures as might never again come together in England during his lifetime; but he said he could not have enjoyed them while a parishioner was counting on seeing him. This trifling incident is mentioned to show how thorough and unselfish he was in his parish work, which in this case could so easily have been passed over for three days to any neighboring clergyman. Among the letters of the year is one to Mrs. Gaskell about her life of Charlotte Brontë:

"Be sure that the book will do good. It will shame literary people into some stronger belief that a simple, virtuous, practical home life is consistent with high imaginative genius; and it will shame, too, the prudery of a not over cleanly, though carefully whitewashed age, into believing that purity is now (as in all ages till now) quite compatible with the knowledge of evil. I confess that the book has made me ashamed of myself. 'Jane Eyre' I hardly looked into, very seldom reading a work of fiction — yours, indeed, and Thackeray's are the only ones I care to open. 'Shirley' disgusted me at the opening: and I gave up the writer and her books with the notion that she was a person who liked coarseness. How I misjudged her! and how thankful I am that I never put a word of my misconceptions into print, or recorded my misjudgments of one who is a whole heaven above me. Well have you done your work, and given us the picture of a valiant woman made perfect by sufferings. I shall now read carefully and lovingly every word she has written."

TO JOHN BULLAR, ESQ.

". . . If I have neglected answering notes, forgive me. I have been careless! but I have been harried, living my double life of writing and parish work, and were it not for my guardian angel of a wife I should never *write* an answer to a letter though I walk about with the answer in my head for a week. But now the weary book is done; have patience with me, and try me again."

Feb. 8, 1857. — " I enjoy your letters very much, indeed more than I dare confess to myself. For I am the strangest jumble of superstition and of a reverence for scientific induction which forbids me (simply for want of certain facts) to believe heaps of things in which I see no *à priori* impossibility. I want to believe all Jung Stilling's pneumatology, all Elliotson's mesmerism. Yea, I would gladly believe in deevs and peris, elves and fairies, if I could. I would even gladly believe half of those monk and nun miracles and visions with which I have gorged myself more than perhaps most men in England, and which (as psychological and physiological studies) have been invaluable to me — but I can't. What is a poor wretch to do, who, disbelieving the existence of matter far more firmly than Bishop Berkeley, is accessible to no hints from anything but matter? A mystic in theory, and an ultra-materialist in practice — who, if I saw a ghost to-morrow, should chat quietly with it, and take out pen, ink, and paper to get an exact description of the phenomenon on the spot, what shall I do? I fear sometimes that I shall end by a desperate lunge into one extreme or the other. I should have done so long ago (for this battle has gone on in me since childhood), had I not seen something of a compromise in what Maurice has taught me.

"But after all, what is speculation to practice? What does God require of us, but to do justly, to love mercy, and to walk humbly with Him? The longer I live this seems to me more important, and all other questions less so. If we can but live the simple right life —

"Do the work that's nearest,
Though it's dull at whiles;
Helping, when we meet them,
Lame dogs over stiles;' —

why, then we shall be better than ghosts; for a ghost is but a soul, and we are soul and body too; and there have the advantage, for aught we know; and if not, what matter?"

March 19, 1857. — " Many thanks for your favorable opinion of the book ('Two Years Ago'); but I fear you take Tom Thurnall for a better man than he was, and must beg you not to pare my man to suit your own favorable conception; but consider that *that* is the sort of man I want to draw, and you must take him as you find him. My experience is, that men of his character (like all strong men till God's grace takes full possession of them) are weak upon one point . . . — everything can they stand but that; and the more they restrain themselves from prudential motives, the more sudden and violent is the temptation when it comes. I have indicated as delicately as I could the worldwide fact, which all know and all ignore; had I not done so, Thurnall would have been a mere chimera fit only for a young lady's novel.

"I feel deeply the change in one's imagination during the last twenty years. As a child I never could distinguish dreams from imaginations, imaginations from waking impressions; and was often thought to be romancing when I was relating a real impression. In ill health from overwork about 16 to 18, I had spectral illusions often (one as clear as any of Nicolai's), accompanied with frightful nervous excitability, and inability to settle to any work, though always working at something in a fierce, desultory way. At twenty I found out tobacco. The spectres vanished; the power of dull application arose; and for the first time in my life I began to be master of my own brain. Now, I am in general the most prosaic and matter-of-fact of parsons. I cannot dream if I try. I go to my brain as to a storehouse or carpenter's shop, from which I take out coolly what I want, and put it into the best shape I can. The German mode of thought, and feeling, and writing, such as you find in Jean Paul or Novalis, lies behind me, as 'boy's love,' belonging to an era when 'the spirits of the prophets' were not yet 'subject to the prophets.' Whether this be right or wrong, I know not; but I confess the fact; — and if we ever get a week together, I fear that you will think me a most dull and frivolous fellow, who cares for nothing but to romp with your children,

To an Independent 59

and pick flowers and study the weather *usque ad nauseam*. But here lies the difference between us. Your work is utterly of the head; and you go for amusement to fancy, to imagination, to metaphysic. My work, whether parish or writing, lies just in the sphere wherein you play: and if I played in that sphere too, I should go mad, or soften my brain, like poor Southey. So when I play, I think about nothing; ride, fish, chat with the farmers over the crops, examine beetles and worms, and forget that I have a heart as much as I can. . . ."

To W. E. FRANKS, ESQ.—". . . I am delighted to hear about your work among the Crystal Palace men; and I think that, with them, things read *vivâ voce* will have more effect than any tracts. The human voice and eye give a realit, to the thought, provided the voice and eye be real and earnest also. I saw this much in the noble work which my friend, Miss Marsh, did among the navvies at the Crystal Palace, when they were starting for the Crimea. So work on, '*getrost und wohlgemuth*,' as the Germans say, and cast thy bread on the waters, for thou wilt find it after many days. . . ."

". . . As to your being an Independent, sir; what's that to me? provided you — as I see well you do — do justly and love mercy, and walk humbly with your God. I don't think you will ever find the freedom in your communion which you would in ours — the freest, thank God, in the world: but I should be a second Ham if I had no respect for the Independents. For why? My forefathers were Independents, and fought by Cromwell's side at Naseby and Marston Moor; and what is more, lost broad acres for their Puritanism. The younger brother of an ancestor of mine was one of the original Pilgrim Fathers, so I am full of old

Puritan blood, though I have utterly — indeed, our family have for generations thrown off their Calvinism: yet I glory in the morale, the God-fearing valor and earnestness of the old heroes, and trust I should have believed with them had I lived in their day, for want of any better belief. But it will not do now, as you have found already. The bed is too short and the cloak too narrow."

TO TOM HUGHES, ESQ.

June 12, 1857. — "Eight and thirty years old am I this day, Tummas; whereof twenty-two were spent in pain, in woe, and vanitie; and sixteen in very great happiness, such as few men deserve, and I don't deserve at all. And now I feel like old Jacob, 'with my staff I passed over Jordan, and now I am become two bands' — for why? I actually could n't get home from Hastings except in two relays, what with servants, tutor, and governess. Well, Tom, God has been very good to me; and I can't help feeling a hope that I may fight a good fight yet before I die, and get something done. I've done little enough yet. The best work ever I've done has been my plain parish work, and that I've done miserably ill, cowardly and idly of late, and bullying and second-hand dogmatic of old; but perhaps I shall get training enough to go into the ring before I die; and if not, I trust one's not going to be idle up there, Tom. Surely as long as there's a devil or devils, even an ass or asses, in the universe, one will have to turn out to the *reveille* now and then, wherever one is, and satisfy one's $\theta \upsilon \mu \acute{o} \varsigma$ 'rage' or 'pluck,' which Plato averreth (for why, he'd have been a wraxling man, and therefore was a philosopher, and the king of 'em) to be the root of all virtue. Why not, Tom? May n't we?

"Now to business, Tommy, which is fish. O that I

Tom Brown

could go to Lambourne Monday! But I preach in town Sunday, and have three good fellows a dying in my parish, so that I must be at home Monday afternoon. I think the boys will catch nought. The fish will be glutted with the fly, and attendant Naiads pitying, holding basins under their noses: mortal aldermanic they were Wednesday here. I caught a fairish lot on the Caperer, which they took as a relish to the heavy fly; but the moment they were ashore the Mayflies came up. On a Dover steamer in a chopping sea was cleanly to it. Poor carnal parties! Why should n't they tuck while they can? Mayflies come to them at Whitsuntide, as club-feasts do to the clods, to give them one jolly blow out in the year, and it 's a pleasure to look at them. That 's why good fishing days always fall on Sundays, Tom, to give the poor fish a good day's appetite (dinner always ready), and nobody to catch them while they 're enjoying it. Also make a note of this. A party with doubtful h's, and commercial demeanor, appears on Wednesday on our little stream, and kills awfully. Throws a beautiful line, and catches more than I have in a day for this two years here; fly, a little green drake, with a ridiculous tufted bright yellow wing, like nothing as ever was. Stood aghast; went home and dreamed all the spiders' webs by the stream were full of thousands of them, the most beautiful yellow ephemeræ with green peacock-tail heads. Oh the beauty of them; and was n't I riled when I found it was all for fancy? But won't I 'realoirioize,' as the Scots parsons say, those little fellows next year, and apply them to the part affected? . . ."

To THE SAME. — " I have often been minded to write to you about 'Tom Brown.'[1] I have puffed it every-

[1] Mr. Kingsley corrected the first proof of "Tom Brown's School Days " for his old friend; but he was not entirely satisfied with the sequel, "Tom Brown at Oxford." (M. K.)

where I went, but I soon found how true the adage is that good wine needs no bush, for every one had read it already, and from every one, from the fine lady on her throne, to the red-coat on his cock-horse, and the school-boy on his forrum (as our Irish brethren call it), I have heard but one word, and that is, that it is the jolliest book they ever read. Among a knot of redcoats at the cover-side, some very fast fellow said, 'If I had had such a book in my boyhood, I should have been a better man now!' and more than one capped his sentiment frankly. Now is n't it a comfort to your old bones to have written such a book, and a comfort to see that fellows are in a humor to take it in? So far from finding men of our rank in a bad vein, or sighing over the times and prospects of the rising generation, I can't help thinking they are very teachable, humble, honest fellows, who want to know what's right, and if they don't go and do it, still think the worse of themselves therefor. I remark now, that with hounds, and in fast company, I never hear an oath, and that, too, is a sign of self-restraint. Moreover, drinking is gone out, and, good God, what a blessing! I have good hopes of our class, and better than of the class below. They are effeminate, and that makes them sensual. Pietists of all ages (George Fox, my dear friend, among the worst) never made a greater mistake than in fancying that by keeping down manly $θυμός$, which Plato saith is the root of all virtue, they could keep down sensuality. They were dear good old fools. However, the day of 'Pietism' is gone, and 'Tom Brown' is a heavy stone in its grave. 'Him no get up again after that,' as the niggers say of a buried obi-man. I am trying to polish the poems: but Maurice's holidays make me idle; he has come home healthier and jollier than ever he was in his life, and is truly a noble boy. Sell your last coat and buy a spoon. I have a spoon of huge size (Farlow his make). I killed

Recreation

forty pounds' weight of pike, &c., on it the other day, at Strathfieldsaye, to the astonishment and delight of ——, who cut small jokes on 'a spoon at each end,' &c., but altered his note when he saw the melancholies coming ashore, one every ten minutes, and would try his own hand. I have killed heaps of big pike round with it. I tried it in Lord Eversley's lakes on Monday, when the fish would n't have even his fly. Capricious party is Jaques. Next day killed a seven pounder at Hurst. . . . We had a pretty thing on Friday with Garth's, the first run I 've seen this year. Out of the Clay Vale below Tilney Hall, pace as good as could be, fields three acres each, fences awful, then over Hazeley Heath to Bramshill, shoved him through a false cast, and a streamer over Hartford Bridge flat, into an unlucky earth. Time fifty-five minutes, falls plentiful, started thirty, and came in eight, and did n't the old mare go? Oh, Tom, she is a comfort; even when a bank broke into a lane, and we tumbled down, she hops up again before I 'd time to fall off, and away like a four-year old, and if you can get a horse through that clay vale, why, then you can get him 'mostwards;' leastwise so I find, for a black region it is, and if you ain't in the same field with the hounds, you don't know whether you are in the same parish, what with hedges, and trees, and woods, and all supernumerary vegetations. Actually I was pounded in a ''taty-garden,' so awful is the amount of green stuff in these parts. Come and see me, and take the old mare out, and if you don't break her neck, she won't break yours.[1]

---

[1] Some time, however, after the letter was written this mare nearly did succeed in breaking her own neck and her master's. Coming up to a high park gate, her rider leaned forward to open it with his hunting-whip. Either he must have touched her with the spur by accident, or she must have thought he wanted her to jump it, for she rose suddenly under him, but was too close to clear it, even if it were possible, and caught her knees under the top

GO HARK!

'Yon sound 's neither sheep bell nor bark,
    They 're running — they 're running, Go hark!
The sport may be lost by a moment's delay,
    So whip up the puppies and scurry away.
Dash down through the cover by dingle and dell,
There 's a gate at the bottom — I know it full well;
And they 're running — they 're running,
        Go hark!

    They 're running — they 're running, Go hark!
    One fence and we 're out at the park;
    Sit down in your saddles and race at the brook,
    Then smash at the bullfinch; no time for a look.
Leave cravens and skirters to dangle behind,
He 's away for the moors, in the teeth of the wind,
And they 're running — they 're running,
        Go hark!

    They 're running — they 're running, Go hark!
    Let them run on and run till it 's dark!
    Well with them we are, and well with them we 'll be,
    While there 's wind in our horses and daylight to see:
Then shog along homeward, chat over the fight,
And hear in our dreams the sweet music all night
Of — They 're running — they 're running,
        Go hark!'"   C. K.

To Lord——: Eversley, *June* 8, 1857.—"... As for the question of 'evil,' on which I know as little as all the rest of mankind, I agree with you on the whole. Evil, as such, has no existence; but men can and do

rail. Both turned complete somersaults, falling on their backs on the other side on to a hard gravel road; fortunately clear of each other. The Rector was stunned for a moment; but, in telling the story afterwards, used to say with a grim chuckle that he could hardly help laughing when he came to, for there was the mare sitting up on her haunches, like a great brown dog, moving her neck slowly from side to side as if to make certain that her head was on. (M. K.)

Love Beyond the Grave 65

resist God's will, and break the law, which is appointed for them, and so punish themselves by getting into disharmony with their own constitution and that of the universe; just as a wheel in a piece of machinery punishes itself when it gets out of gear. I may be wrong, but so it seems to me. My conception of God's Providence, meanwhile, is, that He is, by a divine irony, lovingly, baffling all the lawlessness and self-will of the spirits whom He has made, and turning it into means for their education, as a father does with his children. Whether they take the lesson which He offers, depends on them; but the chances would seem, I should have said, to be in favor of God's proving too good an instructor to lose finally any of His pupils. The world thinks differently, you know, but I am content to be in the minority, for the few years of life which remain to me, to find myself, I trust, in the majority, when I come into the other world. . . . Pray let us hear again of Lady ——'s state. You may guess how deeply I sympathize with you. But I believe one never truly understands the blessed mystery of marriage till one has nursed a sick wife, nor understands, either, what treasures women are. . . ."

To THE SAME. — *July* 12. — " We were utterly shocked at your letter. We knew nothing about it. Who can feel for you more deeply than I, who have had the same danger in prospect in past times, and found it, even at a distance, too horrible to contemplate? But believe that those who are gone are nearer us than ever; and that if (as I surely believe) they do sorrow over the mishaps and misdeeds of those whom they leave behind, they do not sorrow in vain. Their sympathy is a further education for them, and a pledge, too, of help — I believe of final deliverance — for those on whom they look down in love. . . . God bless you, and give you strength. Again, I feel for you and with you utterly."

When "Two Years Ago" came out, it was bitterly attacked by the religious press; and its author accused of Pantheism, Rationalism, &c. But it did the work he meant it to do, as the following letters — a few only out of many he received — will show. The first is from the chaplain of a Queen's ship off Nova Scotia:

HALIFAX. — ". . . My purpose in writing to you is partly for encouragement in the preaching of views to which I am becoming the more and more attached, and partly to tell you how much your books are liked by naval men. . . . I know one instance of an officer, who is a man of cultivated mind, and yet he told me that until he had read 'Two Years Ago,' he had never said his prayers (for years past) except when in trouble. It would fill up this letter altogether, were I to tell you of all the praises I hear from every one of my messmates who have read this book. I consider it a duty to get them all to read it, and 'Westward Ho!' I have got them both for the sick quarters. . . . My preaching since I have read your 'Sermons for the Times,' speaks more of love than ever; I always held the same opinions, but was afraid of the preaching of them. . . . I have a Bible class for the men, which I tried in the 'cock-pit' and failed; on the main-deck, and failed; and at last, taking a lesson from 'Two Years Ago,' I resolved to go to the men instead of expecting them to come to me — and thus, I have at last succeeded. . . ."

A friend writes to him to tell him the effect the book had had on a distinguished member of one of our universities, who had had no settled faith for years:

"I write for your soul's comfort. Poor dear * * * attributed his being convinced of sin, and driven to seek

Christ the Lord and Saviour, to your last book, especially that fearful account of Elsley Vavasour's chase across the mountain, and Tom Thurnall's experience in the Russian dungeon. He had always said to me that he never could understand what was meant by the sense of sin as spoken of in the Bible, and by Maurice in his Theological Essays. But one night, about six weeks before his death, when he awoke in pain and darkness in the middle of the night, the remembrance of that terrible isolation which you had described in these passages came upon him in awful horror, and drove him to seek help from God. No one who knew * * * before that time and after it could fail to see how great the change was that was wrought in him. He only spoke of it to me once, and as I knew how distasteful to him was all self-analysis, at least to others, I never reopened the matter, but after his death I found he had said the same thing to * * * . . . I know how Mrs. Kingsley would prize such a fact in connection with such a man."

Another letter, asking his explanation of " fire and worms," of which he speaks as " one of the saddest and most interesting he had ever read," from a stranger who had found a gospel of deliverance in the view of God's character and hopes of the final destiny of man implied in " Two Years Ago," began thus:

" SIR, — Mr. B—— was my confessor. Dr. P—— is now. Nevertheless, I read all your books, and yesterday, in the midst of 'Two Years Ago,' I knelt down and said, ' At last, O God, I love thee ! for I know that Thou art good ! ' . . ."

" DEAR SIR OR MADAM (for your signature is not sufficiently legible for me to determine which of the two you are)," he replies, — "When I read of worms and fire, I suppose that they either are worms and fire literally, or are some things which so resemble in their action worms and fire, as to be best described by these terms metaphorically; to be what is vulgarly called 'a spiritual fire,' and 'spiritual worms.' Whether of the two they be, this at least is certain:

"The office of worms in this world is to prevent, while they seem to accelerate, putrefaction, and thereby to prevent infectious epidemics; to devour decaying matter, and render it thereby innoxious; finally, to transmute it into new, living, and healthy organisms. The office of fire in this world is much the same, to devour dead matter, all but the ash or inorganic constituents, which are left as manure (and the very best) for some future crop. I know no other worms, no other fire, on earth, than these beneficent ones. I expect none other elsewhere, unless every creature of God is not good, and to be received with thanksgiving. If they be a literal fire and worms, then they must be this or nothing. If a metaphorical fire and worms, an '*ignis immaterialis*,' such as the old fathers talked of, then they must be like this, or Scripture (and the Lord himself) is using words at random, or in a deceptive sense.

"The use of fire for torture, an utterly unnatural and monstrous abuse of that 'element,' sprang up among men of devilish and unnatural cruelty. It remained for a later age to adopt the belief of those Rabbis who crucified our Lord, that God would abuse the powers of fire (for ever!) for the same fiendish purposes for which they abused it for an hour or two, in the case of some shrieking and writhing victim.

"The torture of worms, Herodotus tells us, was tried now and then by old Persian despots. The mind of man has as yet so far recoiled from imputing so refined a barbarity to the Supreme Being, as to suppose in some confused inconsistent way, that the fire of course is fire; but the worm — they don't know about. A fire which cannot be quenched, a worm which cannot die, I see existing, whether they be those or not of which our Lord spoke. I consider them among the most blessed revelations of the Gospel. I fancy that I see them burning and devouring everywhere in the spiritual world, as their analogues do in the physical. I know that they have done so on me, and that their operation, though exquisitely painful, is most healthful. I see the world trying to quench and kill them; I know too well that I often do the same ineffectually. But in the comfort that the worm cannot die, and the fire cannot be quenched, I look calmly forward through endless ages, to my own future and the future of that world whereof it is written, 'He shall reign till He hath put all His enemies under His feet. The last enemy that shall be destroyed is death.' And again, ' Death and hell shall be cast into the lake of fire.'

" Of the parable of the sheep and goats, I have only to say, that our Lord speaks it expressly of nations, and that neither you nor I are a nation, therefore the parable need give us no present selfish disquiet, though it may set us on reading Gibbon's ' Decline and Fall,' as showing how our Lord's words came true fully and literally ; set us thinking what a nation means, and whether it be not better to help to save England, than to try to deliver each ' his own life for a prey,' ' that this ruin may not lie upon our hand.' This would naturally set us on reading the Hebrew prophets, to whom, as to the rest of the Old Testament writers, the rabbinical Tartarus was unknown, and in due time we should come to that verse in Isaiah concerning the worm and the fire, which our Lord quotes in the Gospels, and to other words about the fire of God, and its effect on nations and individuals, from which we might rise up with more reverence than before, for the letter of

Holy Scripture, especially if, as churchmen, we held that the Old Testament was not contrary to the New. . . ."

And now, as the details from India poured in, though he had no relatives or personal friends engaged in the mutiny, the agony of his mind was terrible, and he writes to Mr. Maurice and to Mr. Bullar:

"I can think of nothing but these Indian massacres. The moral problems they involve make me half wild. Night and day the heaven seems black to me, though I never was so prosperous and blest in my life as I am now. I can hardly bear to look at a woman or child — even at my own sometimes. They raise such horrible images, from which I can't escape. What does it all mean? Christ is King, nevertheless! I tell my people so. I should do — I dare not think what — if I did not believe so. But I want sorely some one to tell me that he believes it too. Do write to me and give me a clue out of this valley of the shadow of death. . . ."

". . . Do not talk to me about India, and the future of India, till you can explain the past — the past six months. O Bullar, no man knows, or shall know, what thoughts they have cost me. . . . Meanwhile, I feel as if I could dogmatize no more. I dare say you are right and I wrong. I have no heart, at least, to continue any argument, while my brain is filled with images fresh out of hell and the shambles. Show me what security I have that my wife, my children should not suffer, from some unexpected outbreak of devils, what other wives and children have suffered, and then I shall sleep quiet, without longing that they were safe out of a world where such things are possible.

"You may think me sinful for having such thoughts. My experience is, that when they come, one must face them, do battle with them deliberately, be patient if they worst one for a while. For by all such things men live, in these is the life of the spirit. Only by going down into hell can one rise again the third day. I have been in hell many times in my life; therefore, perhaps, have I had some small power of influencing human hearts. But I never have looked hell so close in the face as I have been doing of late. Wherefore I hope thereby to get fresh power to rise, and to lift others heavenward. But the power has not come yet. . . . And I can only cry, 'O Lord, in thee have I trusted, let me never be confounded. Wherefore should the wicked say, where is now his God?' But while I write now, and while I fret most, there comes to me an inner voice, saying — What matter if *thou* art confounded? *God is not.* Only believe firmly that God is at least as good as thou, with thy 'finite reason,' canst conceive: and He will make thee at last able to conceive how good He is, and thou shalt have the one perfect blessing of seeing God. You will say I am inconsistent. So I am; and so, if read honestly, are David's Psalms. Yet that very inconsistency is what brings them home to every human heart for ever. The words of a man in real doubt and real darkness, crying for light, and not crying in vain. As I trust I shall not. God bless you."

At this time he was preaching a series of sermons on the Creed. On the Day of Humiliation for the Indian Massacres, he had reached the article of faith " In Jesus Christ His Only Son Our Lord." His text was Ps. ii. 1-4. The beginning was like " a cry of agony to God," as he spoke of

". . . those stories which turn women's blood cold with horror, and turn men's blood hot with indignation and rage, and make them long to go out to fight, and die if need be, avenging those innocent women and children. . . .

Do we not say in our hearts, Can this earth belong to God? Can He care for mankind? For men, and men's sufferings, that is a slight matter comparatively. These Englishmen have, as it were, leapt on the back of this great Indian Nation and tamed it, and bitted it, and guided it, and ruled it; but if the horse throws his rider, that is the rider's own business. He took his choice when he mounted and he must abide by it. . . . But the poor women and children! Oh! my God, what have they done? . . . Is it true, O God, that Thou beholdest ungodliness and wrong? Is it true that Thou art set in the throne judging right? Is it true that Thou art loving to every man, and Thy mercy over all Thy works? Is it true that to Thy Son Jesus Christ — He who took little children in His arms and blessed them — power is given in Heaven and earth? . . ."

And then the Creed, in all its grand significance, seemed to answer and quiet all questionings.

"And what have these horrors to do with the Apostle's Creed? My friends, I believe they have everything to do with it, or rather I believe it has everything to do with them. I, for one, could not face the thought of all that has happened in India, unless I could say with heart and soul, 'I believe in Jesus Christ, God's only Son, OUR LORD.' We must believe it is true, or believe nothing at all. . . . Quietly, but firmly, as we think of these massacres, we must say to ourselves, I believe in Jesus Christ, God's only Son, OUR LORD. . . . In spite of all appearances — horrors, cruelties — I believe that Jesus Christ is just as tender, compassionate, careful, loving, merciful, as He was. . . . In spite of the seeming misgovernment of things, although the world seems at moments masterless, and all things going blindfold by chance and passion, ignorance and mistake, yet I believe in OUR LORD. I believe that He is the Lord of those poor dead women and

Humor Divine

children, the Lord of soldiers who are fighting to avenge them; the Lord of heathen rebels, the Lord of India and Lord of England, and Lord of Earth and Heaven, and yet He governs all right well, and will govern till He has put all enemies under His feet. . . ."

While preparing for the press a volume of poems, which he had promised for Christmas, he was suddenly called upon for an article on sanitary reform, and he writes to Mr. J. Parker, his publisher:

". . . Of course I will do it. A bit of sanitary reform work is a sacred duty, from which I dare no more turn away than from knocking down a murderer whom I saw killing a woman. However, if I do — no poems at Christmas, young man; remember that. . . . I will throw my whole soul into it, please God, and forget India in Cholera. That's better than rhyming, surely."

TO REV. GEORGE HENSLOWE

[Who had written to him as to the possibility of a sense of humor in the Creator.]

EVERSLEY: *Sept.* 11, 1857. — " I cannot see how your notions can be gainsaid, save by those who have a lurking belief that God is the devil, after all — a sort of unjust and exacting Zeus, against whom they would rebel if they had Prometheus' courage: but not having that, must flatter him instead.

"The matter presents itself to me thus. I see humor in animals, *e. g.*, a crab and a monkey, a parrot, a crow. I don't find this the result of a low organization. In each of these four cases the animal is of the highest belonging to his class. Well, there the fact is; if I see it, God must see it also, or I must have more insight than God into God's own works. *Q. E. Abs.* Then comes a deeper question. God sees it: but is He affected by it? I think we could give no answer to this, save on the ground of a Son of God, who is that image of the Father in whom man is created. If the New Testament be true, we have a right to say of humor, as of all other universally human faculties — *Hominis est = Ergo Christi est = Ergo Dei est.*

"I must accept this in its fulness, to whatever *seemingly* startling and dangerous result it may lead me, or my theology and my anthropology part company, and then, being philosophically unable to turn Manichee (whether Calvinist or Romanist), the modern Pantheism would be the only alternative; from which homeless and bottomless pit of immoral and unphilosophical private judgment may God deliver us and all mankind. And you will see that into that Pantheism men will rush more and more till they learn to face the plain statement of the creed, 'And He was made man,' and the Catholic belief, that as the Son of man, He sits now ἐν (τοῖς) οὐρανοῖς, and on the very throne of God. Face the seemingly coarse anthropomorphism of the Old Testament, and believe that the New Testament, so far from narrowing it, widens and deepens it. This is my only hope and stay, while I see belief and practice alike rocking and reeling to decay. May God keep it alive in me and in you, recollecting always that to do the simple right thing which lies at our feet, is better than to have ascended into the third heaven, and to have all γνῶσις and all mysteries."

To J. BULLAR, ESQ. — "I am glad you have broached a subject with which I now never trouble any one. That 'associations' are a failure, because the working men are not fit for them, I confess. That any law of political economy or of nature has been broken by them, or by Mr. Maurice, is what I never could perceive. . . .

Humor Divine 75

"The being who merely obeys the laws of nature is *ipso facto* a brute beast. The privilege of a man is to counteract (not break) one law of nature by another. In the exercise of that power stands all art, invention, polity, progress. . . .

"Now, what I complain of in political economy up to this time — what, indeed, earned for it Fourier's bitter epithet of the '*Science du néant.*' . . . It says, There are laws of nature concerning economy, therefore you must leave them alone to do what they like with you and society! Just as if I were to say, You got the cholera by laws of nature, therefore you must submit to cholera; you walk on the ground by laws of nature, therefore you must never go upstairs. Indeed, I am inclined to deny to political economy, as yet, the name of a science. It is as yet merely in its analytic stage; explaining the causes of phenomena which already exist. To be a true science, it must pass on into the synthetic stage, and learn how, by using the laws which it has discovered, and counteracting them by others when necessary, to produce new forms of society. As yet political economy has produced nothing. It has merely said '*Laissez-faire!*'

"Now, I am not complaining of it. I consider the analytic work of the political economists of the last hundred years as invaluable. It forms the subject-matter for all future social science, and he who is ignorant of it builds on air. I only complain of their saying, 'You must not attempt to counteract these laws. You must allow chance and selfishness to rule the fortunes of the human race.' And this they do say.

"Now, as for any schemes of Maurice's or mine — it is a slight matter whether they have failed or not. But this I say, because I believe that the failure of a hundred schemes would not alter my conviction, that they are attempts in the right direction; and I shall die in hope, not having received the promises, but beholding them afar off, and confessing myself a stranger and a pilgrim in a world of *laissez-faire*. For it is my belief that not self-interest, but self-sacrifice, is the only law upon which human society can be grounded with any hope of prosperity and permanence. That self-interest is a law of nature I know well. That it ought to be the root law of human society I deny, unless society is to sink down again into a Roman empire, and a cage of wild beasts. . . . I shall resist it, as I do any other snare of the devil; for if I once believed it I must carry it out. I must give up all which I have learnt most precious concerning political freedom, all which keeps me content with the world, because I look forward to a nobler state of humanity; and I must become as thorough a despotist and imperialist as Strafford himself. . . . So I am content to have failed. I have learned in the experiment priceless truths concerning myself, my fellow-men, and the City of God, which is eternal in the heavens, for ever coming down among men, and actualizing itself more and more in every succeeding age. I see one work to be done ere I die, in which (men are beginning to discover) Nature must be counteracted, lest she prove a curse and a destroyer, not a blessing and a mother; and that is, Sanitary Reform. Politics and political economy may go their way for me. If I can help to save the lives of a few thousand working people and their children, I may earn the blessing of God."

. . . .

"Mind I am not dogmatizing," he says to the same friend. "I only know that I know nothing, but with a hope that Christ, who is the Son of Man, will tell me piecemeal, if I be patient and watchful, what I am, and what man is."

CHAPTER XVII

1858

AGED 39

EVERSLEY WORK — DIPHTHERIA — LECTURES AND SERMONS AT ALDERSHOT — BLESSING THE COLORS OF THE 22D REGIMENT — STAFF COLLEGE — ADVANCED THINKERS — LETTER FROM COLONEL STRANGE — ESAU AND JACOB — POEMS AND SANTA MAURA — BIRTH OF HIS SON GRENVILLE — SECOND VISIT TO YORKSHIRE — CORRESPONDENCE WITH MR. HULLAH ON SONGS — IN YORKSHIRE — GROUNDS OF FAITH — LETTERS ON MIRACLES TO SIR WILLIAM COPE — A HAPPY CHRISTMAS

"He was what he was, not by virtue of his office, but by virtue of what God had made him in himself. He was, we might almost say, a layman in the guise or disguise of a clergyman — fishing with the fishermen, hunting with the huntsmen, able to hold his own in tent and camp, with courtier or with soldier; an example that a genial companion may be a Christian gentleman — that a Christian clergyman need not be a member of a separate caste, and a stranger to the common interests of his countrymen. Yet, human genial layman as he was, he still was not the less — nay, he was ten times more — a pastor than he would have been had he shut himself out from the haunts and walks of men. He was sent by Providence, as it were, 'far off to the Gentiles' — far off, not to other lands or other races of mankind, but far off from the usual sphere of minister or priest, 'to fresh woods and pastures new,' to find fresh worlds of thoughts and wild tracts of character, in which he found a response to himself, because he gave a response to them."   A. P. STANLEY
(Funeral Sermon on Canon Kingsley).

"Yet he was courteous still to every wight,
And loved all that did to armes incline."
                                        SPENSER.

THIS was a year of severe work and anxiety, for he could not afford a curate, and diphtheria, then a new disease in England, had appeared and created a panic in the neighborhood. To him it was a new enemy to be hated, and fought against, as it was his wont to hate and fight against every form of disease, which arose, as he suspected this to do, from malaria, and other preventable causes. Its prevalence among children deeply affected and excited him, and he took counsel with medical men, as to how to meet it in its earliest symptoms. When it reached Eversley, some might have smiled at seeing him, going in and out of the cottages with great bottles of gargle under his arm, and teaching the people — men, women, and children — to gargle their throats, as a preventive; but he did it in terrible grim earnest, acting as he did on Thomas Carlyle's principle, " Wheresoever thou findest disorder, there is thy eternal enemy; attack him swiftly, subdue him, make order of him."

His work for the Hants and Wilts Education Society, to which he had bound himself to give so many lectures annually, in lieu of subscription, was heavy: he lectured on local Geology, on the Days of the Week, Eyes and No Eyes, on Jack of Newbury, and Flodden Field; in those, days seldom repeating the same lecture.

The position of Eversley with regard to Aldershot and Sandhurst, brought him more and more in contact with military men, and widened his sphere of influence. The society of soldiers as a class was congenial to him. " Next to my own farmers and laborers," he writes to a friend, " the officers of Aldershot and Sandhurst are the people for whom I feel and think and write." He inherited much of the soldier's spirit, as he inherited soldier blood; the few of his direct ancestors'

Sermons at Aldershot 79

portraits that have survived the wreck of his family, are all men in uniform, including Colonel Kingsley, who was in the battle of Naseby, and General Kingsley, Governor of Fort William, colonel of the 20th Regiment, who fought at Minden. He had himself, at one time, thought of the army as a profession, and had spent much time as a boy in drawing plans of fortifications; and even after he took holy orders it was a constant occupation to him, in all his walks and rides, to be planning fortifications. There is scarcely a hill-side within twenty miles of Eversley, the strong and weak points of which in attack and defence during a possible invasion, he has not gone over with as great an intensity of thought and interest as if the enemy were really at hand; and no soldier could have read and re-read Hannibal's campaigns, Creasy's Sixteen Decisive Battles, the records of Sir Charles Napier's Indian warfare, or Sir William's magnificent history of the Peninsular War, with keener appreciation, his poet's imagination enabling him to fill up the picture and realize the scene, where his knowledge of mere military detail failed. Hence the honor he esteemed it to be invited to preach to the troops at Aldershot, and to lecture to military men there and at Woolwich. His eyes would kindle and fill with tears as he recalled the impression made on him on Whitsunday, 1858, by the sound heard for the first time, and never to be forgotten, of the clank of the officers' swords and spurs, and the regular tramp of the men as they marched into church, stirring him like the sound of a trumpet. He lectured this year, too, to the troops in camp on Cortez. He camped out one summer's night with the

Guards on Cove Common. He blessed the new colors presented by Mrs. William Napier to her father's grand old regiment, the 22nd, and after the ceremony, went round the ranks, and was introduced by Mrs. Napier to many old veterans who had survived from the great Indian battles. That too was a red-letter day in his calendar, as he called it. His sermons at Aldershot brought many officers over to Eversley Church, and led to the formation of friendships which were very dear to him.

"I shall never," said Captain Congreve, "forget the genial, happy, unreserved intercourse of those Sunday afternoons, and I never strolled home to mess without feeling that I had come away wiser and better from the contact with that clear and kindly mind. He essentially loved men and manly pursuits, and perhaps liked soldiers, as being a class among whom manly feeling and manly virtues were cultivated. The Staff College was then in its infancy, and had perhaps gathered together a few of the best educated, hardest working, and most ambitious young men in the service. Mr. Kingsley was very soon a welcome and an honored guest at our mess. He entered into our studies, popularized our geology, and was an able critic on questions of military history. Not only that, however, — head work needs physical relaxation. He told us the best meets of the hounds, the nearest cut to the covers, the best trout streams, and the home of the largest pike. Many an hour have I spent pleasantly and profitably on the College lakes with him. Every fly that lit on the boat-side, every bit of weed that we fished up, every note of wood-bird, was suggestive of some pretty bit of information on the habits, and growth, and breeding of the thousand unnoticed forms of life around."

Advanced Thinkers

During the earlier years of the Staff College, Sandhurst, of which his valued friend General W. Napier was commandant, he was often invited over there. The following reminiscence from an officer will show that when at mess he never shrunk from showing his colors:

"We had among us one or two so-called 'advanced thinkers,' men who were inclined to ridicule religion somewhat. I remember once the conversation at mess took that direction, and Mr. Kingsley stopped it at once and for ever in the pleasantest, and at the same time most effectual manner, by pointing out how unmanly and ungenerous it was to endeavor to weaken a faith which was a trusted support to one's friends. He said 'it was impossible to use arguments of this kind without causing pain to some, and even if a man could hope to produce conviction, it could only be by taking from his convert much of the present joy of his life. Would any brave man desire to do that for the mere sake of a rhetorical triumph?' There was the regular little apology, 'Forgot for a moment that there was a clergyman at the table,' &c.

"'All right, never mind; but you must not apologize on that ground. We are paid to fight those arguments as you soldiers are to do another sort of fighting, and if a clergyman is worth his salt, you will always find him ready to try a fall with you. Besides, it is better for your friends, if they are to have the poison, to have the antidote in the same spoon.'"

A remarkable letter from Colonel Strange of the Royal Artillery, written from Quebec in 1876, explains Mr. Kingsley's influence from the soldier's point of view:

"My name," he says, "is not worthy to be linked with Mr. Kingsley's, except as a mere unit among the thousands of soldiers to whom he made Christianity possible, being one of them in spirit himself, perhaps the noblest. He invented no new Gospel, but showed them the real courage, the manliness of our Christ reflected somewhat in himself unconsciously. Is it necessary to explain to you that for ages the majority of soldiers had dimly tried to do their duty with the grim creed alone, that 'every bullet has its billet,' and after ——? The circumstances that made the Puritan soldiers died with them. The modern soldier had to choose between what, rightly or wrongly, seemed to them a Christ with all the manliness carefully eliminated, and a creed that culminated in sentimental revivals, that would not stand the rough usage of the camp, except in a few cases, and those happily were generally called away in all their genuine burning zeal before the cold shade of peaceful monotony had more severely tried a faith that fed on excitement. It is not hard to find a creed for a soldier to die with, it seems to me — at least I have seen Mahomet's answer well. A creed to live by is a very different thing. The only alternative to the beautiful evangelical Christianity of such happy soldiers as Hedley Vicars (Havelock was a Puritan out of his age), the extreme evangelical doctrine to which most men are constitutionally averse, was the slavish Roman, or what seemed an unpractical emasculate æsthetic imitation. The average soldier found no rest, no place in modern Christianity, until our apostle tore off the shreds and patches, with which for ages the Divine figure of the God-man had been obscured; He who found no such faith in Israel as that of the centurion. These are solemn themes, and I have handled them perhaps roughly, not from want of respect for the brave and good men who have lived and died in both extremes.

I would have learnt very little from Charles Kingsley if I had not learnt to respect both John Bunyan and Ignatius Loyola, the soldier priest! Feebly and foolishly perhaps I have tried to explain to you the reasons why soldiers had such sympathy with him who sympathized with them, and has given to thousands, I believe (for I have heard private soldiers speak of his books), the most priceless gift that man can bestow upon his brother. Long years ago in India, before I ever saw him, I wrote to thank him, anonymously, for what I and others of my comrades owed him. I think it would be just and useful if a few sermons and extracts from his works could be printed for soldiers' libraries. . . ."[1]

To a clergyman, who, in a review, had called him " a muscular Christian," Mr. Kingsley writes as follows:

October 19, 1858. — " DEAR SIR, — A common reviewer, however complimentary or abusive, would have elicited no answer from me; but in your notice of me, there is, over and above undeserved kind words, an evident earnestness to speak the truth and do good, which makes me write frankly to you. You have used that, to me, painful, if not offensive, term, 'Muscular Christianity.' My dear Sir, I know of no Christianity save one, which is the likeness of Christ, and the same for all men, viz., to be transformed into Christ's likeness, and to consecrate to His service, as far as may be, all the powers of body, soul, and spirit, regenerate and purified in His Spirit. All I wish to do is, to say to the strong and healthy man, even though he be not very learned, or wise, or even delicate-minded — in the æsthetic sense: 'You, too, can serve God with the

---

[1] To carry out Colonel Strange's wish, a small cheap volume was compiled by Mrs. Kingsley and published under the title of " True Words for Brave Men."

powers which He has given you. He will call you to account for them, just as much as He will call the parson, or the devout lady.'

"You seem to be of the same mind as some good-natured youth, who, in reviewing me the other day, said that I must never have known aught but good health, never had an ache in my life. As if one could know health, without having known sickness — or joy, without having known sorrow! . . . May God grant that you may never go through what I have done of sickness, weakness, misery, physical, mental, spiritual. You fancy that I cannot sympathize with the struggles of an earnest spirit fettered, tormented, crushed to the very earth by bodily weakness and sickness. If I did not, I were indeed a stupid and a bad man; for my life for fifteen years was nothing else but that struggle. But what if, when God gave to me suddenly and strangely health of body and peace of mind, I learnt what a priceless blessing that *corpus sanum* was, and how it helped — humiliating as the confession may be to spiritual pride — to the producing of *mentem sanam*? What if I felt bound to tell those who had enjoyed all their life that health which was new to me, what a debt they owed to God, how they must and how they might pay that debt? Whom have I wronged in so doing? What, too, if it has pleased God that I should have been born and bred and have lived ever since in the tents of Esau? What if — by no choice of my own — my relations and friends should have been the hunters and fighters? What if, during a weakly youth, I was forced to watch — for it was always before my eyes — Esau rejoicing in his strength, and casting away his birthright for a mess of pottage? What if, by long living with him, I have learnt to love him as my own soul, to understand him, his capabilities and weaknesses? Whom have I wronged therein? What if I said to myself, Jacob has a blessing, but Esau has one also, though his birthright be not his; and what blessing he has, he shall know of, that he may earn it? Jacob can do well enough without me. He has some 15,000 clergy, besides dissenting preachers, taking care of him (though he is pretty well able to take care of himself, and understands sharp practice as well as he did in his father Isaac's time), and telling him that he is the only ideal; and that Esau is a poor, profane blackguard, only fit to have his blood poured out like water on Crimean battle-fields, while Jacob sits comfortably at home, making money, and listening to those who preach smooth things to him? And what if, when I tried, I found that Esau would listen to me; that he had a heart as well as Jacob; that he would come to hear me preach, would ask my advice, would tell me his sorrows, would talk to me about his mother, and what he had learnt at his mother's knee, because he felt that I was at least one of like passions as himself, who had been tempted on all points like as he was, *and with many sins?* What if he told me at the same time that he could not listen to Jacob's private chaplains; that he did not understand them, nor they him; that he looked on them with alternate fear and contempt? If I said to myself more and more clearly as the years rolled on, I will live for Esau and with Esau; — if I be called a gluttonous man and a wine-bibber, the friend of publicans and sinners, there is One above me who was called the same, and to Him I commit myself and my work; — it is enough for me that He knows my purpose, and that on Crimean battle-fields and Indian marches, poor Esau has died with a clearer conscience and a lighter heart for the words which I have spoken to him. If I have said this, whom have I wronged? I have no grudge against Jacob and his preachers; only when I read the 17th verse of the 3rd chapter of Revelations, I tremble for him, and for England, knowing well that on Jacob depends the well-being of England, whether physical, intellectual, or spiritual, and that my poor Esau is at best food for powder. God help him!

"But surely there is room in God's kingdom for him, and for one parson; though, thank God, there is more than one who will teach him what God requires of him. Therefore my mind is made up. As long as Esau comes to me as to a friend; and as long as Esau's mother comes to me to save her child from his own passions and appetites — would God that I could do it! — so long shall I labor at that which, if I cannot do it well, seems to me the only thing which I can do. . . ."

He published his poems this year "in exceeding fear only after long solicitations," he says, "and I am more dissatisfied with them than any critic can be." Among them was "Santa Maura" — a story little known, which affected some readers deeply. It led to his first acquaintance with Dr. Monsell, vicar of Egham, who wrote to express his gratitude for its teaching to himself, and his wish to have it printed separately:

"As a tract to be slipt into the hands of the suffering. . . . It would strengthen and brace up to high endeavors and endurings many who now little dream of what real endurance for the love of Christ means. . . . What it has done for me I am sure it will do for thousands, and therefore I have ventured to tell you how God has blessed it to me. . . ."

Mr. Kingsley's answer is characteristic:

". . . Would to God that I could *be* the persons that I can conceive. If you wish to pray against a burden and temptation, pray against that awful gift (for it is

Santa Maura 87

a purely involuntary gift) of imagination, which alternately flatters and torments its possessor, — flatters him by making him fancy that he possesses the virtues which he can imagine in others; torments him, because it makes him feel in himself a capacity for every imaginable form of vice. Yet if it be a gift of God's (and it cannot be a gift of the devil's) it must bring some good, and perhaps the good is the capacity for sympathy with blackguards, 'publicans and sinners,' as we now euphemize them in sermons, trying, as usual, to avoid the tremendous meaning of the words by borrowing from an old English translation. To see into the inner life of these; to know their disease, not from books, but from inward and scientific anatomy, imagination may help a man. If it does that for me I shall not regret it; though it is, selfishly speaking, the most humiliating and tormenting of all talents."

To REV. F. D. MAURICE. — "I am delighted that you are satisfied with 'St. Maura.' Nothing which I ever wrote came so out of the depths of my soul as that, or caused me during writing (it was all done in a day and a night), a poetic fervor such as I never felt before or since. It seemed to me a sort of inspiration which I could not resist; and the way to do it came before me clearly and instantly, as nothing else ever has done — to embody the highest spiritual nobleness in the greatest possible simplicity of a young village girl, and exhibit the martyr element, not only free from that celibate element which is so jumbled up with it in the old myths, but brought out and brightened by marriage love. That story, as it stands in the Acta SS., has always been my *experimentum crucis* of the false connection between martyrdom and celibacy. But enough of this selfish prosing. . . . I have said my say for the time. Now I want to sit down and become a learner, not a teacher, for I am chiefly impressed with my own profound ignorance and hasty assumption on every possible subject. . . ."

To B. LEWIS, ESQ. — " As for the *human* element in 'Santa Maura,' it seems to me that wherever human beings are concerned, there cannot well help being a human element, if folks have eyes to see it, which the martyrologists certainly had not, and, indeed, refused to have. It stirs a sad smile in me, that in the nineteenth century, after Christian men had been believing in the Incarnation, they should be welcoming the human element in the stories of their own heroes, as a new thought — but with a certain fear and distrust — as if, however pleasant and interesting to find Santa Maura, or Saint Any-one-else, a human being, it was n't quite right and proper. Excuse me, dear sir, I 'm not laughing at *you;* but at the world in general. Your feeling is that, I suppose, of most pious people : only more kindly expressed. Verily, it is 'a mad world, my masters.' "

To J. LUDLOW, ESQ. — " You are not wise in rating my work high. I feel in myself a deficiency of discursive fancy. . . . I know I can put into singing words the plain things I see and feel ; but all that faculty which Alexander Smith has (and nothing else) — and which Shakespeare had more than any man — the power of metaphor and analogue — the intuitive vision of connections between all things in heaven and earth, which poets *must* have, is very weak in me ; and therefore I shall never be a great poet. And what matter? I will do what I can ; but I believe you are quite right in saying that my poetry is all of me which will last. Except, perhaps, ' Hypatia.' I don't know how to thank you for your review. Cordiality is very comfortable, while one is sickened by the futilities of critics. Every one flatly contradicting the other, both when praising and when blaming ! I never saw till now how worthless opinions

Our Song

of the press are. For if A, B, C, D, flatly contradict each other, one or more must be wrong, eh? And which is the one to believe? For instance, A says I finish carefully, and of art prepense, but want instinctive musical ear. B, that I have natural melody, but am slovenly, and so on. What is to be learned from such criticism? Yet I would gladly take a hint from any man. I long for a guide; but where is there one?"

To JOHN HULLAH, ESQ. — "I only heard your 'Three Fishers' sung a few weeks ago, and was much delighted. It was the only setting which I have heard which at all rendered what I wanted to say, and entered into the real feeling of the words. And there seemed to me in it much true music, simple, noble, and original. . . . I feel more and more inclined to suspect that they [the Poems] are what I can do best, and that I am only likely to get myself into the wars by meddling with politics and lofty matters, only to be handled by Disraelis and Clanricardes. . . . Do as you like about 'The Last Buccaneer.' You have made it rollicking, you say. My idea of the music, as I wrote it, was a doleful sentimental bawl, as of a wooden-legged sailor. I hardly think a rollicking tune suits the worn-out old man, unless you fancy him a thorough blackguard, which I did n't want; I tried to give a human feeling all through, by a touch of poetry and sadness in the poor old ruffian. Had I been a composer I should have tried to express this, and with a half-comic manner. How to do that in poetry I know. Of music I know nought. . . . Boucan signified, if I recollect right, a wooden stage, which the mahogany cutters put up round one of the giant swamp mahoganies when they were about to fell it. Moreover, it meant a stage on which they and the logwood cutters and bull-hunters slept. Moreover, one on which they dried the strips of beef, on which they lived like beasts of prey, and were so called boucaniers, or what you will . . . I am much pleased to hear of the success of the song, 'Oh! that we two were Maying.' But I take no share of the credit. Words are nought without music and singing. . . . I have not been at a concert this ten years: seldom in London, and then always over-busy, and getting 'no amusement' there. My amusement is green fields and clear trout streams, and the gallop through the winter fir-woods; and perhaps this free healthy life makes my little lark's pipe all the fresher and clearer when it tries a song."

His youngest son, Grenville Arthur, for whom, in course of time, "The Water-Babies" and "Madam How" were written, was born this spring, and named after his godfather, Dean Stanley, and Sir Richard Grenville, one of the heroes of "Westward Ho!" from whom Mrs. Kingsley's family claimed descent.

A few days' fishing at Newbury produced the "Chalk Streams Studies" (Prose Idylls) and in the summer a new novel was projected,[1] on the Pilgrimage of Grace, which made it necessary for him to go into Yorkshire for a week to identify places and names. From the house of his kind friend, Mr. W. E. Forster, he writes:

TO HIS WIFE. WHARFSIDE, *July*, 1858. — "At a most delicious place, and enjoying good society and a good library. . . . Tell the children I have just seen oh! I don't know what I hav' n't seen — the largest waterwheel in England, making light summer overcoats for the Yankees and Germans. I am in a state of bewilderment — such machinery as no tongue can describe, about three acres of mills and a whole village of people,

[1] It was only roughly sketched out; but the press of other work prevented his taking it up seriously. (M. K.)

looking healthy, rosy, and happy; such a charming half-time school for the children, library for the men, &c. Tell R. I saw the wool as it came off the sheep's back in Leicestershire, followed it till it was turned into an 'alpaca' coat, and I don't care to see conjuring or magic after that. The country is glorious. . . ."

"We had a delightful day at Bolton yesterday, and saw the Abbey. Tell R. I jumped over the Strid where young Romilly was drowned. Make her learn Wordsworth's ballad on it, 'What is Good for a Bootless Bene?' We go off to-morrow for a walking excursion into the High Craven. This is the most noble and beautiful of counties. I have got such flowers!"

"All that I have heard of the grandeur of Godale Scar and Malham Cove was, I found, not exaggerated. The awful cliff filling up the valley with a sheer cross wall of 280 feet, and from beneath a black lip at the foot, the whole river Air coming up, clear as crystal, from unknown abysses. Its real source is, I suppose, in the great lake above, Malham Tarn, on which I am going to-morrow. Last night we went up Ingleborough, 2380, and saw the whole world to the west, the lake mountains, and the western sea beyond Lancaster and Morecambe Bay for miles. The people are the finest I ever saw — tall, noble, laconic, often very handsome. Very musical too, the women with the sweetest voices in speech which I have ever heard. . . . Thanks for the dear letters. What you say about subjectivity being so delicious is so womanly; *you* ought to feel that, and I perhaps ought to feel, as I do, the value of the outward world; and so you can help me, and I you, and both together make one humanity. . . . I long to be back. I feel restless and reckless away from home, and all the more because I have no time for 'subjectivity.' My days are spent in taking in *facts*, and plenty of them I have got. The book grows on me. I see my way now as clear as day.

How I will write when I get home. Love to R., M., and Baby."

To MR. C. K. PAUL. — "Will you thank Mrs. * * * most heartily for all she has found out for me. . . . But let her understand — if it be any comfort to her — that I shall in this book do the northern Catholics ample justice; that Robert and Christopher Aske, both good Romanists, are my heroes, and Robert the Rebel my special hero. I can't withdraw what I said in 'Westward Ho!' because it is true. Romanism under the Jesuits became a different thing from what it had been before. Of course Mrs. * * * does not know that, and why should she? But I fear she will be as angry as ever, though really she is most merciful and liberal, at my treatment of the monks. I love the old Catholic Laity: I did full justice to their behavior at the Armada juncture; but I know too much of those shavelings, and the worst is, *I* know, as Wolsey knew, and every one knew, things one dare n't tell the world, much less a woman. So judgment must go by default, as I cannot plead, for decency's sake. Still, tell her that had I been born and bred a Yorkshire Catholic, I should probably — unless I had been a coward — have fought the last drop at Robert Aske's side. But this philosophy only gives one a habit of feeling for every one, without feeling with them, and I can now love Robert Aske, though I think him as wrong as man can be, who is a good man and true."

To J. BULLAR, ESQ. — "If I believed what you say, about 'not setting up our reason as the test by which we will try God's government of the world,' I should be much frightened; for I should find myself beginning to disbelieve in the Bible and in Christianity. I don't want to set up my private reasoning, or to say, nothing is

Grounds of Faith 93

true but what I can find arguments for — No man less. I cannot even study physical science without finding insoluble puzzles at every step. But by Reason (in the highest sense), by that moral sense common to all men, I must try God's dealings, because — 1. I cannot otherwise love, or trust God, or even imagine to myself His goodness. 2. Because He bids me do so, in the Bible more and more as the Gospel develops, and in the New Testament appeals entirely by Christ to that moral sense in man. The doctrine of Christ and His apostles is, that man is made in God's likeness, and that therefore man's goodness, justice, love, are patterns of God's, and mirrors in which he may see what his heavenly Father is like. The doctrine of Christ and His apostles is, that Christ's incarnation proves this. That Christ manifested the Father, and showed to men the exact likeness of God's character, not by being a good angel, or good anything else, save a good man. And, therefore, when you impute to God feelings or acts which would be inhuman in any and every sense in you or me, you deny the meaning of our Lord's incarnation.

"I know the Calvinists do not hold this, any more than the Papists. And I know that they have great excuses for the belief, great excuses for taking shelter (as you seem inclined to do, as I long to do and dare not) behind what Fourier calls *les voiles d'airain*, and making the truth that God's 'ways are not as our ways' an excuse for imputing to God ways of which we should be ashamed. But I know, too, that this doctrine has deeply immoral consequences. That it has emboldened men who really wished to be good themselves, to impute to God pride, and vanity, selfishness, obstinacy, spite, cruelty, deceitfulness. The God of Calvin, the God in whom Augustine learnt to believe in his old age, is a being who inspires me with no love — with anything but love. If I discovered that He were indeed ruler of this world, and of mankind, then I should hope — I dare not trust — that I should have faith enough in the everlasting right to prophesy, with Prometheus on his rock, the downfall of the unjust Zeus.

"I have staked all my belief on this, Bullar. If I have to give it up, I must begin to reconsider every phenomena in man, heaven, and earth; and the only escape which I as yet foresee would be into the Ahriman and Ormuzd creed of the old Zend-a-vesta. I know well that God's ways are not as our ways, or any man's; but how? Because, I believe and trust, God fulfils the very ideal which I know I ought to fulfil, and do not. What use in my trying to give up my own ways, and go to God's ways, if God's ways be ways I cannot go, and more, ought not to go, and should be wicked if I were like God? Strange paradox!

"The God and the Christ whom the Bible reveal to me, I love, I glory in. I am jealous for their honor, and though I obey them not, yet I can bear to love the thought that they are right, though I be wrong; they beautiful and noble, though I be ugly and mean, and therefore I am jealous for them. Any fact which seems to reflect on their honor, tortures me. . . ."

TO SIR WILLIAM COPE

EVERSLEY RECTORY: *December* 19, 1858. — "I cannot find, by index, the passage which your friend quotes from St. Augustine, '*Sermones ad Fratres in Eremo,*' the 37th, &c., &c. But I do find, as I thought I should, the curious and valuable chapter ('*De Civitate Dei,*' *Lib. XVI., Cap.* 8) in which he discusses the question of Sciapods, Monopods, Monoculi, Androgynæ, and other monsters, and concludes, philosophically enough, that one is not bound to believe that they exist, and that if they do exist, it is not proven that they are men. The only monsters similar to the 'men whose heads do grow beneath their shoulders,' of Shakespeare, which he mentions there, are the Cynocephali, which he boldly says are animals, and no doubt he is right, the Cynocephalus being nothing but the great gregarious baboon of Africa. He speaks as having seen them, and doubtless had. I have run my eye over the miracles which he mentions as having occurred under his own eyes. . . . I find but three. . . . That he saw and believed these three there can be no doubt. The other stories which he tells rest on the same evidence as most other post-scriptural ones. God forbid that I should deny them. How can I limit the wonders of grace, who find daily the wonders of nature beyond my comprehension or expectation? Only, knowing from mediæval records, and still more from the stories of the Indian massacres (which, as fields for judging of evidence, I have looked into somewhat closely), how very difficult it is to get at truth, when people have once made up their minds what they would like to be true; knowing this, I say, I think one may, without irreverence, preserve a '*stoic epoché*' on the matter, reserving one's judgment for more light, and meanwhile neither affirming nor denying."

Christmas Eve, 1858. — "The Frobenius edition of 'St. Augustine,' which I have, says that *all* the '*Ep. ad Fratres in Eremo*' are spurious. . . . The style is utterly unlike Augustine's, and in places very weak, which *he* never is. I am glad to find them spurious, for on receiving your second letter, I said to myself thus — perhaps too much after the fashion of a German critic — *I will not believe* that the man who wrote the chapter on Monsters in the 'City of God,' ever wrote the passage * * * attributes to him. I know from reason that passage to be a *direct lie*. I will not believe that Augustine ever told one. . . . But the part of your letter which deserves a long answer, longer than I can give, is what you say about natural science and Buckland. It is exceedingly comfortable to me, who knew nothing of him, as proving him to have been the wise man I always believed him. As for the fact — my doctrine has been for years, if I may speak of myself — that *'omnia exeunt in mysterium'* (a saying, I think, attributed to Augustine); that below all natural phenomena, we come to a transcendental — in plain English, a miraculous ground. I argued this once with Professor H., who supported the materialist view, and is a consummate philosopher; and I did not find that he shook me in the least. This belief was first forced on me by investigating the generation of certain polypes of a very low order. I found absolute Divine miracle at the bottom of all; and no *cause*, save that of a supremely *imaginative* (if I may so speak), as well as Almighty mind, carrying out its own ideas; but gravitation, or the simplest law, will show the same truth. What *efficient cause* is there that all matter should attract matter? The only answer is, that God has so willed; and if we come to *final* causes, there is no better answer than the old mystic one, that God has imprest the Law of *Love*, which is the law of His own being, on matter, that it may be a type of the spiritual world when healthy, and of the kingdom of heaven. I am deeply touched by what you say as to the miracles of grace. It is all true, and most necessary to be preached now — to me as well as to others; for one is apt to forget grace in nature, the unseen in the seen. As you say, — after the crowning miracle of this most blessed night, all miracles are possible. The miracle of this night was possible because God's love was absolute, infinite, unconquerable, able to condescend to anything, that good might be done; and who (who calls himself a true philosopher) dare limit that Love and power by any Laws of Time? Miracles, in the vulgar acceptation of the term, may have ceased. But only for a time. I

A Happy Christmas

cannot but believe that, should there come once more in the Church's history, a '*dignus Deo vindice nodus*,' we should have miracles once more, and find them, not arbitrary infractions, but the highest development of that will of God whose lowest manifestations we call the Laws of Nature, though really they are no Laws of Nature, but merely customs of God; which He can alter as and when He will.

"Excuse my thus running on. But this Christmas night is the one of all the year which sets a physicist, as I am, on facing the fact of miracle; and which delivers him from the bonds of sense and custom, by reminding him of God made man. That you and I and all belonging to us may reap the full benefit o that arch-miracle is my prayer. What better one can I have?"

On New Year's Eve he writes to Mr. Maurice:

"We have had a most blessed Christmas. F. well enough to enjoy our Christmas parish party, and work in the garden again; and your godson come home with an admirable character and two prizes. My cup runs over. God grant that I may *not throw it over*, as I expect surely to do some day, by my own laziness, thankless-ness, and self-indulgence."

CHAPTER XVIII

1859

AGED 40

SANITARY WORK — FIRST SERMON AT BUCKINGHAM PALACE — QUEEN'S CHAPLAINCY — FIRST VISIT TO WINDSOR — LETTER TO AN ATHEIST—TO ARTISTS—CHARLES BENNETT, FREDERICK SHIELDS — LADIES' SANITARY ASSOCIATION — EXHAUSTED BRAIN — POLLUTION OF RIVERS — THE ETERNITY OF MARRIAGE.

" What would become of mankind if the arena where must be fought out the great battle of right against wrong should be deserted by the champions of the good cause with — disguise it as we may — the selfish motive of rendering easier to their souls the struggle which all earnest men must wage to the end against their own infirmities ? Rather did he emulate the heroism of those who, throwing themselves into the press of human affairs, strike with all their might, and to their last hour, against ignorance, folly, oppression, and are able to say with Sir Galahad:

'So pass I hostel, hall, and grange,
By bridge and ford, by park and pale;
All armed I ride, whate'er betide,
Until I find the holy grail.'

And those who thus fight on to the end, content to die in their harness, and in the ranks of the faithful, will also be enabled to say with the pure knight:

'And stricken by an angel's hand
This mortal armor that I wear,
This weight and size, this form and eyes,
Are touched, are turned, to finest air.' "

LIFE OF SIR WILLIAM NAPIER.

AS years went on he devoted time, thought, and influence more and more to sanitary science; the laws of health, the deliverance of men's bodies and homes from disease and dirt,

Sanitary Work 99

and their inevitable consequences of drunkenness, sin, and misery, physical and spiritual, became more important in his eyes than any Political reforms.

"I am going to throw myself into this movement," he writes to a lady who had established a convalescent home for children. "I am tired of most things in the world. Of sanitary reform I shall never grow tired. No one can accuse a man of being sentimental over it, or of doing too much in it. There can be no mistake about the saving of human lives, and the training up a healthy generation. God bless you and all good ladies who have discovered that human beings have bodies as well as souls and that the state of the soul too often depends on that of the body."

To J. B. Esq.]—"I see more and more that we shall work no deliverance till we teach people a little more common physical knowledge, and I hail the Prince's noble speech at Aberdeen as a sign that he sees his way clearly and deeply. I have refused this winter to lecture on anything but the laws of health; and shall try henceforth to teach a sound theology through physics."

This year, 1859, was an altogether important one to him. On Palm Sunday he preached for the first time before the Queen and the Prince Consort at Buckingham Palace, and was shortly afterwards made one of Her Majesty's chaplains in ordinary. He now took his turn as preacher at the Chapels Royal, St. James's and Whitehall, and once a year before the Queen in the private chapel at Windsor. In the autumn he was presented to the Queen and the Prince Consort, and to the Crown Prince and Princess of Prussia, then staying at Windsor, and from that hour to his dying day he received marks of royal kindness and condescension, the memory of which will be an heirloom to his children. To a man of his fine imagination and deep loyalty, who had sounded the depths of society, and whose increasing popularity as an author, and power as a preacher, had given him a large acquaintance with all ranks, this new phase in his life seemed to come just to complete the cycle of his experiences. But while its result was, in a certain sense, to establish his position and enlarge his influence, on his own character it had a humbling rather than exalting effect. From this time there was a marked difference in the tone of the public press, religious and otherwise, towards him; and though he still waged war as heretofore against bigotry, ignorance, and intolerance, and was himself unchanged, the attacks on him from outside were less frequent. The events of the year, uninteresting to the outer world, but each important in giving color to his own daily life and leaving its mark on his heart and imagination, are soon told. He sent his eldest son to Wellington College, which had opened in the winter, and where the scheme of education, owing to the wise influence of the Prince Consort, was more consonant to his own views for his son (being of a wider and more modern character) than that of the older and more venerable public schools. He was present at the marriage of his friend Max Müller and a beloved niece.[1] His acquaintance with

[1] The G. to whom the lines were written beginning:
"A hasty jest I once let fall,
As jests are wont to be, untrue." — To G., "Poems."

To an Atheist

Lord Cranworth and with Lord Carnarvon, which soon deepened into attachment, was made this year. Dean Stanley paid his first visit to Eversley. In the autumn he and his wife spent a few days with Mr. and Mrs. Tennyson in the Isle of Wight, but having no curate, his holiday was short, and more than once this year he broke down from overwork. He shrunk from the bustle of London, refused all sermons there, and withdrew from politics. Notwithstanding fair prospects and outward distinction, he clung more and more passionately to his country home — the "far off look," the longing for rest and reality, and for the unfolding of the mystery of life, grew stronger upon him, and, though always bright and cheerful with his children, he said more frequently to his wife, "How blessed it will be when it is all over to lie down in that dear churchyard together!"

"I have not been to town," he writes, "for more than two days in the last nine months. I see no chance of preaching there, I am happy to say, for a long time, save next Sunday, when I preach to the Queen. As for politics, I heed them not."

. . . .

To T. HUGHES, ESQ., *June* 12*th*. — "This is my fortieth birthday. What a long life I have lived! and silly fellows that review me say that I can never have known ill-health or sorrow. I have known enough to make me feel very old — happy as I am now; and I am very happy. . . ."

Among his many correspondents was the editor of an Atheist newspaper in a northern manufacturing town, an intelligent artisan, who told him of the interest with which he and men of his class had read aloud "Alton Locke," "Yeast," and "Hypatia," on Sunday evenings. "Such perusal," he added, "makes us better men," to which Mr. Kingsley replied:

"MY DEAR SIR, — I should have answered so frank and manly a letter before, but my father's sudden illness called me away from home. I hope that you and your friends will not always remain Atheists. . . . It is a barren, heartless, hopeless creed, as a creed — though a man may live long in it without being heartless or hopeless himself. Still, he will never be the man he ought to have been; and therefore it is bad for him and not good. But what I want to say to you is this, and I do want to say it. Whatever doubt or doctrinal Atheism you and your friends may have, don't fall into moral Atheism. Don't forget the Eternal Goodness, whatever name you may call it. *I call it God.* Or if you even deny an Eternal Goodness, don't forget or neglect such goodness as you find in yourselves — not an honest — a manly, a loving, a generous, a patient feeling. For your own sakes, if not for God's sake, keep alive in you the sense of what is, and you know to be, good, noble, and beautiful. I don't mean beautiful in 'art,' but beautiful in morals. If you will keep that moral sense — that sense of the beauty of goodness, and of man's absolute duty to be good, then all will be as God wills, and all will come right at last. But if you lose that — if you begin to say, 'Why should not I be quarrelsome and revengeful? why should I not be conceited and insolent? why should I not be selfish and grasping?' then you will be Atheists indeed, and what to say to you I shall not know. But from your letter, and from the very look of your hand-writing, I augur better things; and even hope that you will not think me impertinent if I send you a volume of my own

To Atheists

Sermons to think over manfully and fairly. It seems to me (but I may flatter myself) that you cannot like, as you say you do, my books, and yet be what I call moral Atheists. Mind, if there is anything in this letter which offends you, don't take fire, but write and ask me (if you think it worth while) what I mean. In looking it through I see several things which (owing to the perversion of religious phrases in these days) you may misunderstand, and take your friend for your foe.

"At all events, I am, yours faithfully,
"CHARLES KINGSLEY."

Artists now often consulted him, and among them the late Charles Henry Bennett, a man full of genius, then on the staff of "Punch." Finding he was in need, and had a difficulty in getting a publisher for his Illustrated Pilgrim's Progress, Mr. Kingsley wrote and gave him a preface for it, upon which Messrs. Longmans accepted it.

To C. H. BENNETT, ESQ. — ". . . I feel as deeply as you our want of a fitting illustration of the great Puritan Epic, and agree in every word which you say about past attempts. Your own plan is certainly the right one, only in trying for imaginative freedom, do not lose sight of beauty of form. I am, in taste, a strong classicist, contrary to the reigning school of Ruskin, Pugin, and the pre-Raphaelites, and wait quietly for the world to come round to me again. But it is perfectly possible to combine Greek health and accuracy of form with German freedom of imagination, even with German grotesqueness. I say Greek and German (*i.e.*, fifteenth and sixteenth century German) because those two are the only two root-schools in the world. I know no such combination of both as in Kaulbach. His illustrations of Reinecke Fuchs are in my eyes the finest designs (save those of three or four great Italians of the sixteenth century), which the world has ever seen. Any man desiring to do an enduring work must study, copy, and surpass them.

"Now in Bunyan, there is a strong German (Albert Dürer) element which you must express, viz., 1st, a tendency to the grotesque in imagination; 2nd, a tendency to spiritual portraiture of the highest kind, in which an ideal character is brought out, not by abstracting all individual traits (the Academy plan), but by throwing in strong individual traits drawn from common life. This, indeed, has been the manner of the highest masters, both in poetry and painting, *e. g.*, Shakespeare and Dante; and the portraits, and even heroic figures of Leonardo, Raphael, Michael Angelo, Sebastian del Piombo, Bronzino, the two latter with Titian the triumvirate of portrait-painting. You find the same in Correggio. He never idealizes, *i. e.*, abstracts in a portrait, seldom in any place. You would know the glorious 'Venus' of the National Gallery if you met her in the street. So this element you have a full right to employ. But there is another, of which Bunyan, as a Puritan tinker, was not conscious, though he had it in his heart, that is, classic grace and purity of form. He had it in his heart, as much as Spenser. His women, his Mr. Greatheart, his Faithful, his shepherds, can only be truly represented in a lofty and delicate outline, otherwise the ideal beauty which lifts them into a supernatural and eternal world is lost, and they become mere good folks of the seventeenth century. Some illustrators, feeling this, have tried to mediævalize them. Silly fellows! What has Bunyan to do with the Middle Age? He writes for all ages, he is full of an eternal humanity, and that eternal humanity can only be represented by something of the eternal form which you find in Greek statues. I don't mean that you are to Grecianize their dress, any more than mediævalize it. No. And here comes an important question.

"Truly to illustrate a poem, you must put the visions on paper as they appeared to the mind of the seer himself. Now we know that Bunyan saw these people in his mind's eye, as dressed in the garb of his own century. It is very graceful, and I should keep to it, not only for historic truth's sake, but because in no other way can you express Bunyan's leading idea, that the same supernatural world which was close to old prophets and martyrs was close to him; that the devil who whispered in the ears of Judas, whispered in the ears of a cavalier over his dice, or a Presbyterian minister in his Geneva gown. Take these hints as meant, kindly."

Another artist, Mr. F. Shields, of Manchester, who consulted him on the same subject, speaks of —

"his helpful words — how helpful to me at the period I could be eloquent in telling, since they were the first words of kindly help which fell to my lot from one whose sympathy I prized, and who could, when in ill health, write so large an answer to the inquiries of a stranger. . . ."

To apply to himself Mr. Kingsley's own words in speaking of Mr. Maurice's work, one may say that —

"It was his humility and self-distrust, combined so strangely with manful strength and sternness, which drew to him humble souls, self-distrustful souls, who, like him, were full of the 'Divine discontent' — who lived as perhaps all men should live — angry with themselves, ashamed of themselves, and more and more angry and ashamed as their own ideal grew, and with it their own consciousness of defection from that ideal."

To F. SHIELDS, ESQ. — " . . . I think that you much overrate the disuse of armor in Bunyan's day. When the 'Pilgrim's Progress' was written it was much gone out, but in Bunyan's boyhood he must have seen everywhere old armor hanging up in every gentleman or burgher's house (he would to his dying day, but) which had been worn and used by the generation before him. Allowing, as we must, in every human being for the reverence for early impressions, I think his mind would have pictured to him simply the Elizabethan and James I.'s armor, which he saw hanging in all noble houses, and in which he may have, as a boy, seen gentlemen joust, for tilting was not extinct in his boyhood. As for this co-existing with slop breeches (what we now call knickerbockers are nothing else), I think you will find, as now, that country fashions changed slower than town. The puffed trunk-hose of 1580-1600 co-existed with the finest cap-à-pie armor of proof. They gradually in the country, where they were ill made, became slops, *i. e.*, knickerbockers. By that time almost loose and short cavalier breeks had superseded them in the court — but what matter? The change is far less than that during 1815-1855. The anachronism of putting complete armor by the side of one drest as Christian is in the frontispiece of the original edition of the 'P. P.' is far less than putting you by the side of a Life-Guards' officer in 1855; far less, again, than putting a clod of my parish, drest as he would have been in A.D. 1100, in smock frock and leather gaiters, by the side of you or me. Therefore use without fear the beautiful armor of the later years of Elizabeth and the beginning of James I., and all will be right, and shock nobody. As for shields, I should use the same time. Shields were common among serving-men in James I. There are several in the Tower, fitted with a pistol to be fired from the inside, and a long spike. All are round. I

Frederick Shields 107

believe that 'sword and buckler play' was a common thing among the country folk in Bunyan's time. Give your man, therefore, a circular shield, such as he would have seen in his boyhood, or even later, among the retainers of noble houses. As for the cruelties practised on Faithful, — for the sake of humanity don't talk of that. The Puritans were very cruel in the North American colonies; horribly cruel, though nowhere else. But in Bunyan's time the pages of Morland, and others, show us that in Piedmont, not to mention the Thirty Years' War in Germany, horrors were being transacted which no pen can describe nor pencil draw. Dear old Oliver Cromwell stopped them in Piedmont, when he told the Pope that unless they were stopped English cannon should be heard at the gates of the Vatican. But no cruelty to man or woman that you dare draw can equal what was going on on the Continent from Papist to Protestant during Bunyan's lifetime. I have now told you all I can. I am very unwell, and forbid to work . . . but what I send I send with all good wishes to any man who will be true to art and to his author."

" . . . God has given you a great talent, whereby you may get an honest livelihood. Take *that* as God's call to you, and follow it out. As for the sins of youth, what says the 130th Psalm? 'If Thou, Lord, were extreme to mark what is done amiss, who could abide it?' But there is mercy with Him, therefore shall He be feared. And how to fear God I know not better than by working on at the speciality which He has given us, trusting to Him to make it of use to His creatures — if He needs us — and if He does not, perhaps so much the better for us. He can do His work without our help. Therefore fret not nor be of doubtful mind. But just do the duty which lies nearest — which seems to me to be to draw as you are drawing now."

In July he spoke at the first meeting of the Ladies' Sanitary Association, which he characterized as —

"One of the noblest, most right-minded, straightforward, and practical conceptions that he had come across for some years. . . . If ladies believe with me," he says, " that the most precious thing in the world is a human being, that the lowest, and poorest, and most degraded of human beings is better than all the dumb animals in the world; that there is an infinite, priceless capability in that creature, degraded as it may be — a capability of virtue, and of social and industrial use, which, if it is taken in time, may be developed up to a pitch, of which, at first sight the child gives no hint whatsoever. . . . Then, perhaps, they may think with me that it is a duty, one of the noblest of duties, to see that every child that is born into this great nation of England be developed to the highest pitch to which we can develop him, in physical strength and in beauty, as well as in intellect and in virtue.

" . . . Sanitary Reform, as it is called, or, in plain English, the art of health, is so very recent a discovery, as all true physical science is, that we ourselves and our own class know very little about it, and practise it very ill. And this Society, I do hope, will bear in mind that it is not simply to affect the working man, not only to go into the foul alley; but it is to go to the door of the farmer, to the door of the shopkeeper, ay, to the door of ladies and gentlemen of the same rank as ourselves. Women can do in that work what men cannot do. Private correspondence, private conversation, private example, may do what no legislation can do. I am struck more and more with the amount of disease and death I see around me in all classes, which no sanitary legislation whatsoever could touch, unless you had a complete house-to-house visitation of a government officer, with powers to enter every house, to drain and ventilate it, and not only do that, but to regulate the clothes and the diet of every inhabitant, and that among all ranks. I can conceive of nothing short of that, which would be absurd and impossible and most harmful, that would stop the present amount of disease and death, without some such private exertion on the part of women, above all of mothers, as I do hope will spring from this Institution. . . .

". . . Oh! it is a distressing thing to see children die. God gives the most beautiful and precious thing that earth can have, and we just take it and cast it away; we cast our pearls upon the dunghill, and leave them. A dying child is to me one of the most dreadful sights in the world. A dying man, a man dying on the field of battle, that is a small sight; he has taken his chance; he has had his excitement, he has had his glory, if that will be any consolation to him; if he is a wise man, he has the feeling that he is doing his duty by his country, and by his Queen. It does not horrify or shock me to see a man dying in a good old age. . . . But it does shock me, it does make me feel that the world is indeed out of joint, to see a child die.' I believe it to be a priceless boon to the child to have lived for a week, or a day. . . .

. . . .

". . . We talk of the loss of human life in war. We are the fools of smoke and noise; because there are cannon-balls and gunpowder, and red coats, and because it costs a great deal of money, and makes a great deal of noise in the papers, we think — What so terrible as war? I will tell you what is ten times, and ten thousand times, more terrible than war, and that is — outraged Nature. . . . Nature, insidious, inexpensive, silent, sends no roar of cannon, no glitter of arms to do her work; she gives no warning note of preparation; she has no protocol, nor any diplomatic advances, whereby she warns her enemy that war is coming. . . . By the very same laws by which every blade of grass grows, and every insect springs to life in the sunbeam, she kills, and kills, and kills, and is never tired of killing, till she has taught man the terrible lesson he is so slow to learn, that Nature is only conquered by obeying her. Man has his courtesies of war, and his chivalries of war: he does not strike the unarmed man; he spares the woman and the child. But Nature is fierce when she is offended, as she is bounteous and kind when she is obeyed. She spares neither woman nor child. She has no pity: for some awful, but most good reason, she is not allowed to have any pity. Silently she strikes the sleeping child, with as little remorse as she would strike the strong man, with the musket or the pickaxe, in his hand. Ah, would to God that some man had the pictorial eloquence to put before the mothers of England the mass of preventible suffering, the mass of preventible agony of mind and body, which exists in England year after year! And would that some man had the logical eloquence to make them understand that it is in their power, in the power of the mothers and wives of the higher class, I will not say to stop it all, — God only knows that, — but to stop, as I believe, three-fourths of it. . . . It is in your power, ladies, and it is so easy. You might save several lives apiece, if you choose, without, I believe, interfering with your daily business, or with your daily pleasure, or, if you choose, with your daily frivolities, in any way whatsoever. . . . Will you learn how easy it is to be earnest in life; how every one of you, amid all the artificial complications of English society in the nineteenth century, can find a work to do, and a noble work to do, chivalrous work to do, — just as chivalrous as if you lived in any old fairy land, such as Spenser talked of in his 'Faerie Queene;' how you can be as true a knight-errant or lady-errant in

Sanitary Association

the present century, as if you had lived far away in the dark ages of violence and rapine? Will you, I ask, learn this? Will you learn to be in earnest, and use the position, and the station, and the talent that God has given you, to save alive those who should live? And will you remember that it is not the will of your Father that is in Heaven that one little one that plays in the kennel outside should perish, either in body or in soul?[1] . . ."

It shocked him to hear people talk of the blessing of death in childhood, and in a letter to his wife says:

"I do not know what to make of the boy's case; but one must hope for the real best, and humanly speaking the best is that he should live. I cannot but regard death as a fearful evil, and the more 'fit for Heaven' the boy is, the more he is wanted on earth. As for his escaping sin by an early death, one feels sad at hearing Christians talk so. Who has made him what he is but God, and is He not able to perfect His work, and keep that committed to Him? When people talk thus they detract from the boy's goodness, by making it out the fruits of mere natural temperament, and of ignorance of harm, which (according to them) would not stand the realities of that life of which God's apostle has said, 'Count it all *joy* when ye fall into divers temptations.' Therefore pray that he may live. If it is right to give him medicine to cure him, it is more right to pray to God to cure him. . . ."

His work at this time was incessant, his energy consuming; and he seldom returned from speech or lecture without showing that so much actual life had gone out of him — not only from the strain

[1] "Massacre of the Innocents," published, by the Ladies' Sanitary Association.

of brain and heart, but from his painful consciousness of the antagonism which his startling mode of stating things called out in his hearers. He was doing three full services on the Sunday with no help; and the letters now printed give a most inadequate idea of the labor of his life, of the calls on his sympathy, and of the different attitudes in which he had to put his mind according to the variety of subjects on which he was asked for sympathy of counsel, or called upon to do battle.

He wrote by urgent request a preface to the "Fool of Quality," a book to which he attached a high value.

"I am," he says to the Editor, "as one desperate and pre-done with work of various kinds at once. Meanwhile, believe me ready and willing to do full justice to one who seems to me more and more one of our forgotten worthies. . . ."

To JOHN BULLER, ESQ. — ". . . I have not yet found time to read Mansell, and don't know whether I shall. I have made up my own mind about the matter, as you may see from my last volume of sermons,[1] and am not going to alter my tune. But I am drawing back into silence, for the purpose of renewing the attack on a new and unexpected side — that of physical science. I have long begun to see that our advanced physics can only be made to stand on realist ground; and I am going, I trust, to get them up carefully enough to enforce my own belief some ten years hence. I am in no hurry. There is plenty of life in me, and your kind fears are groundless. I had been, by continual creation, using the gray matter of the back of the head a little too fast,

[1] Town and Country Sermons.

Pollution of Rivers

till it got hot and aching; and I found that the novel which I had been wearily trying to write was twaddle and a·failure. So I have just stopped, and shall write nothing but sermons, and read hard. I find my receptive wits as clear as ever they were in my life, and my digestive wits also. I am only like a spider who has spun all his silk, and must sit still and secrete more. Since I stopped writing this last month my head has got cool, and the ache in my limbs gone off, and this bitter bracing weather suits me perfectly. I believe a week's real north-easter would make me young again."

To LORD ROBERT MONTAGU. — "Don't talk about the Thames. I have thought and written much on it some years since, but have given it up in despair. There is no adequate demand for the sewage. Till you can awaken farmers, nothing can be done. My last dream is, to have the sewage conveyed along the line of rail by pipes, giving the railway companies an interest therein, and so to fertilize, especially the barrens of Surrey and Berkshire. But while railways are ruining themselves by frantic competition they have neither time nor money for such projects. . . . What I think you should do, in order to produce any effect, is to ascertain — 1. What demand for liquid sewage there is among the farmers of the neighborhood of London. Have guano and superphosphate really beaten sewage out of the field of superior facility of carriage? I suspect they have for the time being; there is no chance of the phosphatic beds of the green-sand being exhausted for many years; or the guano islands either. 2. What facilities or hindrances have been given to the carriage of liquid sewage by the great metropolitan sewers now making? This I do not know, and this you must ascertain. My scheme has always been to have arterial pipes along the railway lines. But the railway companies have no money to start such arteries, and private companies could not do it, unless they were sure of a demand from the farmers contiguous to the lines, which demand is *in nubibus*. . . .

"As to revivals, I don't wonder at revivalists taking to drink. Calvinism has become so unreal — so afraid of itself — so apologetic about its own peculiar doctrines, on which alone it stands, that revivals now must be windy flarings up in the socket of the dying candle. All revivals of religion which I ever read of, which produced a permanent effect, owed their strength to the introduction of some new element, derived from the actual modern consciousness, and explaining some fresh facts in or round man; *e. g.*, the revivals of the Franciscans and Dominicans — those of the Reformation and of Wesley.

"We may see such things ere we die. At present revivals are mere threshings of the old chaff, to see if a grain of corn be still there."

To JOHN BULLAR, ESQ. — "You are the kindest of men. Two letters come ere I answer one. But I have been hunted from pillar to post. There really is very little the matter with me, except what is called in country fellows 'idleness.' I never call it so. If they say to me, 'Jem is a slack hand, he won't do no work; and if he tries, he hain't no heart, but gies out at mowing or pitching like any chicken,' then I answer, 'Very well; you leave Jem alone: he won't live long if you hurry him!' Whereon they ask, 'And what's wrong wi' he, then?' To which I answer solemnly, 'Deficient vitality.' Which shuts them up; and is also a true and correct answer. I am a slack hand now. I can't think; I can't write; I can't run; I can't ride — I have neither wit, nerve, nor strength for anything; and if I try I get a hot head, and my arms and legs begin to ache. I was so ten years ago: worse than now. I have learnt by that last attack, and have, thank God, pulled up in time.

Exhausted Brain

Your letters are full of practical wisdom, as usual. Almost the best hint in them is the folly of trying to cure mental fatigue by bodily. I tried that experiment a fortnight ago, and was miserably ill for three days. When I came to think I saw I was an ass. I had used up the gray matter of my brain by thought, and then had used up still more by violent volition, running to hounds on foot, and leaping hedges and ditches for five hours, calling the same fresh air and exercise! I was a great fool, and found it out. . . . One thing I should like, that you would come and stay with me — on the understanding that neither of us is to speak a word of sense during the visit. Oh life — life, life! why do folks cling to this half existence, and call that life?

> '"T is life, not death, for which I pant,
> 'T is life, whereof my nerves are scant,
> More life and fuller that I want.'

". . . I wish I could see your father once! I like to look in the faces of strong good men, and to hear the tones of their voice. I don't mind what they say. It is the men themselves I love to contemplate. And I know one more strong good man than I did — and that is the Prince Consort. I love that man. . . ."

To W. FULLER MAITLAND, ESQ., *August* 9, 1859. — "How gladly would I come with you; but, alas! I have already spent all my journey-money and spare time for the year; I must stay at home and work peaceably. I think I shall never get to Scotland. I have three or four invitations every year, each pleasanter than the other, and cannot, cannot go. However, "Life is not all beer and skittles," as my friend Tom Brown remarks; and I suppose if it was good for me to go North, a door would be opened, as the old Puritans would say.

"So go, and shoot infinite grouse, and think on me

whose sporting will be confined to catching vile chub at Mattingley."

To ——— ———, Esq. — "As to Matt. xxii. 24-28. ... It seems to me that we must look at it from the standpoint of the Sadducees, and therefore of Our Lord as condescending to them. It is a hideous case in itself. ... I conceive the Jews had no higher notion than this of the relation of the sexes. Perhaps no eastern people ever had. The conception of a love-match belongs to our Teutonic race, and was our heritage (so Tacitus says with awe and astonishment) when we were heathens in the German forests. You will find nothing of it in Scripture, after the first chapter of Genesis, save a glimpse thereof (but only a glimpse) in St. Paul's Epistle to the Ephesians. To me, who believe the Gospel of St. John, and believe therefore that Jesus Christ, the Word of God, was the light and life of my German forefathers, as well as of the Jews, there is nothing strange in this. I only say, Christ has taught us something about wedlock, which He did not teach the Jews; that He taught it is proved by its fruits, for what has produced more of nobleness, more of practical good, in the human race, than the chivalrous idea of wedlock, which our Teutonic race holds, and which the Romance or Popish races of Europe have never to this day grasped with any firm hold? Therefore all I can say about the text is . . . (about such marriages in the world to come) that it has nought to do with me and my wife. I know that if immortality is to include in my case identity of person, I shall feel to her for ever what I feel now. That feeling may be developed in ways which I do not expect; it may have provided for it forms of expression very different from any which are among the holiest sacraments of life: of that I take no care. The union I believe to be as eternal as my own soul. I have no rule

Eternity of Marriage 117

to say in what other pair of lovers it may or may not be eternal. I leave all in the hands of a good God; and can so far trust His Son Jesus Christ Our Lord as to be sure that He knew the best method of protesting against the old Jewish error (which Popish casuists still formally assert) that the first end of marriage is the procreation of children, and thereby laid the true foundation for the emancipation of woman. . . .

To J. BULLAR, ESQ.—". . . Matthew xxii. 30, has been to me always a comfort. I am so well and really married on earth, that I should be exceedingly sorry to be married again in heaven. All I can say is, if I do not love my wife, body and soul, as well there as I do here, then there is neither resurrection of my body or of my soul, but of some other, and I shall not be I. Therefore, whatsoever the passage means, it can't mean what monks make it. Ten years ago I asked in 'Yeast' the question which my favorite old monk legends (from which I have learnt volumes) forced on me, 'Who told you that the angelic life was single?' and I have found no answer yet. . . ."

A letter on the eternity of marriage, written some years before, comes in fitly here.

". . . 'In heaven they neither marry nor are given in marriage, but are as the angels of God!'—And how are the angels of God in heaven? Is there no love among them? If the law which makes two beings unite themselves, and crave to unite themselves, in body, soul, and spirit, be the law of earth — of pure humanity — if, so far from being established by the Fall, this law has been the one from which the Fall has made mankind deflect most in every possible way; if the restoration of purity and the restoration of this law are synonymous; if love be of the spirit — the vastest and simplest exercise of will of which we can conceive — then why should not this law hold in the spiritual world as well as in the natural? In heaven they neither marry nor are given in marriage; but is not marriage the mere approximation to a unity which shall be perfect in heaven? Read what Milton says of angels' love in Books VI. and VII. and take comfort. What if many have been alone on earth? may they not find their kindred spirit in heaven, and be united to it by a tie still deeper than marriage? And shall not we be re-united in heaven by that still deeper tie? Surely on earth God has loved, Christ the lord has loved — some more than others — why should we not do the same in heaven, and yet love all? Here the natural body can but strive to express its love — its desire of union. Will not one of the properties of the spiritual body be, that it will be able to express that which the natural body only tries to express? Is this a sensual view of heaven? — then are the two last chapters of the Revelations most sensual. They tell, not only of the perfection of humanity, with all its joys and wishes and properties, but of matter! They tell of trees, and fruit, and rivers — of gold and gems, and all beautiful and glorious material things. Isaiah tells of beasts and birds and little children in that new earth. Who shall say that the number of living beings is filled up? Why is heaven to be one vast lazy retrospect? Why is not eternity to have action and change, yet both, like God's, compatible with rest and immutability? This earth is but one minor planet of a minor system: are there no more worlds? Will there not be incident and action springing from these when the fate of this world is decided? Has the Evil Spirit touched this alone? . . .

"These are matters too high for us, therefore we will leave them alone; but is flatly denying their existence and possibility leaving them alone? . . . It is more humble, more rational, to believe the possibility of all things than to doubt the possibility of one thing. . . . And what if earthly love seems so delicious that all

Eternity of Marriage

change in it would seem a change for the worse? Shall we repine? What does reason (and faith, which is reason exercised on the invisible) require of us, but to conclude that, if there is change, there will be something better there? Here are two truths —

"1st. Body is that which expresses the spirit to which it is joined; therefore, the more perfectly spiritual the body, the better it will express the spirit joined to it.

"2nd. The expression of love produces happiness; therefore, the more perfect the expression the greater the happiness! And, therefore, bliss greater than any we can know here awaits us in heaven. And does not the course of nature point to this? . . . What else is the meaning of old age? when the bodily powers die, while the love increases. What does that point to, but to a restoration of the body when mortality is swallowed up of life? Is not that mortality of the body, sent us mercifully by God, to teach us that our love is spiritual, and therefore will be able to express itself in any state of existence? . . . Do not these thoughts take away from all earthly bliss the poisoning thought, 'all this must end'? . . . Do I undervalue earthly bliss? No! I enhance it when I make it the sacrament of a higher union! Will not .his thought give more exquisite delight, will it not tear off the thorn from every rose and sweeten every nectar cup to perfect security of blessedness, in this life, to feel that there is more in store for us — that all expressions of love here are but dim shadows of a union which shall be perfect, if we will but work here, so as to work out our salvation!"

. . . .

"My views of second marriage are peculiar. I consider that it is allowed . . . but from the beginning it was not so, and will not be so, some day, when the might of love becomes generally appreciated! Perhaps that will never be, till the earth is renewed. . . . "

CHAPTER XIX

1860–62

AGED 41–43

PROFESSORSHIP OF MODERN HISTORY — DEATH OF HIS FATHER AND OF MRS. ANTHONY FROUDE — PLANTING THE CHURCHYARD — VISIT TO IRELAND — FIRST SALMON KILLED — WET SUMMER — SERMON ON WEATHER — ON PRAYER — LETTER FROM SIR CHARLES LYELL — RESIDENCE IN CAMBRIDGE — INAUGURAL LECTURE IN THE SENATE HOUSE — REMINISCENCES OF AN UNDERGRADUATE — LECTURES TO THE PRINCE OF WALES — ESSAYS AND REVIEWS — CHILDREN'S EMPLOYMENT COMMISSION — DEATH OF THE PRINCE CONSORT — THE WATER-BABIES — INSTALLATION ODE AT CAMBRIDGE — VISIT TO SCOTLAND — BRITISH ASSOCIATION — LORD DUNDREARY — DEGRADATION THEORY — AMERICAN LECTURES — THE PROFESSOR AND THE BOATS — COTTON FAMINE IN LANCASHIRE.

"The best reward for having wrought well already, is to have more to do: and he that has been faithful over a few things, must find his account in being made ruler over many things. That is the true and heroical rest which only is worthy of gentlemen, and sons of God. And for those who, either in this world, or the world to come, look for idleness, and hope that God shall feed them with pleasant things, as it were with a spoon, Amyas, I count them cowards and base, even though they call themselves saints and elect. . . . Do thou thy duty like a man to thy country, thy Queen, and thy God, and count thy life a worthless thing, as did the holy men of old."

WESTWARD HO! Chapter vii.

IN 1860 Mr. Kingsley's name was mentioned to Lord Palmerston, then Prime Minister, for the Regius professorship of Modern History at Cambridge, which Sir James Stephen had lately

Professorship of History

resigned. When the vacant chair was offered to him, he accepted it with extreme diffidence; and in the spring he went up to the University to take his M.A. degree, which he had not been able to afford as yet. Dr. Whewell, who was then Master of Trinity, received him most kindly. Having been one of those who had disapproved most emphatically of "Alton Locke" when it was first published, his generosity on this occasion, and his steady friendship henceforward up to the date of his own death in 1866, laid the new Professor under a deep debt of gratitude. His own feelings are best told in letters to his wife:

TRINITY, CAMBRIDGE, *May 22*, 1860.—". . . It is like a dream. Most beautiful. My windows look into Trinity Walks—the finest green walks in England, now full of flags and tents for a tulip show. I had a pleasant party of men to meet me last night. After breakfast I go to Magdalene, then to the Senate House; then to dinner in hall at Magdalene. . . . All this is so very awful and humbling to me. I cannot bear to think of my own unworthiness. . . ."

. . . . . .

"I have been thinking and praying a good deal over my future life. A new era has opened for me: I feel much older, anxious, and full of responsibility; but more cheerful and settled than I have done for a long time. All that book-writing and struggling is over, and a settled position and work is before me. Would that it were done, the children settled in life, and kindly death near to set one off again with a new start somewhere else. I should like the only epitaph on our tomb to be Thekla's:

'We have lived and loved,'
'We live and love.'"

Early in the winter, his father, the Rector of Chelsea, to whom he had ever been a devoted son, died, and from that hour till her death in 1873, the care of his widowed mother was one of his most nobly fulfilled duties. He speaks of the death of parents as —

". . . the awful feeling of having the roots which connect one with the last generation seemingly torn up, and having to say 'Now *I* am the root, I stand self-supported, with no older stature to rest on.' And then one *must* believe that God is the God of Abraham, and that all live to Him, and that we are no more isolated and self-supported than when we were children on our mother's bosom."

To REV. J. MONTAGU. — ". . . Forgive me for my silence, for I and my brothers are now wearily watching my father's death-bed — long and lingering. Miserable to see life prolonged when all that makes it worth having (physically) is gone, and never to know from day to day whether the end is to come in six hours or six weeks. But he is all right and safe, and death for him would be a pure and simple blessing. James Montagu, never pray for a long life. Better die in the flower of one's age, than go through what I have seen him go through in the last few days. . . ."

"MY DARLING BOY," he writes to his eldest son at school, — "Poor Grandpapa is dead, and gone to heaven. You must always think of him lovingly; and remember this about him, Maurice, and copy it — that he was a *gentleman*, and never did in his life, or even thought, a mean or false thing, and therefore has left behind him many friends, and not an enemy on earth. Yes, dear boy, if it should please God that you should help to build up the old family again, bear in mind that

Planting the Churchyard

honesty and *modesty*, the two marks of a gentleman, are the only way to do it. . . . Mother sends you a thousand loves. . . .

"Your own Daddy,   C. K."

His churchyard at Eversley was enlarged at this time. It had long been his wish to make it an arboretum, and gradually to gather together rare shrubs and evergreens, so that it should be truly a *Gottes-acker* in a double sense; and he took this opportunity of planting an avenue of Irish yews from the gate to the church door. His wife was then at Chelsea with his widowed mother; and he writes to her:

". . . I can understand your being unhappy leaving us and this delicious place again. It does look too blessed for a man to spend his life in. I have been making it blessed-er in the last thirty hours, with a good will; for I and B. (his church-warden) have been working with our own hands, as hard as the four men we have got on. We have planted all the shrubs in the churchyard. We have gravelled the new path with fine gravel, and edged it with turf; we have levelled, delved, planned, and plotted. M. is trimming up unsightly graves, and we shall be all right and ready for the Bishop to consecrate. Altogether I am delighted at the result, and feel better, thanks to two days' hard work with pick and spade, than I have done for a fortnight. . . . But I cannot bear working and planning at improvements without you; it seems but half a life; and I am leaving everything I can to be done after you come back. Oh! when shall we settle down here in peace? Patience, though. — It wants three weeks to spring, and we may, by God's blessing, get back here in time to see the spring unfold around us, and all mend and thrive. After all, how few troubles we have ! for God gives with one hand, if He takes away with the other. . . . I found a new competitor for the corner of the new ground, just under our great fir-tree, which I had always marked out for you and me, in dear old Bannister (a farmer), who had been telling M. that he wanted to be buried close to me. So I have kept a corner for ourselves; and then he comes at our feet, and by our side —— insists on lying. Be it so. If we could see the children grown up, and the History[1] written, what do I need, or you either, below?"

The vacant space by the side of his own proposed grave was soon filled up, for before long another heavy sorrow came — and one to whom he had been more than a brother for the last sixteen years, his wife's sister, Charlotte, wife of Anthony Froude, was laid there under the shade of the fir-trees she loved so well. Her grave was to him during the remainder of his own life a sacred spot, where he would go almost daily to commune in spirit with the dead, where flowers were always kept blooming, and where on Sunday morning he would himself superintend the decorations — the cross and wreaths of choice flowers placed by loving hands upon it.

No book was written this year, his spare time being given to the preparation of his inaugural lecture at Cambridge, and the course of lectures which was to follow it. By command of the Prince Consort, he preached the annual sermon

[1] Before his appointment at Cambridge he had begun a "School History of England," of which only the three first chapters were written. There is no harm now in mentioning that the reason for giving it up was that Mr. Kingsley learned that Charles Dickens was engaged on a similar work.

First Salmon

for the Trinity House, of which H. R. H. was then Master. He preached also at Whitehall, Windsor Castle, and St. James's; and was made chaplain to the Civil Service Volunteers. A few weeks' rest in Ireland with Mr. Froude, helped him greatly in preparing for his Cambridge work, and from Markree Castle, where he killed his first salmon, a new and long coveted experience in life, he writes home:

July 4.—"... I have done the deed at last—killed a real actual live salmon, over five pounds' weight. This place is full of glory—very lovely, and well kept up. . . .

"But I am haunted by the human chimpanzees I saw along that hundred miles of horrible country. I don't believe they are our fault. I believe there are not only many more of them than of old, but that they are happier, better, more comfortably fed and lodged under our rule than they ever were. But to see white chimpanzees is dreadful; if they were black, one would not feel it so much, but their skins, except where tanned by exposure, are as white as ours. . . ."

July 5.—"... I had magnificent sport this morning—five salmon killed (biggest, seven pounds), and another huge fellow ran right away to sea, carrying me after him waist deep in water, and was lost, after running 200 yards, by fouling a ship's hawser! There is nothing like it. The excitement is maddening, and the exertion very severe. . . . But the country which I have come through moves me even to tears. It is a land of ruins and of the dead. You cannot conceive to English eyes the first shock of ruined cottages; and when it goes on to whole hamlets, the effect is most depressing. I suppose it had to be done, with poor-rates twenty shillings in the pound, and the people dying of starvation, and the cottier system had to be stopped; but what an amount of human misery each of those unroofed hamlets stands for! . . ."

The summer of 1860 was a very wet one. Rain fell almost incessantly for three months. The farmers were frightened, and the clergy all over the country began to use the prayer against rain. Mr. Kingsley did not do so; for the cholera had long been threatening England, and his knowledge of physical and sanitary science told him how beneficial this heavy rain was — a gift from God at that particular moment to ward off the enemy which was at hand, by cleansing drains, sweeping away refuse, and giving the poor an abundance of sweet clean water. All this he explained to his own people by preaching them a sermon on Matt. vii. 9-11, which was published under the title of "Why should we pray for fair weather?" of which he thus speaks:

"A certain sermon of mine about the rains, which shocked the clergy of all denominations, pleased deeply, thank God, my own laborers and farmers. They first thanked me heartily for it, and begged for copies of it. I then began to see (what I ought to have seen long before) that the belief in a good and just God is the foundation, if not of a scientific habit of mind, still of a habit of mind into which science can fall, and seed, and bring forth fruit in good ground."

"How do we know," he says in this sermon, "that in praying God to take away these rains, we are not asking Him to send the cholera in the year to come? I am of opinion that we are. I think, I have thought long, that one or two more dry summers, keeping the springs at their late low level, would have inevitably brought back the cholera, or some other kind of pesti-

Sermon on Weather

lence: but even if that particular guess be wrong, this I believe, and this I will preach, that every drop of rain which is falling now is likely to be not a plague and a punishment, but a blessing and a boon to England and to Englishmen.

"Now, perhaps, you may understand better why I said that I was afraid of being presumptuous in praying for fine weather. I do not blame any one for so doing: God forbid. Who am I, to judge another? To his own master each man stands or falls. All I say is, that looking at the matter as I do, it would be presumptuous in me; and I do not wish to do it, unless I am commanded by my bishop, in which case my duty is to obey orders. But I do shrink from praying for fine weather on my own responsibility. . . ."

. . . .

The sermon was strongly commented on by the religious press, and he had numerous letters on the subject from the clergy and others, who misunderstood, and therefore resented, his views on prayer in general. He sent copies of it to several scientific men, who naturally agreed with his opinion. "Accept my sincere and hearty thanks for your sermon," says Professor Owen, "in which you alone — so far as I know — in your calling, have had the honesty and courage to utter the truth in reference to its subject; the words will not be spoken in vain. . . ."

"On my return from the Continent," wrote Sir Charles Lyell, "I find here your excellent sermon on the prayer for rain, sent to me, I presume, by your direction, and for which I return you many thanks. Two weeks ago, I happened to remark to a stranger, who was sitting next me at a *table d'hôte* at Rudoldtstadt in Thuringia, that I feared the rains must have been doing a great deal of mischief. He turned out to be a scientific man from Berlin, and replied, 'I should think they were much needed to replenish the springs, after three years of drought.' I immediately felt that I had made an idle and thoughtless speech. Some thirty years ago I was told at Bonn of two processions of peasants, who had climbed to the top of the Peter's Berg, one composed of vine-dressers, who were intending to return thanks for sunshine, and pray for its continuance: the others from a corn district, wanting the drought to cease and the rain to fall. Each were eager to get possession of the shrine of St. Peter's Chapel before the other, to secure the saint's good offices, so they came to blows with fists and sticks, much to the amusement of the Protestant heretics at Bonn, who, I hope, did not, by such prayers as you allude to, commit the same solecism, occasionally, only less coarsely carried out into action."

To —— ——, ESQ.— "I think you have misunderstood me in one important point. You ignore the fact that I do tell people to pray—only telling them what to pray for. The longer I live, the more I see that the Lord's Prayer is the pattern for all prayers, and whether it be consistent with that to ask that God should alter the course of the universe, in the same breath that we say—Thy will be done on earth—judge you. I do not forbid praying for special things—God forbid! I do it myself—I cannot help doing it, any more than a child in the dark can help calling for its mother. Only it seems to me (I do not dogmatize, but only say it *seems*) that when we pray 'Grant this day that we run into no kind of danger,' we ought to lay our stress on the '*run*' rather than on the '*danger;*' to ask God not to take away the danger, by altering the course of nature; but to give us light and guidance whereby to avoid it.

All prayers for forgiveness, teaching, strength, guidance, whether for ourselves or others, must be good. They concern the spiritual world of moral agents, having free will and capable of inspiration from the spirit of God — the laws whereof are totally different from those of the physical world. You mistake me again, then, when you class me with the mechanical philosophers. I have combated them in every book I have ever written. I am now hard at work protesting against their views being applied to History in my inaugural lecture, wherein I assert that the Hebrew prophets knew more of the laws of history than all the Comtes and Positivists put together. I fully admit all that you say about God's using natural plagues, locusts, earthquakes, pestilence, &c., as national punishments for national sins. . . . But that does not prevent my asserting man's power and right to abolish those natural plagues, when he has learnt how to do it. To pray against them, as long as he cannot conquer them, is natural, and not to be blamed. But when God has answered his prayer, in a deeper and fuller sense than he dreamed of, by teaching him how to protect himself against these plagues, it is very wrong and ungrateful to God, to go on praying as if God had not answered. The Russian has a right to pray against the locust-swarms as long as he does not know (what we do) that by tilling the waste lands instead of leaving them in wild turf, he would destroy the locust larvæ. But when he has found out that, let him till and thank God. So with our prayer against rain. I do not blame our forefathers for putting it in. God forbid! It rather marks a precious step forward in our theology. For till the time when that prayer was inserted, the general belief of Christendom had been, that the devil and witches were the usual producers of storms, and blights, and all that hurt the crops; and it was (as I believe) the very inspiration of God which kept the good man who wrote that prayer from saying anything about the devils and witches, and referring the whole question to God alone. Now, I believe that that prayer has been answered most fully, and in this way. We have learnt and ought, in the last two hundred years, to conquer the weather. We know now that if we cut down our superabundant timber, drain our land, and use an improved agriculture, a wet season, instead of bringing (as it did two hundred years ago) famine to man and beasts, does little or no harm, and we have taken the lesson. . . . Does a wet season hurt England in the present state of agriculture? I prophesied, No. . . . I saw the crops of England fairly housed, and in quantity, it seems, above the average, though the rains did not stop. Recollect that, dear sir. God did not answer those prayers. At the very time that some good men in their haste were thanking God in churches for having stopped the rains, they returned as heavily as ever; and we had the painful spectacle one Sunday, of one diocese praying that the rains might stop, and another thanking God for having stopped them. But the rains went on; and are you aware what they have done? Have you read the Registrar-General's reports for the last quarter? If not, you can hardly judge the matter. But this the rains have done. They have saved (by the returns compared with those of the same quarter last year) in the three months ending October, 18,000 English lives, besides the seeds of future disease. The doctors and apothecaries have been saying they never had so little to do — and the only persons, as far as I can find, who will suffer, are the brewers and hop-growers, who have been making huge profits of late, and can very well afford to make less this year. . . ."

To Rev. ——— ———. — "I feel very deeply the difficulties which you put, as corollaries from my sermon on the weather; nevertheless, I can and do pray, and hope that I always shall pray. I do not pretend to see my (logical) way clearly on this most subtle and important point; but this I see — that trials cannot be put into the same category as natural phenomena. Trials are part of our spiritual education — chastisements to teach us somewhat; and if we learn the lesson beforehand, we may pray to have the sin forgiven, and the chastisement remitted; and even if we have not, we can, and in effect do cry out of the darkness to the boundless love of God, by an instinct more rational and divine than all logic. And this may apply even to natural phenomena. To pray that there may not be a thunderstorm is to me presumptuous, because the thunderstorm will not come unless it is wanted. To pray that the particular lightning-flash may not strike my child, is not presumptuous. It is only asking God that a peculiar combination of circumstances which will bring my child under the influence of the laws of electricity may not take place; and that God can and does arrange by a perpetual providence every circumstance whatsoever, so making laws take effect only when and where He chooses, I believe utterly. It may be answered, 'If it be right for the child to be struck, it will be; if not, not!' I know that — I believe that. Everybody does who is pious. Even those who believe in a quite magical effect from prayer, will say, and rightly, when their prayers are not answered, 'It is God's will, it ought not to have been answered, therefore it was not!' All are driven to this; yet all pray, and should pray. It is one of those paradoxes which no science can explain. All we can do is, to eliminate from our prayers, as much as we can, all of self-will and selfishness, and study and copy the Lord's Prayer, praying 'after that manner.' This is a poor answer: but if you be an honest man, you would sooner have an honest half-answer than a dishonest whole one."

In the autumn the new Professor went up to Cambridge with his family till Christmas. "It is with a feeling of awe, almost of fear, that I find myself in such a place on such an errand," he said when he delivered his inaugural lecture,[1] "The Limits of Exact Science applied to History," in the crowded senate-house on the 12th of November. The lecture was listened to with profound attention, and most kindly received by all ranks in the university. It was followed by his first course of public lectures, "The Roman and the Teuton," to a class of upwards of one hundred undergraduates, who gave him an enthusiastic welcome. One of them, now a professor in the University of Cape Town, thus recalls this time:

"One of the charms of going into residence at Cambridge in October, 1860, was the fact that Kingsley was coming up as Professor of Modern History. I remember the thrill one felt as one November evening a man announced "in Hall" — 'Kingsley is come; I saw him to-day in the streets; my father knows him, and I knew him in a moment.' The man whose father knew Kingsley was a man to be envied, and to be asked to one's rooms at once. I remember there was a warm discussion as to some of the Professor's supposed views, and within a few days after he had stood up in the senate-house and delivered his inaugural lecture, men who were opposed to him began to say, ' Whether we agree with this or that, we like Kingsley.' And so it was; every creature that came near to him began to love him;—one could so thoroughly trust him;—he rang so thoroughly true; one felt instinctively there was not

[1] Now published as an Introduction to "The Roman and the Teuton," with preface by Max Müller.

Undergraduate Reminiscences 133

the slightest bit of affectation about the man — inside and outside moved together.

"Then he began to lecture and we undergraduates to crowd his room. We crowded him out of room after room, till he had to have the largest of all the schools, and we crowded that — crammed it. For undergraduates are an affectionate race, and every one of us who wished to live as a man ought to live, felt that the Professor of Modern History was a friend indeed. Tutors and fellows and lecturers came too, and sat on the same benches with undergraduates. And often and often, as he told a story of heroism, of evil conquered by good, or uttered one of his noble sayings that rang through us like trumpet-calls, loud and sudden cheers would break out irresistibly — spontaneously; and wild young fellows' eyes would be full of manly, noble tears. And again and again, as the audience dispersed, a hearer has said, 'Kingsley is right — I'm wrong — my life is a cowardly life — I'll turn over a new leaf, so help me God.' And many a lad did it too. Kingsley preached without seeming to do so. History was his text. The men and women of History were the words that built up his sermon. He loved men and women, you felt that. He never *sneered* at their faults. He had a deep, sad pity for them: he would even laugh a little, good-humoredly, at the comical side of some of them, for he was full of humor: but anything like a sneer one never heard. Hence, partly, his great power. Again, he had such a warm, passionate admiration for fine deeds. His eye used to glisten, his voice in its remarkable sea-like modulations to swell like an organ as he recounted something great, till his audience listened — quiet, spell-bound, fixed, till the climax came, and then rushed into a cheer before they were well aware of it. He was so modest and humble he could not *bear* our cheers. He would beckon for quiet;

and then in a broken voice and with dreadful stammering say, 'Gentlemen, you must not do it. I cannot lecture to you if you do.' But it was no good — we did not mean to cheer — we could not *help* it. Had Kingsley had to lecture upon broom-handles, he would have done more good than many men would do with the most 'suggestive themes.' His own noble, gallant, God-fearing, loving soul shone through everything, and we felt it was good to be with him. He made us read too. He taught us how to read. History was the story of God's men and women in the past, for the men and women living now. He lighted it up and showed us its true unity. But I must end with him in his lecture-room. I should like to have had time to tell about him at our sports, but I have not. Men all over the world have thanked God for the lessons of manliness, charity, and godliness they learned in the room of the Professor of Modern History. Amongst other things they learned this great lesson — and it is a good one — to love heartily and deeply (so that even now after fifteen years the recollection of him moves one to tears) — to love a great and good man."

"His lectures," Professor Max Müller says, "were more largely attended than any in Cambridge, and they produced a permanent impression on many a young mind. They contain" (speaking of "The Roman and the Teuton," which were more severely criticised than any) "the thoughts of a poet and a moralist, a politician, a theologian, and before all, of a friend and counsellor of young men while reading for them and with them one of the most awful periods in the history of mankind, the agonies of a dying empire, and the birth of new nationalities. History was but his text, his chief aim

Lectures to the Prince of Wales

was that of the teacher and preacher; and as an eloquent interpreter of the purposes of history before an audience of young men to whom history is but too often a mere succession of events to be learnt by heart and to be ready against periodical examinations, he achieved what he wished to achieve. . . . According to the unanimous testimony of those who heard them delivered, they stirred up the interest of young men, and made them ask for books which undergraduates had never asked for before at the university library."

The year 1861 opened upon the Professor with new and grave responsibilities, for in addition to his public class he had to give private lectures to the Prince of Wales; but his indomitable determination enabled him to get through his work, bravely and cheerfully, though often with weary body and exhausted brain, while his childlike faith in God kept him free from the irritability so common to all highly-strung natures, under the pressure of new circumstances. On the 2nd of January, he received, through Mr. H. Fisher, a message from the Prince Consort on the subject of his son's studies, to which he replied:

"Do me the kindness to inform the Prince Consort that his wishes are, of course, commands to me. I shall have great pleasure in putting myself into Dr. Whewell's hands as to the formation of a special class for His Royal Highness. . . . I put myself entirely into your hands, both as the expounder of the Prince Consort's wishes, and as the Prince of Wales's tutor. The responsibility is too solemn and too sudden for me to act in any way upon my own private judgment in the matter. The first question which I have to ask is — up to what year in the eighteenth century I ought to extend my lectures?"

The class was formed of eleven undergraduates, and early in February the Prince of Wales settled at Madingley, from whence he rode in three times a week to Mr. Kingsley's house, for lectures, twice with the class, and once to go through a *résumé* of the week's work alone. During the course of the academical year the Professor carried his pupils from the reign of William III. to that of George IV.; at the end of each term setting questions for the Prince, which were always most satisfactorily answered. Throughout this time the sense of responsibility which would otherwise have been overpowering, was relieved not only by the intense interest of the work, in which he was allowed perfect freedom of speech, but by the attention, courtesy, and intelligence of his royal pupil, whose kindness to him then and in after-life made him not only the Prince's loyal, but his most attached servant.

When "Essays and Reviews" came out, he writes to Oxford his impression of the attitude of Cambridge:

To REV. A. P. STANLEY, *Feb.* 19, 1861. — "Cambridge lies in magnificent repose, and shaking lazy ears stares at her more nervous elder sister and asks what it is all about. She will not persecute the authors of the Essays; and what is more, any scraps of the Simeonite party, now moribund here, who try to get up a persecution, will be let alone — and left to persecute on their own hook. That is the Cambridge danger. Cool indifferentism: not to the doctrines, but to the means of fighting for them. The atmosphere is the most liberal (save 'Bohemia') which I ever lived in. And it is a liberality (not like that of Bohemia, of want of principle or creed), but of real scholarly largeness and lovingness between men who disagree. We 'live and let live' here, I find to my delight. But with that will come the feeling — in which, I confess, I share — what the plague had these men to do, starting a guerilla raid into the enemy's country, on their own responsibility?

"Next. There is little or nothing, says Cambridge, in that book which we have not all of us been through already. Doubts, denials, destructions — we have faced them till we are tired of them. But we have faced them in silence, hoping to find a positive solution. Here comes a book which states all the old doubts and difficulties, and gives us nothing instead. Here are men still pulling down, with far weaker hands than the Germans, from whom they borrow, and building up *nothing* instead. So we will preserve a stoic calm. We wish them all well. We will see fair play for them, according to the forms of English law and public opinion. But they must fight their own battle. We cannot be responsible for other men's campaigns."

To BISHOP SUMNER. — "MY LORD, — I have received a circular from the archdeacon, asking me to sign an address to your lordship in reference to the 'Essays and Reviews,' of miserable notoriety. That address I declined to sign upon a question of archidiaconal jurisdiction.[1] . . . But in justice to your lordship, and to

[1] He was jealous on principle of archidiaconal interference, lest it should "end by becoming an inquisitorial superintendence of parishes fatal to the position of free rectors, which he held to be one of the greatest safeguards and blessings of the Church of England."

myself, I must tell you what I thought myself bound not to tell the archdeacon in his official capacity. I should be sorry that you should think that I agreed with a book whose publication I have deeply deplored, and have more reason to deplore every day. I deplore it first, for itself; second, for the storm which I saw it would raise. For itself. With the exception of Dr. Temple's essay, in which I can see nothing heterodox, be his theory right or wrong, all the essays deny but do not affirm. The doubts and puzzles which they raise afresh have passed through the mind of every thinking man in the last twenty-five years.... I confess to having thrust the book away in disgust, as saying once again, very weakly, what I had long put out of sight and mind, in the practical realities of parish work. When my new curate came back to me after ordination, having heard your lordship's allusion to these 'Essays and Reviews,' and asked me whether he should read them, I told him 'By no means. They will disturb your mind with questions which you are too young to solve. Stick to the old truths and the old paths, and learn their divineness by sick-beds and in every-day work, and do not darken your mind with intellectual puzzles, which may breed disbelief, but can never breed vital religion, or practical usefulness.' As for my own opinions, my lord, they are sufficiently known. The volumes of sermons which I have published are, I am sure, a sufficient guarantee to you, as they are to the public, that I keep to the orthodox faith, and the orthodox formulæ, without tormenting my soul, or my hearers, with fruitless argument on things which we shall never know, save by taking our Bible in hand like little children, and obeying it. The effect at the Universities will be very bad; for young men are only too glad to fly off on intellectual disquisitions, from the plain requirements of Christian faith and duty, and therefore I could have

Children's Employment 139

wished that the book had been passed by in silence, as what it is, a very weak and inconsiderable book."

To T. HUGHES, ESQ. — ". . . I have yet hope, for the Church of England, if men will only do (whether for or against us or the Essays) what you bid them, say what they *do* believe and not what they don't. But it is difficult to make men do that; and for this reason. If you ask the religionist what he believes, he answers you pat enough — but mere formulæ out of a book, the slang of his school, which he has not translated into his own native tongue, and which he would not recognize as his creed were it translated for him. . . . For me, I bide my time. I have always asserted, rather than denied. I have nothing more to say now than what I have said in print a dozen times. . . . My soul is moved by the abominations which this Children's Employment Commission is said to have brought to light. I am minded to speak earnestly about it in my Chapel-Royal Sermon,[1] if between now and then I can get facts

---

[1] He did preach on the revelations made by the Employment Commission, both at the Chapel Royal, St. James's, and before the Queen in the private chapel at Windsor, and in these striking words:

"Meanwhile we are sorry (for we English are a kind-hearted people) for the victims of our luxury and neglect. Sorry for the thousands whom we let die every year by preventable diseases, because we are either too busy or too comfortable to save their lives. Sorry for the thousands who are used up yearly in certain trades, in ministering to our comfort, even our very frivolities and luxuries. Sorry for the Sheffield grinders, who go to work as to certain death; who count how many years they have left, and say, ' A short life and a merry one — let us eat and drink, for to-morrow we die.' Sorry for the people whose lower jaws decay away in lucifer-match factories. Sorry for the miseries and wrongs which this Children's Employment Commission has revealed. Sorry for the diseases of artificial-flower makers. Sorry for the boys working in glasshouses whole days and nights on end without rest, laboring in the very fire, and wearying themselves for very vanity. Vanity, indeed! If, after an amount

enough to speak with authority, and also can hear what is likely to be done about it next session. Now, can you tell me aught? or tell me how to find out aught? Do give me a lift, and you shall find that 'still in my ashes live the wonted fires.'"

". . . I hear that you are bothered and disappointed. Do remember if you lose heart about your work in London, that none of it is *lost*. That the good of every good deed remains, and breeds, and works on for ever; and that all that fails and is lost is the outside shell of the thing, which perhaps might have been better done, but, better or worse, has nothing to do with the real spiritual good which you have done to men's hearts — and of that, dear Tom, you have done a very great deal; for which God will surely repay you in His own way and time. . . ."

His professional duties with the Prince of Wales obliged him to keep all the terms at Cambridge, and he left his parish under the superintendence of the Rev. Septimus Hansard (afterwards Rector of Bethnal Green), who tenderly recalls his impression of Mr. Kingsley's character at that time:

"Never can I forget his free and friendly talks with me, in that dear, dear old study — his deep earnestness

of gallant toil which nothing but the indomitable courage of an Englishman could endure, they grow up animals and heathens. We are sorry for them all, as the giant is for the worm on which he treads. Alas! poor worm! But the giant must walk on. *He* is necessary to the universe, and the worm is not. So we are sorry for half an hour; and glad, too (for we are a kind-hearted people) to hear that charitable people or the government are going to do something to alleviate these miseries. And then we return, too many of us, each to his own ambition or his own luxury, comforting ourselves with the thought that we did not make the world, and we are not responsible for it. . . ." — Water of Life, Sermon XIII.

Death of the Prince Consort

on all questions of the day, his faithful hope for the future, his utter detestation and abhorrence of sin and wrong-doing, and especially of all little, mean, dirty sins, which most men gloss over; and then his heartiness and playfulness, and his sympathy for the poor and needy; and, more striking to those who only knew of him by his writings, his Christ-like toleration for those who differed with him in opinion, and his sweet gentleness. . . . Naturally and by principle averse from quarrelling, he was ever ready to fight in the cause of justice to the poor, the oppressed and the suffering, and the weak. The Revelation of His Master's life — THE Revelation of Christ — had penetrated Charles Kingsley through and through. . . ."

The year was ended sadly by the death of the Prince Consort, which threw a gloom all over England, and was to Mr. Kingsley a personal loss, which he deeply felt:

> " Can we forget one friend,
> Can we forget one face,
> Which cheered us toward our end,
> Which nerved us for our race?
> Oh sad to toil, and yet forego
> One presence which has made us know
> To God-like souls how deep our debt!
> We would not, if we could, forget."[1]

"I remember," said a friend, "how Kingsley was affected by it, as at the loss of a personal friend. We walked over the next day to Madingley, and met, on the way, more than one of the young associates of the Prince of Wales. I can never forget, nor probably will those who were addressed forget, the earnest, solemn, and agitated tones in which he spoke of the Prince Consort's care for his son, and the duty which lay on

[1] Installation Ode, Cambridge, 1862.

them, the Prince of Wales's young friends, to see that they did all in their power to enforce the wise counsel of him who was dead."

To SIR CHARLES BUNBURY. — "As for the death of the Prince Consort, I can say nothing. Words fail me utterly. What little I could say, I put into a sermon for my own parishioners. . . . I need not say how we regretted not being able to accept your kind invitation. But the heavy work of last term, and the frightful catastrophe with which it ended, sent us all home to rest, if rest is possible, when, on coming home, one finds fresh arrears of work waiting for one, which ought to have been finished off months since. The feeling of being always behindhand, do what one will, is second only in torment to that of debt. I long to find myself once again talking over with you ' the stones which tell no lies.' "

The opening of 1862 found him once more settled at Eversley, and thankful to return to parish work after the heavy duties and responsibilities of such a year at Cambridge as could never come again. But the change of scene and work had done him good. His mind was particularly vigorous this year; and one spring morning, while sitting at breakfast, his wife reminded him of an old promise, "Rose, Maurice, and Mary have got their book, and baby must have his." He made no answer, but got up at once and went into his study, locking the door. In half an hour he returned with the story of little Tom. This was the first chapter of "The Water-Babies," written off without a flaw. The whole book was more like an inspiration than a composition, and seemed to flow naturally out of his brain and heart, lightening both of a burden

The Water Babies 143

without exhausting either. Nothing helped the books and sermons more than the silence and solitude of a few days' fishing, which he could now indulge in. "The Water Babies," especially, have the freshness and fragrance of the sea-breeze and the riverside in almost every page.

"When you read the book," he writes to Mr. Maurice, "I hope you will see that I have not been idling my time away. I have tried, in all sorts of queer ways, to make children and grown folks understand that there is a quite miraculous and divine element underlying all physical nature; and that nobody knows anything about anything, in the sense in which they may know God in Christ, and right and wrong. And if I have wrapped up my parable in seeming Tom-fooleries, it is because so only could I get the pill swallowed by a generation who are not believing, with anything like their whole heart, in the Living God. Meanwhile, remember that the physical science in the book is *not* nonsense, but accurate earnest, as far as I dare speak yet."

In the summer the Duke of Devonshire was installed at Cambridge as Chancellor of the University, in the place of the Prince Consort; and the Professor of Modern History wrote an installation ode, which was set to music by Sir William Sterndale Bennett. Their work together was a great mutual interest. "Music and words were well received, and followed," said the Professor of Music, by a "ringing cheer for Professor Kingsley," who was unable to be present. A month's holiday in Scotland with his wife and eldest boy this year, and visits to The Grange, where Lord Ashburton gathered round him a brilliant society: Thomas Carlyle, Bishop Wilberforce, the Duke and Duchess of Argyll, Lord Houghton, Mr. Venables, Mr. E. Ellice, &c., &c., were a great refreshment to him. He writes to his mother from —

INVERARAY CASTLE, *August* 21. — " The loveliest spot I ever saw — large lawns and enormous timber on the shores of a salt-water loch, with moor and mountain before and behind. We had the grandest drive yesterday through Glencroe, from Loch Lomond at Tarbet to Inveraray round the head of Loch Fyne. . . . If you examine the picture enclosed, carefully, on the extreme top of the extreme left, you behold the hill of Dunnaquoich, or the drinking-cup, which has a watch-tower on his top, for speculation after the thieves of those parts, and is about 500 feet high, with enormous pine and beech to his top, and views angelical. Beneath it you see the Castle of the Maccallum More. Between the hill and the castle, you would perceive, if it were visible, the river Aray, which contains now far more salmon than water; wherefore not being able to catch them fairly, we gaff them in narrow places. Beyond Dunnaquoich runs up Glen Shiray, which contains the Dhu Loch, which again contains salmon, salmon trout, brown trout, salmo-ferox, sythe, lythe, herrings, sticklebacks, flounders, grayling (on my honor I ain't lying), and all other known and unknown fresh and salt-water fish, jumbled together in thousands. Such a piece of fishing I never saw in my life. . . ."

The visit to Inveraray was one of the bright memories and green spots of his life, combining as it did not only beautiful scenery, but intellectual, scientific, and spiritual communings with his host and hostess on the highest, holiest themes. Such holidays were few and far between

Lord Dundreary Lecture 145

in his life of labor, and when they came he could give himself up to them, "thanks," as he would say,

"to my blessed habit of intensity, which has been my greatest help in life. I go at what I am about as if there was nothing else in the world for the time being. That's the secret of all hard-working men; but most of them can't carry it into their amusements. Luckily for me, I can stop from all work, at short notice, and turn head over heels in the sight of all creation for a spell."

He returned to Cambridge for his autumn course of lectures, and for the meeting of the British Association — the first he had ever attended. The zoölogical and geological sections were those which naturally attracted him; and the acquaintances he now made, the distinguished men he met, made this an era in his life, and gave a fresh impetus to his scientific studies. He was present at the famous tournament between Professor Owen and Professor Huxley on the Hippocampus question, which led to his writing the following little squib for circulation among his friends.

SPEECH OF LORD DUNDREARY IN SECTION D. ON FRIDAY LAST, ON THE GREAT HIPPOCAMPUS QUESTION.

CAMBRIDGE: *October*, 1862. — "Mr. President and Gentlemen, I mean Ladies and Mr. President, I am sure that all ladies and gentlemen will see the matter just as I do; and I am sure we're all very much obliged to these scientific gentlemen for quarrelling — no — I don't mean that, that would n't be charitable, and it's a sin to steal a pin: but I mean for letting us hear them quarrel, and so eloquently, too; though, of course, we don't understand what is the matter, and which is in the right; but of course we were very much delighted, and, I may say, quite interested, to find that we had all hippopotamuses in our brains. Of course they're right, you know, because seeing's believing.

"Certainly, I never felt one in mine; but perhaps it's dead, and so didn't stir, and then of course, it don't count, you know. A dead dog is as good as a live lion. Stop — no. A live lion is as good as a dead dog — no, that won't do again. There's a mistake somewhere. What was I saying? Oh, hippopotamuses. Well, I say, perhaps mine's dead. They say hippopotamuses feed on water. No, I don't think that, because teetotallers feed on water, and they are always lean; and the hippo's fat, at least in the Zoo. Live in water, it must be; and there's none in my brain. There was when I was a baby, my aunt says; but they tapped me; so I suppose the hippopotamus died of drought. No — stop. It wasn't a hippopotamus after all, it was hip — hip — not hip, hip, hurrah, you know, that comes after dinner, and the section hasn't dined, at least since last night, and the Cambridge wine is very good, I will say that. No. I recollect now. Hippocampus it was. Hippocampus, a sea-horse: I learnt that at Eton; hippos, sea, and campus, a horse — no — campus a sea, and hippos, a horse, that's right. Only campus ain't a sea, it's a field, I know that; Campus Martius — I was swished for that at Eton — ought to be again, I believe, if every dog had his day. But at least it's a sea-horse, I know that, because I saw one alive at Malta with the regiment, and it rang a bell. No; it was a canary that rang a bell; but this had a tail like a monkey, and made a noise like a bell. I dare say you won't believe me; but 'pon honor I'm speaking truth — *noblesse oblige*, you know; and it hadn't been taught at all, and perhaps if it had it would n't have learnt: but it did, and it was in a monkey's tail. No, stop, it must have been in its head, because it was in its brain; and every one has brains in his head, unless he's a skeleton; and it curled its tail round things like a monkey, that I know, for I saw it with my own eyes. That was Professor Rolleston's theory, you know. It was Professor Huxley said it was in his tail — not Mr. Huxley's, of course, but the ape's: only apes have no tails, so I don't quite see that. And then the other gentleman who got up last, Mr. Flower, you know, he said that it was all over the ape, everywhere. All over hippocampuses, from head to foot, poor beast, like a dog all over ticks! I wonder why they don't rub bluestone into the back of its neck, as one does to a pointer. Well, then. Where was I? Oh! and Professor Owen said it was n't in apes at all: but only in the order Bimana, that's you and me. Well, he knows best. And they all know best, too, for they are monstrous clever fellows. So one must be right, and all the rest wrong, or else one of them wrong, and all the rest right — you see that? I wonder why they don't toss up about it. If they took a half-crown now, or a shilling, or even a four-penny piece would do, if they magnified it, and tost heads and tails, or Newmarket, if they wanted to be quite sure, why, then there could n't be any dispute among gentlemen after that, of course. Well, then, about men being apes, I say, why should n't it be the other way, and the apes be men? do you see? Because then they might have as many hippocampuses in their brains as they liked, or hippopotamuses either, indeed. I should be glad indeed if it was so, if it was only for my aunt's sake; for she says that her clergyman says, that if anybody ever finds a hippopotamus in a monkey's head, nothing will save her great, great, great — I can't say how great, you see — it's awful to think of — quite enormous grandfather from having been a monkey too; and then what is to become of her precious soul? So, for my aunt's sake, I should be very glad if it could be settled that way, really; and I am sure the scientific gentlemen will take it into consideration, because they are gentlemen, as every one knows, and would not hurt a lady's feelings. The man who would strike a woman, you know — everybody knows that, it's in Shakespeare. And besides, the niggers say that monkeys are men, only they won't work for fear of being made to talk; no, won't talk for fear of being made to work; that's it (right for once, as I live!) and put their hands over their eyes at night for fear of seeing the old gentleman — and I'm sure that's just like a reasonable creature; I used to when I was a little boy; and you see the niggers have lived among them for thousands of years, and are monstrous like them, too, d'ye see, and so they must know best; and then it would be all right.

"Well, then, about a gulf. Professor Huxley says there's a gulf between a man and an ape. I'm sure I'm glad of it, especially if the ape bit; and Professor Owen says there ain't. What? am I wrong, eh? Of course. Yes — beg a thousand pardons, really now. Of course — Professor Owen says there is, and Professor Huxley says there ain't. Well, a fellow can't recollect everything. But I say, if there's a gulf, the ape might get over it and bite one, after all. I know Quintus Curtius jumped over a gulf at Eton — that is, certainly, he jumped in: but that was his fault, you see: if he'd put in more powder he might have cleared it, and then there would have been no gulf between him and an ape. But that don't matter so much, because Professor Huxley said the gulf was bridged over by a structure. Now I am sure I don't wish to be personal, especially after the very handsome way in which Professor Huxley has drunk all our healths. Stop — no. It's we that ought to drink his health, I'm sure, Highland honors and all; but at

Lord Dundreary Lecture 149

the same time I should have been obliged to him if he'd told us a little more about this structure, especially considering what nasty mischievous things apes are. Tore one of my coat tails off at the Zoölogical the other day. He ought — no, I don't say that, because it would seem like dictation, I don't like that; never could do it at school — wrote it down all wrong — got swished — hate dictation : — but I might humbly express that Professor Huxley might have told us a little, you see, about that structure. Was it wood? Was it iron? Was it silver and gold, like London Bridge when Lady Lee danced over it, before it was washed away by a man with a pipe in his mouth? No, stop, I say — That can't be. A man with a pipe in his mouth wash away a bridge? Why, a fellow can't work hard with a pipe in his mouth — everybody knows that — much less wash away a whole bridge. No, it's quite absurd — quite. Only I say, I should like to know something about this structure, if it was only to quiet my aunt. And then, if Professor Huxley can see the structure, why can't Professor Owen? It can't be invisible, you know, unless it was painted invisible green, like Ben Hall's new bridge at Chelsea : only you can see that of course, for you have to pay now when you go over, so I suppose the green ain't the right color. But that's another reason why I want them to toss up — toss up, you see, whether they saw it or not, or which of them should see it, or something of that kind, I'm sure that's the only way to settle; and — oh, by the by, as I said before — only I did n't, but I ought to have — if either of the gentlemen have n't half a crown about them, why, a two-shilling piece might do; though I never carry them myself, for fear of giving one to a keeper; and then he sets you down for a screw, you know. Because, you see, I see, I don't quite see, and no offence to honorable members — learned and eloquent gentlemen,

I mean; and though I don't wish to dictate, I don't quite think ladies and gentlemen quite see either. You see that?"

(The noble lord, who had expressed so accurately the general sense of the meeting, sat down amid loud applause.)

TO PROFESSOR ROLLESTON.

CAMBRIDGE: *October* 12, 1862. — "Many thanks for the paper. It is most satisfactory, and I am glad to see that you incline to my belief, which I hardly dare state in these days, even to those who call themselves spiritual, viz., that the soul of each living being down to the lowest, secretes the body thereof, as a snail secretes its shell, and that the body is nothing more than the expression, in terms of matter, of the stage of development to which the being has arrived. If that is n't awful doctrine, what is? and yet it is in my mind strictly philosophical and strictly orthodox; but I am not going to tell any one what I have just told you. I wish you would *envisager* that gorilla brain for once in a way, and the baboon brain also under the fancy of their being *degraded* forms.

"I shall torment you and your compeers with my degradation theory, till you give me a plain Yes or No from facts."

His professorial lectures were on the History of America, suggested by the Civil War then raging. The following recollections are by one of his class:

"I remember the concluding words of the Lectures on America. 'And now, gentlemen, I have done. And if I can have convinced you that well-doing and

Lecture on America

ill-doing are rewarded and punished in this world, as well as in the world to come, I shall have done you more good than if I had crammed your minds with many dates and facts from Modern History;' and then out broke the wild cheers that told him, and tell him now, if memory is not destroyed, how we loved him. I think he almost sobbed as he sat down amidst the storm; and men on the outskirts of the room handed in their cards by those who were nearer to his rostrum; and we went away feeling that something in our lives was over, and a leaf closed down for ever. It was a feature of his lectures that he had no 'Gyp' at the door to collect cards. He took them all himself. And it was quite a scene to watch the men crowding up at the end of the lecture, and to see him taking cards with both hands."

"How well, too, I remember," again writes the same, "how one dull February afternoon, at Baits-bite Lock, willows bare — river swollen — time, about four o'clock — the light failing — a few enthusiastic undergraduates in pea-jackets and comforters, waiting at the lock for the return of the university boat. The boat has been for a long 'training grind' down to Ely — we are waiting for its return. The ordinary crowd of eight oars are all gone back to Cambridge, and the river is quiet; but his favorite 'north-easter' is just bending the golden reed buds and 'crisping the lazy dyke'— hands are deep in coat pockets, and divers pipes are in requisition, and men keep making short expeditions to the bend of the reach below to see if 'she' is not coming. She is very late. Through the deepening twilight come two figures more; one tall, felt-hatted, great-coatless, with a white comforter, slinging along at a great pace. He is among us before we are well aware of it. In the pipes go into the pockets, and the caps are lifted. He passes down a little below us, and returns smoking a cigar, and goes a little above us and waits. Then the sound of the thrashing oars — up comes the boat — out tumble the men, and she is taken through the lock — they get in. 'Eyes on the stroke!' 'Ready all!' 'Row on all!' and on she goes in the gloom. As she passes him he throws his cigar into the river, and begins to run too. I shall never forget it. The crew are tired and row badly, as they did at Putney afterwards. He ran with us to Grassy Corner. I remember the boat stopped there for an 'Easy all,' and his short comment, 'I'm afraid that won't do, gentlemen.' And it didn't do. . . .

"We all *loved* him; we would have *carried* him back to Cambridge with delight. The boat went on again, and away we ran and left him to his walk. But in many a hall that evening the story was told how he had been running with the boat. . . ."

The cotton famine in the North, which occurred now, roused his indignation, and led to a very heavy correspondence, and to a characteristic letter to the editor of the "Times," for which he was fiercely attacked by manufacturers and the North Country press:

"The thanks of all Wessex men are due to you, for your article of Friday, contrasting the poor rates of Wessex with those of Lancashire. . . .

"The world will now know, that though there has been a great deal of foul linen in Wessex, yet we washed it at home. Whatever our Dorsetshire squires did, they never asked Queen Victoria to open her private purse in order to take their cottagers' blankets out of the pawn-shop. Whatever the Andover guardians did, they never informed England that Andover would do her duty in time; but that till they considered that the time was come, England must do their duty for them.

It pleased us in Wessex to keep our land ill-cultivated and our laborers depressed; but we paid for our hobby ourselves; and sunk in it, as you say, no less than eight millions in the last seventeen years. And now we are asked in addition to our own poor rates to contribute to the poor's rates of Lancashire — for all gifts and subscription of ours will be nothing else than contributions to poor's rates. We shall do it, but 'grudgingly and of necessity,' I am sorry to say, and in anything but the spirit of a 'cheerful giver,' as far as the rate-payers are concerned. How can it be otherwise?

"I know a clergyman who has a living (actual gross, not ratable value) of the huge sum of £600 a year. Out of that he has been paying, for the last twenty years, more than £100 in poor's rates. That is, he has sunk in the relief of the poor more than £2000, besides his subscriptions and private charities. His parishioners have, of course, been paying poor's rates at nearly the same ratio of three shillings and fourpence in the pound. 'And now,' he says, 'I am asked to contribute, and to persuade my parishioners to contribute, to the aid of a county which it appears has been paying poor's rates at less than half that ratio, and which now, if it chose to tax itself by one such a "one and threepenny rate" as we have had often three times in a year, might furnish for its poor £40,000 a week for the next three months. I am asked, too, to contribute clothes and bedding to a district where every pawn-broker's shop is already teeming with clothes and bedding, pawned of course at far less than their real value, and therefore all the more easily redeemable, and thereby to enable the Lancashire pawnbrokers to make their fortunes out of the glut. I shall do it, of course, but under false pretences. I dare not tell my honest farmers the facts of the case. I should rouse their indignation. I should button up their pockets. I should make them say, "Let their poor's rates be judge between them and us. Meanwhile, they may take care of their poor, and we shall take care of ours.'"

"And, meanwhile, let those who see school children [1] robbed of their little savings, and delicate ladies starving themselves into illness, to save here a shilling and there a shilling for the Lancashire folk, and know that in the chain of cause and effect, the actual fate of that hard-wrung shilling will be, to enable some rich man of Lancashire to escape the giving up some tawdry luxury: let them, I beg, exercise the Englishman's right, to give: but while he gives, to grumble, and to remember, that these very Lancashire men have directly helped to cause the present distress and the present war, by their determination to use exclusively slave-grown cotton; developing thereby, alike slavery itself, and the political power of the slave-owners."

To a highly respected mill-owner he writes:

To ———, Esq., of Manchester. — ". . . That I am cross with the Lancashire men I don't deny, and my reason is, that their leaders concealed carefully the broad fact, that the present distress came not merely from the American war, but from the over production of the last few years, and must have happened, more or less, in any case. As to the parsons, I am sure that with all the ignorance and fanaticism of some of them — on which I am as hard as any man — there is no body of men in England who work so hard for others, from the mere knowledge that it is their duty, and no body of men who give half or a quarter as much in charity and other good works, in proportion to their incomes. Sir, the amount of good done, or tried to be done, by hun-

---

[1] The school children of Eversley and many of the poor brought their money weekly to the Rectory for the sufferers in the North.

Cotton Famine

dreds, ay, thousands of parsons, who have to keep up the appearance of gentlemen on the income of a skilled iron workman at Preston or Sheffield, will never be known till the last day.

"I say it with some fear, lest I should be misunderstood. When any gentleman boasts to me that the earnings of his workpeople average 16s. a week, man, woman, and child, I am inclined to answer, so much the worse for them. It is a very great question whether such high wages are a benefit, without a corresponding high education. You must know well (for I do) that most of them do not know what to do with their money, and waste it on drink, on rich food, on finery, &c. God knows, I do not grudge it them; but the waste, and the temptation to coarse self-indulgence, is extreme. And I was quite shocked, knowing how great the earnings had been during the last few years, to find only £270,000 in the Lancashire savings banks. I know the sum struck me as one-fourth what it should have been. Another great evil of your system (if you will excuse me) is, that the children earn wages too nearly equal to those of their parents. Hence the family is broken up, the children are independent too early, boys and girls go off and live in lodgings of their own, and so a great deal of fearful profligacy is engendered; that fact I have from the mouths of masters. Another great evil, by the masters' own account, is that mill-labor effeminates the men, and renders them unfit for any other sort of labor. How far this is true, I know not. But I conceive it to be, if true, a very great evil. That large bodies of men should be employed in exclusively performing day after day the same minute mechanical operation, till their whole intellect is concentrated on it, and their fingers kept delicate for the purpose, is to me shocking. I would gladly see such men emigrate, even though they fared badly at first, because the life of a colonist would, by calling out the whole man, raise them in body and mind enormously.

"Now I say all this without blaming the masters at all. It is merely a result of inevitable circumstance. But when I am told that the Lancashire system is perfect, and ought to be permanent and helped towards permanence by the alms of a whole nation, I answer: It is not perfect at all. It is fortuitous, barbaric, exceptional, transitional. We thank the masters for it, because it has called a great population into existence, who otherwise would not have been born. It has created great wealth. It has civilized, somewhat at least, tens of thousands who would have been languishing in Irish bogs or English workhouses; but, like all things of rapid growth, it is hollow and insecure, and here is its fall. It has collapsed at the first real shock; and what wise men must do, is to help out of it as soon as possible as many workmen as are sufficiently civilized to emigrate to a manlier and healthier sphere of life, and to supply their places, if fresh hands be needed, by less civilized beings, who may be raised and trained in the transitional school of Lancashire work. But I am justly indignant, when I find Mr. * * * *, and the organs of the Manchester school, holding up this Lancashire system (which is no system at all) as the model of human society — taking their stand on it to insult all that four-fifths of England holds dear, — the monarchy, the government, the church, the army, the navy, the landlords, the sturdy agricultural peasant; and after doing more than all the demagogues to set class against class, accusing me of setting class against class, 'under well-known Satanic influences' (the actual words of the 'Morning Star'), because I interfere to see common justice done to the British public and to the Lancashire workman. . . .

"Years since, when I was the only free-trade parson for miles round, I fought a similar battle against landlords and farmers. I have found that by so doing I did not lose their respect. Angry as they were at the time with me, their English justice and common sense confessed me slowly to be in the right; and no one is better friends with squire and farmer now, than I who was looked on as a firebrand once."

CHAPTER XX

1863

AGED 44

FELLOW OF THE GEOLOGICAL SOCIETY — GEOLOGY OF PALESTINE AND THE BIBLE — WORK AT CAMBRIDGE — WELLINGTON COLLEGE MUSEUM — LECTURE AT WELLINGTON — LETTER FROM DR. BENSON — WONDERS OF SCIENCE — MAN AND THE APE — MOCKING BUTTERFLIES — A CHAIN OF SPECIAL PROVIDENCES — TOADS IN ROCKS — PRINCE OF WALES'S WEDDING — D. C. L. DEGREE AT OXFORD — BISHOP COLENSO — SERMONS ON THE PENTATEUCH.

> How seldom, friend, a good great man inherits
> Honor or wealth, with all his toil and pains.
> It sounds like stories from the land of spirits,
> If any man obtain that which he merits,
> Or any merit that which he obtains.
> ——— For shame, dear friend! renounce this canting strain.
> What wouldst thou have the good great man obtain?
> Place, titles, recompense? a gilded chain,
> Or throne of corses that his sword hath slain?
> Hath he not always treasures, always friends,
> The good great man? Three treasures, Love and Light,
> And Calm Thoughts, regular as infant's breath;
> And three firm friends, more sure than day and night,
> Himself, his Maker, and the angel — Death.
>
> COLERIDGE.

PROFESSOR KINGSLEY was this year made a Fellow of the Geological Society — he was proposed by Sir Charles Bunbury, and seconded by Sir Charles Lyell. "To belong to the Geological Society," he writes to the former, "has long been an ambition of mine, but I feel how little I know, and how unworthy I am to mix with the really great men who belong to it. So strongly do I feel this, that if you told me plainly that I had no right to expect such an honor, I should placidly acquiesce in what I already feel to be true." The distinction of F.G.S. came as a counterbalance to his rejection at Oxford for that of a D.C.L. degree, which his friends there had proposed to confer on him. From boyhood geology had been his favorite study; but since he entered the Church it had assumed a deeper importance from the light he believed it must throw on Bible history; and long before any scientific exploration of Palestine was planned, we find him urging it on travellers. The following fragment of a letter, written early in 1853 to Dean Stanley, will show his speculations on the subject:

". . . While you are on your way to the Holy Land, I wish to point out to you the great help you might give to our understanding the prophets, especially Micah and Isaiah, by trying to make out whether there are volcanic features in the country to the southwest of Jerusalem. I need not point out to you the distinct allusion to volcanic phenomena of every kind, with which these two writers connect the drought of Ahaz's time, the great misery of the landholders of Judea, and the final destruction of Sennacherib's army, as well as the desolation of Edom and Moab which occurred about the same time. I have been trying for a long time to arrange them, and also to connect them with the remarkable (though well-known in similar cases) re-appearance of the springs throughout a large part of the country, of which Isaiah speaks (cap. xxx. 25, and also xxxv.). But the travellers, except to the volcano district of Sinai, have been such bad geognosts, that I cannot get enough from them. And, moreover, scientific travellers think themselves bound to ignore the Bible, and 'pious' ones to ignore science. So science suffers from neglecting the history which is ready made for them, and the Bible suffers, being considered to be a mere tale of portents and 'miracles,' even by the pious. Now I want some one like you, to look at these points: (1) The recent volcanic marks in Edom. Isaiah, cap. xxxiv., connects the eruption there with the great events of Hezekiah's time. But no one has worked the country well to the east of the Dead Sea. And no one *will* tell me whether there are marks (as I expect) of recent upheaval, which have caused the disappearance of water in Edom. Oh, for some one to look for *raised* beaches half-way up the cliffs on the east side, and to examine the famous sand-cliff between El-Ghor and the Dead Sea, and tell us whether it bears marks, as I expect, of recent upheaval.

" (2) The liability of Jerusalem to earthquakes. They evidently very seldom shook the city itself; but they did not always spare it. Josephus, Antiq. ix. 10, in fine, connects the Rabbinical legend of Uzziah's attempt to offer sacrifice, with an earthquake which broke the temple roof and hurled a large rock close to the city into the king's garden. See also the passage of Jeremiah, which has now got into Zechariah xiv., 4, 5, whereon Whiston with exquisite *naïveté*, makes the pardonable remark, that "*there seems to have been some considerable resemblance between these historical and prophetical earthquakes.*" The same earthquake seems to me (if you believe, as I think we ought, that Isaiah's lyrics are chronologically arranged) to be spoken of very clearly in Isaiah ii.

" His most important chapter, xxix., speaks of the eruption during Sennacherib's invasion as visiting Jeru-

Geology of the Bible   161

salem with earthquake and flame, and also with tempest; that latter puzzles me as being a crater-volcano-phenomenon, while I can find as yet no craters or lava streams nearer than the country round Tiberias to the north, and Sinai to the south. The flame is a common phenomenon as issuing from earthquake cracks — it did so in Bashan during the great earthquake of 1837. That earthquake, like those of 1759 and 1202, did not affect Jerusalem; the centre of detonation being the volcanic district of Tiberias. And Isaiah in cap. xxvi. 1, and in other places, intimates that Jerusalem, though shaken, would escape.

"But Jerusalem is surrounded by volcanic phenomena. Russegger says that the mountains between Jerusalem and Jordan are full of earthquake-faults. We know of the hot springs of that neighborhood, of the mineral and evidently volcanic fountain of Siloam, and of the periodically 'troubled' pool of Bethesda. Will you, *en passant*, be so good as to see to that ebbing and flowing of the pool of Siloam, which some one wants to make out the consequence of the Arabs damming back the water? It, like the troubling of the lost Bethesda, probably, like it, a strong mineral spring, is among the commonest of volcanic-spring phenomena.

"(3) But my great object of anxiety is, to examine the volcanic traces to the southwest of Jerusalem. Micah, the Morasthite, who lived some twenty-five miles to the south-west, down the valley of Eschol, speaks, cap. i., as if he had seen lava streams with his own eyes. Pray look about there for black trap-dykes, pumice, and crater cones. You are likelier to find craters in the sides and spurs, than on the tops of those limestone hills; often they will stand right out in elevated plains, of which the soil, which you should observe at cuttings and deep lanes, will be full of pumice and slag, and often of little bits of half-burnt rock; if limestone burnt white and crumbly, if silicious, black or red, and hard.

Also little nodules containing crystals of olivine, augite, &c. Also all the way from there to Bethlehem, look for cracks in the earth and in the rocks, and faults and shifts in the strata. Distortions don't count, they are ante-human by whole æons. Also look for big boulders fallen into the valleys, and for any appearance of black trachyte, &c., cropping out, or running down into the valleys. A lava stream will look, atop, like a long dyke of loose stones, more or less over-grown with vegetation. I speak from pretty good experience, having worked a large extinct volcano-district last summer. Basalt of course you will recognize; but it will be recent only if low in valleys, and damming up watercourses.

"Next, please look carefully at the traditionary scene of Sennacherib's slaughter, the valley on the Bethlehem road. . . . It is a shame to ask you to burden yourself with geological specimens, but they might be of immense use in this matter."

He was obliged this year to part with his Cambridge house, for he found the salary of his Professorship did not admit of his keeping up two homes; and henceforth to go up twice a year only, for the time required for his lectures and the examination for degrees. He deeply regretted this necessity, as it prevented his knowing the members of his class personally. From the first he did all he could to bridge over the gulf which in his own day had been a very wide one between dons and students; and during the early years of his residence many charming evenings were spent in easy intercourse between the Professor and his pupils when they came to his house, where he could meet them on equal terms. His influence showed itself by the fact of members of his class writing to consult him after they left

Cambridge on their studies, their professions, and their religious difficulties, proving their perfect confidence in his sympathy.

"Speaking," says one, "from the experience of these three years, there is no comparison between our status of thought now and that of 1860 — chiefly, if not entirely, due to you. We are learning, I trust, to look very differently at our relation to our fellow-men, at those social duties which seldom appear important to young men in our position until we come across a mind like yours to guide us. We are learning above all, I think, to esteem more highly this human nature we have, seeing, as you show us in your books and words, how it has been consecrated and raised by union with the God-made Man. . . . I could not leave Cambridge without testifying to you how much your silent as well as expressed influence is felt among us."

"Excuse a perfect stranger," writes an undergraduate of Jesus College, "but in no other quarter could I hope for a solution of my doubts. . . . I seem to have grasped a truth which came out in every one of your lectures here, that the Governor of the world is a Righteous Governor, and that even our contentions are working out His peace. . . . I make no apology, for I believe your sympathy will be enlisted for me, tossed about as I thus am. . . ."

Wellington College, which was only four miles from Eversley, was a continual interest to him, not only because his eldest son was there, and from his warm friendship with its head-master, afterwards Bishop of Truro and Archbishop of Canterbury; but he loved it for the sake of the Prince Consort, under whose fostering care it had risen into importance.

"In the readiest and yet most modest way," said Dr. Benson, "he helped us wonderfully. His presence looking on helped our games into shape when we began with fifty raw little boys, our football exploits, twelve years after, were as dear to him as to his son, and 'The Kingsley' steeple-chase was the event of the year. But in far higher ways he helped us. He wrote an admirable paper for us, which was widely circulated, on School Museums; he prevailed on the Royal College of Surgeons, on Lady Franklin, and other friends, to present the boys with many exquisite specimens, and started all our collections. His lectures on natural history, and two on geology, were some of the most brilliant things I ever heard. Facts and theories, and speculations, and imaginations of what had been and might be, simply riveted the attention of 200 or 300 boys for an hour and a half or two hours, and many good proverbs of life sparkled among these. Their great effect was that they roused so much interest. At the same time his classification of facts such as the radiation of plants (Heather for instance) from geographical centres, gave substantial grounds for the work which he encouraged. 'Let us make a beginning by knowing one little thing well, and getting roused as to what else is to be known.' Nothing was more delightful too, to our boys, than the way in which he would come and make a little speech at the end of other occasional winter lectures, above all, when, at the close of a lecture of Mr. Barnes's, he harangued us in pure Dorset dialect, to the surprise and delight of the Dorsetshire poet."

One of these lectures has happily been preserved.

June 25, 1863. — " YOUNG GENTLEMEN, — Your headmaster, Dr. Benson, has done me the honor of asking me to say a little to you to-night about the Museum which is in

Lecture at Wellington 165

contemplation, connected with this College, and how far you yourselves can help it. I do so gladly. Anything which brings me in contact with the boys of Wellington College, much more of helping forward their improvement in the slightest degree, I shall always look upon as a very great pleasure and a very serious duty. Let me tell you, then, what I think you may do for the Museum, and how you may improve yourselves by doing it, without interfering with your regular work. Of course, that must never be interfered with. You are sent here to work. All of you here, I suppose, depend for your success in life on your own exertions. None of you are born (luckily for you) with a silver spoon in your mouths, to eat flapdoodle at other people's expense, and live in luxury and idleness. Work you must, and I don't doubt that work you will, and let nothing interfere with your work.

"The first thing for a boy to learn, after obedience and morality, is a habit of observation — a habit of using his eyes. It matters little what you use them on, provided you do use them. They say knowledge is power, and so it is. But only the knowledge which you get by observation. Many a man is very learned in books, and has read for years and years, and yet he is useless. He knows *about* all sorts of things, but he can't *do* them. When you set him to do work, he makes a mess of it. He is what is called a pedant: because he has not used his eyes and ears. He has lived in books. He knows nothing of the world about him, or of men and their ways, and therefore he is left behind in the race of life by many a shrewd fellow who is not half as book-learned as he: but who is a shrewd fellow — who keeps his eyes open — who is always picking up new facts, and turning them to some particular use.

"Now, I don't mean to undervalue book-learning. No man less. All ought to have some of it, and the time which you spend here on it is not a whit too long; but the great use of a public-school education to you, is, not so much to teach you things as to teach you how to *learn* — to give you the noble art of learning, which you can use for yourselves in after-life on any matter to which you choose to turn your mind. And what does the art of learning consist in? First and foremost, in the art of observing. That is, the boy who uses his eyes best on his book, and *observes* the words and letters of his lesson most accurately and carefully, that is the boy who learns his lesson best, I presume. You know, as well as I, how one fellow will sit staring at his book for an hour without knowing a word about it, while another will learn the thing in a quarter of an hour, and why? Because one has actually not *seen* the words. He has been thinking of something else, looking out of the window, repeating the words to himself like a parrot. The other fellow has simply, as we say, 'looked sharp.' He has looked at the lesson with his whole mind, seen it, and seen into it, and therefore knows all about it. Therefore, I say, that everything which helps a boy's powers of observation helps his power of learning; and I know from experience that nothing helps that so much as the study of the world about you, and especially of natural history. To be accustomed to watch for curious objects, to know in a moment when you have come on anything new — which is observation. To be quick at seeing when things are like, and when unlike — which is classification. All that must, and I well know does, help to make a boy shrewd, earnest, accurate, ready for whatever may happen.

"When we were little and good, a long time ago, we used to have a jolly old book called 'Evenings at Home,' in which was a great story called Eyes and No Eyes, and that story was of more use to me than any dozen other stories I ever read. . . .

Lecture at Wellington 167

"And when I read that story, I said to myself, I *will* be Mr. Eyes; I will *not* be Mr. No Eyes, and Mr. Eyes I have tried to be ever since; and Mr. Eyes I advise you, every one of you, to be, if you wish to be happy and successful.

"Ah, my dear boys, if you knew the idle, vacant, useless life which too many young men lead when their day's work is done, and done spiritlessly, and therefore done ill, having nothing to fall back on but the theatre, or billiards, or the gossip at their club, or if they be out in a hot country, everlasting pale ale; and continually tempted to sin, and shame, and ruin, by their own idleness, while they miss opportunities of making valuable discoveries, of distinguishing themselves, and helping themselves forward in life; then you would make it a duty to get a habit of observing, no matter what you observe, and of having at least some healthy and rational pursuit with which to fill up your leisure hours. The study of natural history, of antiquities, of geography, of chemistry, any study which will occupy your minds, may be the means, whether out on some foreign station, or home here, at work in London, of keeping you out of temptation and misery, of which, thank God, you as yet know nothing.

"I am happy to hear that there are many of you who don't need this advice, some who are working well at chemistry, some who have already begun to use your eyes, and to make collections of plants, insects, and birds' eggs. That is good as far as it goes. As for bird-nesting, I think it a manly and excellent pursuit;[1] no one has worked harder at it than I, when I was young, or should like better to go bird-nesting now, if I was not getting rather too stiff and heavy to bark up to a hawk's nest. But see. Because every boy collects for himself,

---

[1] He never allowed his own boys to take more than one, or at most two eggs out of a nest where there were several, lest the mother bird should miss them, and forsake her nest.

there is a great deal of unnecessary destruction of eggs, especially of the small soft-billed birds, which are easiest got, and are the very ones which ought to be spared, on account of their great usefulness to the farmer in destroying insects; and next — Pray, where will nine-tenths of those eggs be seen a few days hence? smashed, and in the dust-hole. And so of the insects and plants. Now, if fellows were collecting for a College Museum, instead of every one for himself, it would save a great deal of waste, and save the things themselves likewise. As for a fellow liking to say, 'I have got this, and I will keep it to myself, I like to have a better collection than any one else,' that is natural enough; but like a great many natural things, rather a *low* feeling, if you will excuse my saying so. Which is better, to keep a thing to yourselves, locked up in your own drawers, or to put into the common stock, for the pleasure of every one? and which is really more honor to you to be able to say to two or three of your friends, 'I have got an egg which you have not,' or to have the egg, or whatever else it may be, in a public collection, to be seen by every one, by boys, years hence, after you are grown up. . . .

". . . There are many of you who have relations abroad, or in other countries, that you will be able to obtain from them rare and curious objects which you could not collect yourselves, and I advise you to turn sturdy beggars, and get hold (by all fair means) of anything and everything worth putting in the Museum. . . . I myself am ready to give as many curious things as I can, out of my own collections. . . . And I believe you will be helped by many real men of science, who will send the Museum such things as are wanted to start it well. To start it well with 'Typical Forms,' by which you can arrange and classify what you find. They will as it were stake out the ground for you, and you must fill up the gaps, and I don't doubt you will do it, and well. I am sure you can, if you will see now here is an opportunity of making a beginning — during the next vacation. . . . What can you do better? I am sure your holidays would be much happier for it. I don't think boys' holidays are in general so very happy. Mine used to be: but why? Because the moment I got home, I went on with the same work in which I employed every half-holiday: natural history and geology. But many boys seem to me in the holidays very much like Jack when he is paid off at Portsmouth. He is suddenly free from the discipline of ship-board. He has plenty of money in his pocket, and he sets to, to have a lark, and makes a fool of himself till his money is spent; and then he is very poor, and sick, and seedy, and cross, and disgusted with himself, and longs to get a fresh ship and go to work again — as a great many fellows, I suspect, long for the holidays to be over. They suddenly change the regular discipline of work for complete idleness, and after the first burst is over, they get very often tired, and stupid, and cross, because they have nothing to do, except eating fruit and tormenting their sisters. How much better for them to have something to do like this. Something which will not tire their minds, because it is quite different from their school work, and therefore a true *amusement*, which lets them cut the muses for a while; and something, too, which they can take a pride in, because it is done of their own free will, and they can look forward to putting their gains in the Museum when they come back, and saying, 'This is my holiday work, this is what I have won for the College since I have been away.' . . . Take this hint for your holidays, and take it too for after life. For I am sure if you get up an interest for this Museum here, you will not lose it when you go away. Many of you will go abroad . . . and you will use the opportunities you will then have to enrich the Museum of the College, and be its benefactors each according to your powers throughout your lives.

"But there is one interest, young gentlemen, which I have more at heart even than the interest of Wellington College, much as I love it, for its own sake and for the sake of that great Prince beneath whose fostering shadow it grew up, and to whom this College, like myself, owes more than we shall either of us ever repay: yet there is an interest which I have still more at heart, and that is the interest of Science herself. Ah, that I could make you understand what an interest that is. The interest of the health, the wealth, the wisdom of generations yet unborn. Ah, that I could make you understand what a noble thing it is to be men of ˹ience; rich with a sound learning which man can neither give nor take away; useful to thousands whom you have never seen, but who may be blessing your name hundreds of years after you are mouldering in the grave, the equals and the companions of the noblest and the most powerful — taking a rank higher than even Queen Victoria herself can give, by right of that knowledge which is power.

"But I must not expect you to see that yet. All I can do is to hope that my fancy may be fulfilled hereafter, that this Museum may be the starting-point of a school of scientific men, few it may be in number, but strong, because bound together by common affection for their College, and their Museum, and each other. Scattered perhaps over the world, but communicating their discoveries to each other without jealousy or dispute, and sending home their prizes to enrich the stores of their old Museum, and to teach the generations of lads who will be learning here, while they are grown men, doing the work of men over the world.

"Ah, that it might so happen. Ah, that even *one* great man of science might be bred up in these halls, one man who should discover a great truth, or do a great deed for the benefit of his fellow-men. . . . If this College could produce but one master of natural knowledge, like Murchison or Lyell, Owen or Huxley, Faraday or Grove, or even one great discoverer, like Ross, or Sturt, or Speke, who has just solved the mystery of ages, the mystery after which Lucan makes Julius Cæsar long, as the highest summit of his ambition: to leave others to conquer nations, while he himself sought for the hidden sources of the Nile. Or, if it ever should produce one man able and learned enough to do such a deed as that of my friend Clements Markham, who penetrated, in the face of danger and death, the trackless forests of the Andes, to bring home thence the plants of Peruvian bark, which transplanted into Hindostan, will save the lives of tens of thousands — English and Hindoos — then, young gentlemen, all the trouble, all the care, which shall have been spent on this Museum — I had almost said, upon this whole College, will have been well repaid."

Dr. Benson's testimony to his friend must not be passed over:

"As I write," he says, "I feel that what I owe him is more than most — many a maxim, 'fresh from life,' many a flash of bright thought are among my possessions for ever — *his* gift. It was a great thing to see his noble words lit up with his noble life, and to see how, great as his gifts were, they were most fully at the service of his humblest parishioners. . . . There was a bold sketch of him in the 'Spectator' in his squire-like aspect, and I think it was true. But I know that an equally true sketch might be made of him as a parish priest who would have delighted George Herbert. The gentle, warm frankness with which he talked on a summer Sunday among the grassy and flowery graves. The happy peace in which he walked, chatting, over to

Bramshill chapel-school, and, after reading the evening
service, preached in his surplice with a chair-back for
his pulpit, on the deeps of the Athanasian Creed; and,
after thanking God for words that brought such truths
so near, bade the villagers mark that the very Creed
which laid such stress on faith, told them that 'they who
did good would go into everlasting life.'—His striding
across the ploughed field to ask a young ploughman in
the distance why he had not been at church on Sunday,
and ending his talk with, 'Now, you know, John, your
wife don't want you lounging in bed half a Sunday
morning. You get up and come to church, and let her
get your Sunday dinner and make the house tidy, and
then you mind your child in the afternoon while *she*
comes to church.' These, and many other scenes, are
brightly before me. The sternness and the gentleness
which he alternated so easily with foolish people—the
great respectfulness of his tone to old folks. His never
remitted visits to sick and helpless, his knowledge of
their every malady, and every change of their hopes
and fears, made the rectory and church at Eversley the
centre of the life of the men as well as their children
and wives. Gypsies on Hartford-bridge flats have told
me they considered Eversley their parish church wherever they went; and for his own parishioners, 'every
man jack of them,' as he said, was a steady churchgoer. But it was no wonder, for I never heard sermons
with which more pains had been taken than those which
he made for his poor people. . . . The awe and reverence of his manner of celebrating the service was striking to any one who knew only his novels. Strangers
several times asked me, who saw him at service in our
own school-chapel, who it was who was so rapt in manner, who bowed so low at the Gloria and the name of
Jesus Christ; and so I too was surprised when he asked
me, before preaching in his church, to use only the

Letter from Dr. Benson

Invocation of the Trinity; and when I observed that he celebrated the communion in the eastward position. This he loyally gave up on the Purchas judgment, 'because I mind the law,' but told me with what regret he discontinued what from his ordination he had always done, believing it the simple direction of the Prayerbook. In our many happy talks we scarcely ever agreed in our estimate of mediæval character or literature, but I learnt much from him. When even St. Bernard was not appreciated by him, it is not surprising that much of the life of those centuries was repulsive, and its religious practice 'pure Buddhism,' as he used to say. At the same time, I never shall forget how he turned over on a person who was declaiming against 'idolatry.' 'Let me tell you, sir,' (he said with that forcible stammer), 'that if you had had a chance you would have done the same, and worse. The first idols were black stones, meteoric stones. And if you'd been a poor naked fellow, scratching up the ground with your nails, when a great lump of pyrites had suddenly half buried itself in the ground within three yards of you, with a horrid noise and smell, don't you think you'd have gone down on your knees to it, and begged it not to do it again, and smoothed it, and oiled it, and anything else?' Greek life and feeling was dear to him in itself, and usually he was penetrated with thankfulness that it formed so large a part of education. 'From that and from the Bible, boys learn what must be learnt among the grandest moral and spiritual reproofs of what is base. Nothing so fearful as to leave curiosity unslaked to help itself.' At other times he doubted. Still, if I measure rightly, he doubted only when he was so possessed with the forest ardor, that he said, 'All politics, all discussions, all philosophies of Europe, are so infinitely little in comparison with those trees out there in the West Indies. Don't you think the brain is a fungoid growth? O! if I could only find an artist to paint a tree as I see it!' In mentioning last this keen enjoyment of his in the earth as it is, I seem to have inverted the due order: but I see it as a solid, truthful background in his soul of all the tenderness and lovingness, and spiritual strength in which he walked about 'convinced,' as a friend once said to me of him, 'that, as a man and as a priest, he had got the devil under, and that it was his bounden duty to keep him there.'"

His time this year was divided between his parish work and the study of science, and in corresponding with scientific men. Mr. Darwin's book on the "Fertilization of Orchids" had opened a new world to him, and made all that he saw around him, if possible, even more full of divine significance than before. He was busy too with observations on Ice action connected with the Bagshot Sands' district. Every fresh fact he gained tended to strengthen his faith; and to Mr. Bates, whose wonderful travels in the Amazons, and whose discoveries of Mocking butterflies filled him with delight and admiration, he writes:

"Anyhow, it is utterly wonderful, and your explanation, though it is the simplest, is the most wonderful of all; because it looks most like an immensely long chapter of accidents, and is really, if true, a chapter of special Providences of Him without whom not a sparrow falls to the ground, and whose greatness, wisdom, and perpetual care I never understood as I have since I became a convert to Darwin's views. For myself, I agree with Dr. Asa Gray, in his admirable pamphlet on Darwin, that the tendency of physical science is 'not

Wonders of Science

towards the omnipotence of Matter, but to the omnipotence of Spirit.'"

"I have been reading," he writes to Mr. Darwin, "with delight and instruction your paper on climbing plants. . . . Ah, that I could begin to study nature anew, now that you have made it to me a live thing, not a dead collection of names. But my work lies elsewhere now. Your work, nevertheless, helps mine at every turn. It is better that the division of labor should be complete, and that each man should do only one thing, while he looks on, as he finds time, at what others are doing, and so gets laws from other sciences which he can apply, as I do, to my own."

TO REV. F. D. MAURICE

"I am very busy working out points of Natural Theology, by the strange light of Huxley, Darwin, and Lyell. I think I shall come to something worth having before I have done. But I am not going to rush into print this seven years, for this reason: The state of the scientific mind is most curious; Darwin is conquering everywhere, and rushing in like a flood, by the mere force of truth and fact. The one or two who hold out are forced to try all sorts of subterfuges as to fact, or else by evoking the *odium theologicum*. . . . But they find that now they have got rid of an interfering God — a master-magician, as I call it — they have to choose between the absolute empire of accident, and a living, immanent, ever-working God. Grove's truly great mind has seized the latter alternative already, on the side of chemistry. Ansted is feeling for it in geology; and so is Lyell; and I, in my small way of zoölogy, am urging it on Huxley, Rolleston, and Bates, who has just discovered facts about certain butterflies in the valley of the Amazon, which have filled me, and, I trust, others, with utter astonishment and awe. Verily, God is great, or else there is no God at all.

"* * * says somewhere, 'the ape's brain is almost exactly like the man's, and so is his throat. See, then, what enormously different results may be produced by the slightest difference in structure!' I tell him 'not a bit; you are putting the cart before the horse, like the rest of the world. If you won't believe my great new doctrine (which, by the bye, is as old as the Greeks), that souls secrete their bodies, as snails do shells, you will remain in outer darkness.... I know an ape's brain and throat are almost exactly like a man's — and what does that prove? That the ape is a fool and a muff, who has tools very nearly as good as a man's, and yet can't use them, while the man can do the most wonderful thing with tools very little better than an ape's. If men had had apes' bodies they would have got on very tolerably with them, because they had men's souls to work the bodies with. While an ape's soul in a man's body would be only a rather more filthy nuisance than he is now. You fancy that the axe uses the workman, I say that the workman uses the axe, and that though he can work rather better with a good tool than a bad one, the great point is, what sort of workman is he — an ape-soul or a human soul?' Whereby you may perceive that I am not going astray into materialism as yet."

"I am bringing up my children," he writes to an old friend, "as naturalists — my boy as both naturalist and sportsman; and then, whether he goes into the army or emigrates, he will have a pursuit to keep him from cards and brandy-pawnee, horse-racing, and the poor of hell...."

To REV. E. PITCAIRN CAMPBELL. — "... Sir Charles Bunbury and I were talking over this evening Sir Alex. Gordon Cumming's toads in a hole, and behold, your

Toads in Rocks

letter anent them! Verily, great things are in these toads' insides, or so strange a coincidence would not have happened. Now, I say to you what I said to him. Toads are rum brutes. Like all batrachians, they breathe through their skins, as well as through their lungs. The instinct (as I have often proved) of the little beggars an inch long, fresh from water and tadpoledom, is to creep foolishly into the dirtiest hole they can find, in old walls, &c., where 99 out of a 100 are eaten by rats and beetles, as I hold — or else the world would have been toadied to utter disgust and horror long ago. Some of these may get down into cracks in rocks, and never get back. The holes may be silted up by mud and sand. The toad may exist and grow in that hole for Heaven knows how long, I daresay for centuries, for I don't think he would want food to grow; oxygen and water he *must* have, but a very little would do. Accordingly, all the cases of toads in a hole which I have investigated have been either in old walls or limestone rocks, which are porous as a sponge, absorb water and air, and give them out slowly, but enough to keep a cold-blooded batrachian alive. Now, Sir Alex. Gordon Cumming's toads have puzzled me. I have read all that he has written, and thought over it, comparing it with all I know, and I think I know almost every case on record, and I am confounded. Will you ask him for me, what is the nature of this conglomerate in which the toads are? I said to-night I would not believe in toads anywhere but in limestone or chalk, *i.e.*, in strongly hydraulic strata. Sir Charles Bunbury corrected me, by saying that certain volcanic rocks, amygdaloid basalts, were as full of holes as limestone, and as strongly hydraulic, and so toads might live in them. If Sir A. G. C. would send us a piece of the rock in which the toads lie, we could tell him more. But that the toads are contemporaneous with the rock, or have got there any way save through cracks now filled up, and so overlooked in the blasting and cutting is, I believe, impossible, and cannot be — though God alone knows what cannot be — and so I wait for further information.

EVERSLEY: *March* 12, 1863. — " Your patterns of flies are excellent (Brown Mackarel especially), and would kill well on chalk on still and bright days. I send you my pet drake for average blowing weather, and a caperer and alder which can't be beat. At Inveraray last August — hardly anything. River like a turnpike road. Salmon asleep. They had to gaff to supply the house. I had one jolly turn, though — poached a 14-pounder with a triangle, had an hour and three quarters of him, and killed him. Gilly and I fell into each other's arms — and regretted we had no whusky ! "

" We are just from the Royal Wedding[1] — at least so I believe. We had (so I seem to remember) excellent places. Mrs. Kingsley in the temporary gallery in the choir. I in the household gallery, both within 15 yards of what, I am inclined to think, was really the Prince and Princess. But I can't swear to it. I am not at all sure that I did not fall asleep in the dear old chapel, with the banners and stalls fresh in my mind, and dream and dream of Edward the Fourth's time. At least, I saw live Knights of the Garter (myths to me till then). I saw real Princesses with diamond crowns, and trains, and fairies holding them up. I saw — what did I not see? And only began to believe my eyes, when I met at the *déjeuner* certain of the knights whom I knew, clothed and in their right mind, like other folk; and of the damsels and fairies many, who, I believe, were also flesh and blood, for they talked and ate with me, and vanished not away.

[1] The Prince of Wales to Alexandra, Princess of Denmark.

"But seriously, one real thing I did see, and felt too — the serious grace and reverent dignity of my dear young Master, whose manner was perfect. And one other real thing — the Queen's sad face, scarred with sorrow, yet determined to be glad. . . . I cannot tell you how auspicious I consider this event, or how happy it has made the Prince's household, who love him because we know him. I hear nothing but golden reports of the Princess from those who have known her long. . . ."

In the summer of this year the Prince and Princess of Wales were present at the Oxford Commemoration, and previously, according to custom, His Royal Highness sent in the names of those on whom he wished the University to bestow the honorary degree of D.C.L. Among them that of Charles Kingsley. Many friends in the University, besides Dean Stanley, Max Müller, &c., would have gladly seen this honor conferred on him; but among the extreme High Church party there were dissentient voices; and Dr. Pusey took the lead in opposing the degree on the ground of Mr. Kingsley's published works, especially "Hypatia," which he considered "*an immoral book*," and one calculated to encourage young men in profligacy and false doctrine — the very charge that twelve years before had been brought against "Yeast" by an Oxford graduate of the same party. If the vote in Convocation had been carried in Mr. Kingsley's favor, it would have been anything but unanimous, and a threat being made of a "non placet" in the theatre at the time of conferring the degree, he decided to retire. "I do not deny," he says in a letter to Dean Stanley, "a great hankering for years past, after an Oxford D.C.L. . . . But all these things are right, and come with a reason, and a purpose, and a meaning; and he who grumbles at them or at worse, believeth not (for the time being at least) in the living God." Again, he said to one who craved to see honor upon honor showered upon him — "Pray, pray take what God does *not* send as *not* good for us, and trust Him to send us what is good. . . ." He never allowed a past disappointment to ruffle his spirit, but would root out the memory of it before it had time to rankle in his mind and sow any seed of envy or malice. He lived on a high level, and to keep there he knew that he must crush down the unforgiving spirit which springs from envy in the hearts of less noble men. His intense faith in the government of God, as shown in the smallest as well as the most important events of life, and in His education of His creatures by each and every one of these events, and a deep sense of his own unworthiness, made him "content" (a word he loved) with what he had already as all too good for him. The following year some of his Oxford friends chivalrously offered to propose his name again for the distinction which he would have valued so much: but he declined, saying that "it was an honor that must be given, not fought for," and that till the imputation of immorality was withdrawn from his book "Hypatia," he could not entertain the offer even in prospect. When asked by Bishop Wilberforce, in 1866, to preach one of a course of Lent sermons in Oxford, he declined that honor too on the same grounds as the degree.

Bishop Colenso's work on the Pentateuch was now the topic of general discussion, which led to Mr. Kingsley's preaching a series of sermons [1] on the subject to his people at Eversley. These he published and dedicated to Dean Stanley.

"All this talk about the Pentateuch," he writes to Mr. Maurice, "is making me feel its unique value and divineness so much more than ever I did, that I burn to say something worth hearing about it, and I cannot help hoping that what I say may be listened to by some of those who know that I shrink from no lengths in physical science. ... I am sure that science and the creeds will shake hands at last, if only people will leave both alone, and I pray that by God's grace perchance I may help them to do so. My only fear is that people will fancy me a verbal-inspiration-monger, which, as you know, I am not; and that I shall, in due time, suffer the fate of most who see both sides, and be considered by both parties a hypocrite and a traitor. ...."

"A reverent and rational liberty in criticism (within the limits of orthodoxy) is," he says in his preface to the "Sermons on the Pentateuch," "I have always supposed, the right of every Cambridge man; and I was therefore the more shocked, for the sake of free thought in my university, at the appearance of a book which claimed and exercised a licence in such questions, which I must (after careful study of it) call anything but rational and reverent. That book seemed dangerous to the University of Cambridge itself, because it was likely to stir up from without attempts to abridge her ancient liberty of thought; but it seemed still more dangerous to the hundreds of thousands without the university, who, being no scholars, must take on trust the historic truth of the Bible. ... It was making many unsettled and un-

[1] "Sermons on the Pentateuch."

happy; it was (even worse) pandering to the cynicism and frivolity of many who were already too cynical and frivolous. . . . I could not but see that, like most other modern books on biblical criticism, it was altogether negative; was possessed too often by that fanaticism of disbelief, which is just as dangerous as the fanaticism of belief; was picking the body of Scripture to pieces so earnestly, that it seemed to forget that Scripture had a spirit as well as a body; or, if it confessed that it had a spirit, asserting that spirit to be one utterly different from the spirit which the Scripture asserts that it possesses. For the Scripture asserts that those who wrote it were moved by the Spirit of God; that it is a record of God's dealings with men, which certain men were inspired to perceive and to write down; whereas the tendency of modern criticism is, without doubt, to assert that Scripture is inspired by the spirit of man; that it contains the thoughts and discoveries of men concerning God, which they wrote down without the inspiration of God, which difference seems to me (and I hope to others) infinite and incalculable, and to involve the question of the whole character, honor, and glory of God. . . .

". . . There is, without a doubt, something in the Old Testament, as well as in the New, quite different in kind, as well as in degree, from the sacred books of any other people: an unique element, which has had an unique effect upon the human heart, life, and civilization. This remains, after all possible deductions for 'ignorance of physical science,' 'errors in numbers and chronology,' 'interpolations,' 'mistakes of transcribers'. . . . there remains that unique element, beside which all these accidents are but as the spots on the sun, compared to the great glory of his life-giving light; and I cannot but still believe, after much thought, that it — the powerful and working element, the inspired and Divine element, which has converted, and still converts millions of souls

On the Pentateuch

— is just that which Christendom in all ages has held it to be — the account of certain 'noble acts' of God's, and not of certain noble thoughts of man; in a word, not merely the moral, but the historic element; and that, therefore, the value of the Bible teaching depends on the truth of the Bible story. That is my belief. Any criticism which tries to rob me of that, I shall look at fairly, but very severely indeed.

"If all that a man wants is a 'religion,' he ought to be able to make a very pretty one for himself, and a fresh one as often as he is tired of the old. But the heart and soul of man wants more than that, as it is written, 'My soul is athirst for *God*, even for the living God.' Those whom I have to teach want a living God, who cares for men, forgives men, saves men from their sins: — and Him I have found in the Bible, and nowhere else, save in the facts of life, which the Bible alone interprets. In the power of man to find out God I will never believe. The religious sentiment or 'God-consciousness,' so much talked of now-a-days, seems to me (as I believe it will to all practical common-sense Englishmen) a faculty not to be depended on, as fallible and corrupt as any other part of human nature; apt, to judge from history, to develop itself into ugly forms, not only without a revelation from God, but too often in spite of one — into polytheisms, idolatries, witchcrafts, Buddhist asceticisms, Phœnician Moloch sacrifices, Popish inquisitions, American spirit-rappings, and what not. The hearts and minds of the sick, the poor, the sorrowing, the truly human, all demand a living God, who has revealed Himself in living acts; a God who has taught mankind by facts, not left them to discover Him by theories and sentiments; a Judge, a Father, a Saviour, an inspirer; in a word, their hearts and minds demand the historic truth of the Bible — of the Old Testament no less than of the New. . . ."

CHAPTER XXI

1864-1865

AGED 45-46

ILLNESS — CONTROVERSY WITH DR. NEWMAN — APOLOGIA — JOURNEY TO THE SOUTH OF FRANCE — BIARRITZ — PAU — NARBONNE — THE SCHOOLBOY'S SEA — BÉZIERS — PONT DU GARD — NISMES — AVIGNON — UNIVERSITY SERMONS AT CAMBRIDGE — LETTER ON THE TRINITY — ON SUBSCRIPTION — SAVONAROLA — THE LITERARY WORLD — WESLEY AND OXFORD — BEWICK'S AUTOBIOGRAPHY — VISIT OF QUEEN EMMA OF THE SANDWICH ISLANDS TO EVERSLEY RECTORY AND WELLINGTON COLLEGE — DEATH OF KING LEOPOLD — LINES WRITTEN AT WINDSOR CASTLE.

" He heeded not reviling tones
Nor sold his heart to idle moans,
Though cursed and scorn'd, and bruised with stones.
. . . .
He seems to hear a Heavenly Friend
And thro' thick veils to apprehend
A labor working to an end."

TENNYSON.

THE severe illness and great physical depression with which this year began were a bad preparation for the storm of controversy which burst upon Mr. Kingsley, and which eventually produced Dr. Newman's famous "Apologia pro vita sua." The whole controversy is before the world, and no allusion would be made to it in these pages, but from the fear that silence might be construed into a tacit acknowledgment of defeat on the main question. This fact, however, must be mentioned, that it was the infor-

The Newman Controversy 185

mation conveyed to Mr. Kingsley of Dr. Newman's being in bad health, depressed, and averse from polemical discussion, coupled with Dr. Newman's own words in the early part of the correspondence, in which he seemed to deprecate controversy, which appealed irresistibly to Mr. Kingsley's chivalrous consideration, and put him to a great disadvantage in the issue.

"It was his righteous indignation," says Dean Stanley, "against what seemed to him the glorification of a tortuous and ambiguous policy, which betrayed him into the only personal controversy in which he was ever entangled, and in which,' matched in unequal conflict with the most subtle and dexterous controversalist of modern times, it is not surprising that for the moment he was apparently worsted, whatever we may think of the ultimate issues that were raised in the struggle, and whatever may be the total results of our experiences, before and after, on the main question over which the combat was fought — on the relation of the human conscience to truth or to authority." [1]

For the right understanding of Mr. Kingsley's conduct throughout, it cannot be too strongly insisted upon, that it was for truth and truth only that he craved and fought. With him the main point at issue was not the personal integrity of Dr. Newman, but the question whether the Roman Catholic priesthood are encouraged or discouraged to pursue "Truth for its own sake." While no one more fully acknowledged the genius and power of his opponent than Mr. Kingsley himself, or was more ready to confess

[1] Funeral Sermon on Canon Kingsley, in Westminster Abbey.

that he had "crossed swords with one who was too strong for him," yet he always felt that the general position which he had taken up against the policy of the Roman Catholic Church, remained unshaken.[1] And among those who watched the conflict there were many, including even some of his personal friends in the Roman Catholic Church, who felt he had right on his side, though they dared not say so openly in face of his powerful antagonist. Private letters, too, of generous sympathy from strangers came to cheer him — from laymen — from clergymen — even from working-men who having come in contact with the teaching of Roman Catholic priests, knew the truth of his statements. Last but not least, a pamphlet was published by the Rev. Frederick Meyrick, entitled "But is not Kingsley right, after all?" This pamphlet was never answered.

---

[1] It may be doubted whether any words of Mr. Kingsley's convey a more serious accusation against the Church of Rome, than Dr. Newman's own, when speaking of the professions of Rome he warns those who make advances to her, that "*we shall find too late that we are in the arms of a pitiless and unnatural relative who will but triumph in the arts which have inveigled us within her reach . . . for in truth she is a church beside herself . . . crafty, obstinate, wilful, malicious, cruel, unnatural as madmen are — or rather she may be said to resemble a demoniac — possessed with principles, thoughts, and tendencies not her own; in outward form and in natural powers what God made her, but ruled by an inexorable spirit who is sovereign in his management over her, and most subtle and most successful in the use of her gifts. Thus she is her real self only in name, and till God vouchsafes to restore her, we must treat her as if she were that evil one who governs her.*" (Prophetical Office of the Church, p. 101.) These words Dr. Newman formally retracted in the advertisement to an "Essay on the Development of Christian Doctrine," but when first published, they expressed his deliberate opinion, and as such were accepted without remonstrance by the High Church party.

For more than a year past Mr. Kingsley had been suffering from illness caused by overwork of brain, and a thorough rest and change of air had long been seriously urged upon him. At this moment, Mr. Froude, who was going to Spain on literary business, invited him to go with him, and he replies:

"DEAREST ANTHONY, — This is too delightful. . . . When you propose, what can I do but accept? . . . I have always felt that one good sea voyage would add ten years to my life. All my friends say, go, but I must not be the least burden to you. Remember that I can amuse myself in any hedge, with plants and insects and a cigar, and that you may leave me anywhere, any long, certain that I shall be busy and happy. I cannot say how the thought of going has put fresh life into me."

To HIS WIFE. — "PARIS: *March* 25. — The splendor of this city is beyond all I could have conceived, and the beautiful neatness and completeness of everything delight my eyes. Verily these French are a civilized people. . . ."

BAYONNE, *March* 26. — "A place utterly unlike anything I ever saw — very picturesque, with the yellow and brown jalousies to the windows, and the shipping at the bottom of the street, and the red-legged soldiers everywhere. I have seen so much since I wrote this morning, I hardly know where to begin. At Coutras, the other side of Bordeaux, I felt at once I was in a new world. Everything a month earlier than with us; the fruit trees in full flower; pink and crimson almond trees by dozens everywhere. The air strangely clear, the houses low-roofed, and covered with purple-ribbed tiles like the old Roman. . . . Into Bordeaux we did not go, but only into the Landes — for which, fancy one hundred miles of Hartford Bridge Flat, with *Pinus maritima* instead of Scotch fir, and a tall delicate heath unknown to me, among the common heath. Little long-wooled sheep, cows you could put under your arm, boys on stilts tending them, with sheepskin coats (wool outside) and sheepskin pads for their 'poor feet,' else they would have to have them asked after, if there was anyone to ask, which there ain't — the only birds magpies. But thrivingness and improvement everywhere; immense new plantations of the pinus, new clearings for cultivation, new smart cottages, beautiful new churches, railway stations laid out with shrubberies of foreign trees. What a go-a-head place France is! It gladdens my heart to look at it. Saw the first cork-trees about forty miles from Bayonne planted, barked all round about nine feet high for the cork. It don't hurt them, in fact they rather like it, and it gives the new wood room to expand. I saw many flowers on the banks I did not know, and maize-fields, with last year's stubble in them, and plenty of our dear English 'lady's smock' in the wet meadows near here, which looked very homey. Coming off the Landes between Morceux and Dax, saw a low ridge of clouds below the other clouds, which were the Pyrenees. I could soon distinguish the line of eternal snow — could see vast *arrêtes* and glaciers blazing in the sun one hundred miles off — gorges that faded into infinite cloud land; peaks just cut off by the lower banks of vapor. It was an awful sight for the first time. They were intensely clear in the rainy atmosphere, and clear all but the tops of a few of the highest. After Dax they faded, as we rounded their lower outworks, which run to the sea. . . . I have just discovered a huge vulture chained to a tree in the courtyard in the rain, sulking, and poking and dripping. . . . They have the most exquisite little yellow oxen here, rather bigger than a donkey. They put brown holland pinafores on their backs, and great sheepskin mats on their heads, where the yoke comes, and persuade them as a great favor to do a little work. But they seem so fond of them that the oxen have much the best of the bargain. God bless you all with all Easter blessings. . . ."

BIARRITZ: *April*, 1864. — " A pleasant day at Biarritz. It was blowing great guns in from dead W.N.W. I never saw a finer sea, rushing through caverns and cracks in a strange sandstone full of nummulities and flat layers of flint. Flowers wonderful. Cliffs covered with white and red stocks, the same as our garden ones, and just as fine. I shall stop here for a week or so, to botanize and breathe sea-champagne. The Basques speak a lingo utterly different from all European languages, which has no analogue, and must have come from a different stock from our ancestors. The women are very pretty — brown aquiline, with low foreheads, and have a quaint fashion of doing up their back hair in a gaudy silk handkerchief, which is cunningly twisted till one great triangular tail stands out stiff behind the left ear. This is a great art. The old ones tie their whole heads up in the handkerchief and look very pretty but browner than apes from wearing no bonnets.

"It has rained to-day, again, 'marling-spikes and copper sheathing,' and the vulture (whom I have sketched much) has been dancing about trying to dry himself, and expanding great concave wings as big as windmill sails. He must be a glorious bird in his native Pyrenees. . . . The hills here are covered with the true Cornish heath, pale blue vernal squills, a great white *Potentilla verna*, and a long blue flower, which seems to me a borage or bugloss. I am drying all

I find. The Spanish mountains are covered with snow, and look magnificent. The rocks are covered with *Echinus lividus*, a sea-urchin that bores in limestone! We are going to chisel some out.

". . . A day as pleasant as one can be without you; sea and rocks wonderful. — A new and most beautiful and curious zoöphite, ditto seaweed. God bless you. I wish I was home again. Yesterday we went to the bar of the Adour, and saw the place where Hope carried the Guards across and made a bridge of boats in the face of 15,000 French. When one sees such things, who dare sneer at old 'Peninsular officers?' To-day I was looking through the glass at the Rhune mountain, which Soult entrenched from top to bottom, and Wellington stormed, yard by yard, with 20,000 men, before he could cross the Bidassoa; and to have taken that mountain seemed a deed of old giants. We drove through Landes yesterday, too, and saw the pine trees hacked for turpentine and a little pot hung to each, with clear turpentine running in, and in the tops of the young trees great social nests of the pitzocampo moth-caterpillar, of which I have got some silk, but dared not open the nest, for their hairs are deadly poison, as the old Romans knew. . . . Oh, the blessed, blessed feeling of having nothing to do! I start sometimes and turn round guiltily, with the thought, 'Surely I ought to be doing something—I have forgotten something,' and then to feel that there is nothing to do even if I wanted! It will make me quite well. . . ."

TO HIS YOUNGEST DAUGHTER

BIARRITZ. — "MY DARLING MARY, — I am going to write you a long letter about all sorts of things. And first, this place is full of the prettiest children I ever saw, very like English, but with dark hair and eyes, and none

At Biarritz

of them look poor or ragged; but so nicely dressed, with striped stockings, which they knit themselves, and Basque shoes, made of canvas, worked with red and purple worsted. There is a little girl here six years old, a chemist's daughter, who knits all her own woollen stockings. All the children go to a school kept by nuns; and I am sure the poor nuns are very kind to them, for they laugh and romp, it seems to me, all day long. In summer most of them wear no shoes or stockings, for they do not want them; but in winter they are wrapped up warm; and I have not seen one ragged child or tramp, or any one who looks miserable. They never wear any bonnets. The little babies wear a white cap, and the children a woollen cap with pretty colors, and the girls a smart handkerchief on their back hair, and the boys and men wear blue and scarlet caps like Scotchmen, just the shape of mushrooms, and a red sash. The oxen here are quite yellow, and so gentle and wise, the men make them do exactly what they like. I will draw you an ox cart when I come home. The banks here are covered with enormous canes, as high as the eaves of our house. They tie one of these to a fir pole, and make a huge long rod, and then go and sit on the rocks and fish for doradas, which are fish with gilt heads. There are the most lovely sweet-smelling purple pinks on the rocks here, and the woods are full of asphodel, great lilies, four feet high, with white and purple flowers. I saw the wood yesterday where the dreadful fight was between the French and English — and over the place where all the brave men lay buried grew one great flower-bed of asphodel. So they 'slept in the meads of asphodel,' like the old Greek heroes in Homer. There were great 'lords and ladies' (arums) there, growing in the bank, twice as big as ours, and not red, but white and primrose — most beautiful. But you cannot think how beautiful the commons are, they are like flower gardens, golden with furze, and white with *potentilla*, and crimson with sweet-smelling Daphne, and blue with the most wonderful blue flower which grows everywhere. I have dried them all.

"Tell your darling mother I am quite well, and will write to her to-morrow. There, that is all I have to say. Tell Grenville they have made a tunnel under the battle-field, for the railroad to go into Spain, and that on the top of the tunnel there is a shaft, and a huge wheel, to pump air into the tunnel, and that I will bring him home a scarlet Basque cap, and you and Rose Basque shoes. . . .   YOUR OWN DADDY."

To HIS WIFE. PAU :—" Writing from a place which, for beauty, beats everything I ever saw, and all the better for finding your dear letter here, and one from Grenville, which I shall answer at once. At its foot, below the beautiful *château* where Henry IV., 'Le Monstre Henri,' was born, a valley of flat grass, filled with poplars, the Gare, a glacier torrent rolling over acres of gray gravel. On the south bank of the town the loveliest *châteaux*, parks, *allées*, flower-gardens, trees full of singing-birds, whose notes are new to me, and trees covered with purple flowers. Wisterias, and yellow Banksia roses over every wall. Frogs barking, rattling, making a dozen noises unknown at home. Opposite, broken wooded hills covered with *châteaux*. Ten miles off, a purple wall with white streaks, which is not the Pyrenees, but is about as high as Snowdon; twenty miles off, an abyss of cloud and snow, which is the Pyrenees. It is a place to live in! a great town, city one ought to say, as it is royal from all ages, and in the loveliest spot one can imagine. We went to the English church, after having all been ill; for why? the water is horrible, I suppose from the great age of the town. So Cane and I flee to the mountains to-

Letters from Pau

morrow. . . . Then Bagnières, Tarbes, Toulouse, Carcassonne, Béziers (all the scenes of the Albigense horrors, which I have wished to realize to myself for years), and so to the Mediterranean. But I have no plans, and don't intend to have any. If I had wits I should tell you about Orthez, and the noble ruin we saw there; one of the Duke's great battle-fields. But you should make R—— read up this country in Napier's 'Peninsular War,' beginning at the passage of the Bidassoa, and following me hither and to Toulouse. How I shall devour it when I get home. . . ."

TO HIS YOUNGEST BOY

PAU. — " MY DEAR LITTLE MAN, — I was quite delighted to get a letter from you so nicely written. Yesterday I went by the railway to a most beautiful place, where I am staying now. A town with an old castle, hundreds of years old, where the great King Henry IV. of France was born, and his cradle is there still, made of a huge tortoise shell. Underneath the castle are beautiful walks and woods — all green, as if it was summer, and roses and flowers, and birds singing — but different from our English birds. But it is quite summer here because it is so far south. Under the castle, by the river, are frogs that make a noise like a rattle, and frogs that bark like toy-dogs, and frogs that climb up trees, and even up the window-panes — they have suckers on their feet, and are quite green like a leaf. Far away, before the castle are the great mountains, ten thousand feet high, covered with snow, and the clouds crawling about their tops. I am going to see them to-morrow, and when I come back I will tell you. But I have been out to-night, and all the frogs are croaking still, and making a horrid noise. Mind and be a good boy and give Baba my love. There is a vulture here in the inn, but he is a little Egyptian vulture, not like the great vulture I saw at Bayonne. Ask mother to show you his picture in the beginning of the bird book. He is called *Neophra Egyptiacus*, and is an ugly fellow, who eats dead horses and sheep. There is his picture. Your own Daddy, "C. KINGSLEY."

To HIS WIFE. — "I have taken a new turn, and my nerve and strength have come back, from three days in the Pyrenees. What I have seen I cannot tell you. Things unspeakable and full of glory. Mountains whose herbage is box, for miles and thousands of feet, then enormous silver firs and beech, up to the eternal snow. We went up to Eaux-Chaudes — a gigantic Lynmouth, with rivers breaking out of limestone caverns hundreds of feet over our heads. There we were told that we must take horses and guides up to the Plateau to see the Pic du Midi. We would n't and drove up to Gabas, and found the mountain air so jolly that we lounged on for an hour — luckily up the right valley, and behold, after *rochers moutonnés*, and moraines, showing the enormous glaciers which are extinct, we came to a down, which we knew by inspiration was the Plateau. We had had a good deal of snow going up — climbed three hundred feet of easy down, and there it was right in front, nine thousand feet high, with the winter snow at the base — the eternal snow holding on by claws and teeth where it could above. I could have looked for hours. I could not speak. I cannot understand it yet. Right and left were other eternal snow-peaks; but very horrible. Great white sheets with black points mingling with the clouds, of a dreariness to haunt one's dreams. I don't like snow mountains. The Pic above is jolly, and sunlit and honest. The flowers were not all out — only in every meadow below *Gentiana verna*, of the most heavenly azure, and huge oxslips: but I have got some beautiful things. To-day we saw Eaux Bonnes — two great eternal snow-peaks there, but not so striking. Butterflies glorious, even now. The common one — the great Camberwell beauty (almost extinct in England), a huge black butterfly with white edge; we could n't catch one. The day before yesterday, at Eaux Chaudes, two bears were fired at, and a wolf seen. With every flock of sheep and girls are one or two enormous mastiffs, which could eat one, and do bark nastily. But when the children call them and introduce them to you formally, they stand to be patted, and eat out of the hand; they are great darlings, and necessary against bears and wolf. So we did everything without the least mishap — nay, with glory — for the folk were astonished at our getting to the Plateau on our own hook. The Mossoos can't walk, you see, and think it an awful thing. A Wellington College boy would trot there in three-quarters of an hour. Last night, *pour comble*, we (or rather I) did something extra — a dear little sucking earthquake, went off crash — bang, just under my bed. I thought something had fallen in the room below, though I wondered why it hove my bed right up. Got out of bed, hearing a woman scream, and hearing no more, guessed it, and went to bed. It shook the whole house and village; but no one minded. They said they had lots of young earthquakes there, but they went off before they had time to grow. Lucky for the place. It was a very queer sensation, and made a most awful noise."

NARBONNE. — "It is strange to be sitting here and writing to you, just as if I had been travelling all my life. The novelty of the thing has worn off, and I long to be home. . . .

" . . . We were yesterday at Carcassonne, a fortified place, whose walls were built by Roman, Visigoth, Mussulman, Romance (*i.e.* Albigense) and then by

French kings. Such a remnant of the old times as I have dreamed of . . . with its wonderful church of St. Nazare, where Roman Corinthian capitals are used by the Romance people — 9–10 century. We went down into real dungeons of the Inquisition, and saw real chains and torture rings, and breathed more freely when we came up into the air, and the guide pointed to the Pyrenees and said, ' *Il n'y a point de démons là.*'

"I shall never forget that place. Narbonne is very curious, once the old Roman capital, then the Albigense. Towers, cathedral, archbishop's palace — all wonderful. Whole quarries of Roman remains. The walls, built by Francis I., who demolished the old Roman and Gothic walls, are a museum of antiquities in themselves. If you want to have a souvenir of Narbonne, read in my lectures Sidonius's account of Theodoric the Visigoth and his court here. His palace is long gone. It probably stood where the archbishop's palace does now. . . ."

NISMES. — ". . . It is all like a pleasant dream. If I had but you and Rose to show it to! But I have no one to share with me the mere pleasure of existence of this sunny South. I am sitting, 8.30, at an open window. Garden, trees, flowers, fountain outside, with people sitting out on the benches already, doing nothing but simply *live*; and more and more will sit there, till 10 to-night; from 7 to 10 the whole population of this great city will be in the streets, not sunning but mooning themselves, quite orderly and happy, listening to music, and cutting their little jokes, along the boulevards, under the beautiful trees these French have the sense to plant. I understand them now. They are not Visigoths, these fellows. They are the descendants of the old Roman Gauls, the lovers of the town, and therefore they make their towns livable and lovable with trees and fountains, and bring the country into the town, while the Teutons take the town out into the country, and love each man his own

At Nismes

garden and park, like us English — the only real Teutons left in the world. But what a country they have made of it, these brave French! For one hundred miles yesterday, what had been poor limestone plain was a garden. A scrap or two I saw of the original vegetation a donkey would have starved on. But they have cleared it all off for ages, ever since the Roman times, and it is one sea of vines, with olive, fig, and mulberry planted among them. Where there is a hill it is exactly like the photographs of the Holy Land and Nazareth — limestone walls, with nothing but vineyards and gray olives planted in them, and raised stone paths about them. The only green thing — for the soil is red, and the vines are only sprouting — is here and there a field of the Roman plant, lucerne, as high as one's knee already. I came by Béziers, where the Inquisitor cried, 'Kill them all, God will know his own,' and they shut them into the Madelaine and killed them all — Catholics as well as Albigenses, till there was not a soul alive in Béziers, and the bones are there to this day!

"But this land is beautiful — as they say, '*Si Dieu venait encore sur la terre, il viendrait demeurer à Béziers,*' and, indeed it is just like, as I have said, the Holy Land. Then we came to immense flats — still in vine and olive, and then to sand-hills, and then upon the tideless shore broke the blue Mediterranean, with the long lateen sails, as in pictures. It was a wonderful feeling to a scholar[1]

---

[1] "There it is at last. The long line of heavenly blue, and over it, far away, the white-peaked lateen sails, and there, close to the rail, beyond the sand-hills, delicate wavelets are breaking for ever on a yellow beach, each in exactly the same place as the one which fell before. One glance shows us children of the Atlantic that we are on a tideless sea.

"There it is, — the sacred sea. The sea of all civilization, and almost all history, girdled by the fairest countries in the world; set there that human beings from all its shores might mingle with each other, and become humane — the sea of Egypt, of Palestine, of Greece, of Italy, of Byzant, of Marseilles, and this Narbonnaise, to see the 'schoolboy's sea' for the first time, and so perfectly, in a glory of sunshine and blue ripple. We ran literally through it for miles between Agde and Cette — tall asphodel growing on the sand-hills, and great white iris and vines. . . .''

" My first impression of the Pont du Gard was one of simple fear. ' It was so high that it was dreadful,' as Ezekiel says. Then I said, again and again, 'A great people and a strong. There hath been none like before them, nor shall be again for many generations.' As, after fifteen miles of the sea of mulberry, olive, and vine, dreary from its very artificial perfection, we turned the corner of the limestone glen, and over the deep blue rock-pool, saw *that thing* hanging between earth and heaven, the blue sky and green woods showing through its bright yellow arches, and all to carry a cubic yard of water to Nismes, twenty miles off, for public baths and sham sea-fights ('*naumachiæ*') in the amphitheatre, which even Charlemagne, when he burnt the Moors out of it, could not destroy. — Then I felt the brute greatness of that Roman people; and an awe fell upon me as it may have fallen on poor Croc, the Rook, king of the Alemans — but that is a long story, — when he came down and tried to destroy this city of the seven hills, and ended in being shown about in an iron cage as *The Rook*. But I doubt not when he and his wild Alemans

'more Roman than Rome herself,' to which we owe the greater part of our own progress; the sea, too, of Algeria, and Carthage, and Cyrene, and fair lands now desolate, surely not to be desolate for ever — the sea of civilization. Not only to the Christian, nor to the classic scholar, but to every man to whom the progress of his race from barbarism toward humanity is dear, should the Mediterranean Sea be one of the most august and precious objects on this globe; and the first sight of it should inspire reverence and delight, as of coming home — home to a rich inheritance in which he has long believed by hearsay, but which he sees at last with his own mortal corporal eyes." — *From Ocean to Sea*, Prose Idylls.

came down to the Pont du Gard they said it was the work of dwarfs — of the devil! We walked up to the top, through groves of *Ilex, Smilax,* and *Coronella* (the first time I have seen it growing), and then we walked across on the top. The masonry is wonderful, and instead of employing the mountain limestone of the hills, they have brought the most splendid Bath oolite from the hills opposite. There are the marks cut by the old fellows — horse-hoofs, hatchets, initials, &c., as fresh as paint. The Emperor has had it all repaired from the same quarries, stone for stone. Now, after 1600 years, they are going to bring the same water into Nismes by it. When we crossed, I was in a new world. *Genista Anglica,* the prickly needle furze of our commons (rare with us), is in great golden bushes; and box, shrubby thyme, a wonderful blue lily, bee-orchis, and asters, white, yellow, purple (which won't dry, for the leaves fall off). — Then wild rosemary, and twenty more plants I never saw. We went below into a natural park of ilex and poplar (two or three sorts), and watched such butterflies and the bridge, till C—— said, 'This is too perfect to last,' which frightened me and made me pray. And there was reason — for such a day I never had in my life of beauty and wonder . . . and yet there is one thing more glorious and precious than the whole material universe, — and that is a woman's love. . . ."

"I stopped at Nismes, and begin again at Avignon. We saw to-day the most wonderful Roman remains. But the remarkable thing was the Roman ladies' baths in a fountain bursting up out of the rock, where, under colonnades, they walked about, in or out of the water as they chose. All is standing, and could be used to-morrow, if the prudery of the priests allowed it. Honor to those Romans; with all their sins, they were the cleanest people the world has ever seen. But to tell you all I saw at

Nismes would take a book. Perhaps it will make one some day. . . . Good-bye. I shall write again from this, the most wonderful place I have yet seen."

AVIGNON: *Sunday.* — "We are still here, under the shadow of that terrible fortress which the Holy Fathers of mankind erected to show men their idea of paternity. A dreadful dungeon on a rock. The vastest pile of stone I ever saw. Men asked for bread, and they gave a stone, most literally. I have seen La Tour de la Glacière, famous for its horrors of 1793, but did not care to enter. The sight here are the walls — very nearly perfect. . . . Did you ever hear of a mistral? It is on this wise. The whole of the air between the Alps and Pyrenees rushes into the Mediterranean from north-west — a three or four days' gale, with a bright blue sky, cold wind, parching and burning, with not dust merely but gravel, flying till the distances are as thick as in an English north-easter. It is a fearful wind, and often damages crops severely; but they say it is healthy and bracing, and so I find it; but the roar and rush, and the dust and dirt, beat anything I ever felt. When one has a gale in England it has the courtesy to water the streets first. To-morrow for the Mediterranean again, *viâ* the plain of Crau, where Zeus threw great stones on the savages, who attacked Hercules as he came back from Spain with Gorgons' heads — a place I have longed to see for years. . . ."

He returned home better, but not well, and worked on. He gave a lecture at Aldershot Camp on the "Study of History," and preached the usual sermons before the Queen at Windsor Castle, and at the Chapels Royal, London. In the autumn, having been selected as one of the preachers at Cambridge for 1865, he was busy preparing four sermons on David. "Wish me

Sermons at Cambridge

well through these university sermons," he writes to Mr. Maurice, "they lie heavy on my sinful soul;" and when the Christmas vacation was over, he went up to Cambridge to deliver them, closing with these words:—

"Therefore rejoice in your youth, for God has given it to you; but remember, that for it, as for each and all of His gifts, God will bring you into judgment. And when the hour of temptation comes, go back — go back, if you would escape — to what you were all taught at your mother's knee, concerning the grace of God; for that alone will keep you safe, or angel or archangel, or any created being safe, in this life and in all lives to come." [1]

"I was present," said a Fellow of a College in Cambridge, "at the University sermons on David, and well remember the crowds of us undergraduates round the church-door before it was opened, all wishing to have a good place to see and hear him, and the rapt attention with which he was listened to, and the thrill of half-expectation, half-amusement, which seemed to go round the church as he uttered the words, 'Muscular Christianity — a clever phrase invented by I know not whom ——.'" [2]

The same friend speaks too of the impression made upon him by "that keen, fiery, worn face;

[1] Sermons on David.
[2] It may be well to quote the rest of this sentence which is omitted: "We have heard much of late about Muscular Christianity. A clever expression, spoken in jest by I know not whom, has been bandied about the world, and supposed by many to represent some new ideal of the christian Character. For myself I do not know what it means. It may mean one of two things. If it mean the first, it is a term somewhat unnecessary, if not somewhat irreverent. If it mean the second, it means something untrue and immoral."

the noble spirit ever fretting its tenement of clay," and how he used to wonder what drew the deep lines in it, which he only came to understand in after years.

The letters of 1865 that have been recovered are few. He was so broken in strength, that to get through the duties of his professorship and his parish was as much, nay, more than he could manage, and in the summer he was forced to leave home with his family for three months' rest and quiet on the coast of Norfolk.

To T. HUGHES, ESQ. — "The doctors forbid my preaching. I gave my Whitehall sermon to the Consumptive Hospital as to an old and dear friend; but I have refused all others. I am getting better after fifteen months of illness, and I hope to be of some use again some day; a sadder and a wiser man, the former, at least, I grow every year. I catch a trout now and then out of my ponds (I am too weak for a day's fishing, and the doctors have absolutely forbidden me my salmon). I have had one or two this year, of three and two pounds, and a brace to-day, near one pound each, so I am not left troutless. . . ."

TO REV. F. D. MAURICE

"Your letter comforted me, for (strange as it may seem for me to say so) the only thing I really care for — the only thing which gives me comfort — is theology, in the strict sense; though God knows I know little enough about it.

"As to the Trinity. You first taught me that the doctrine was a live thing, and not a mere formula to be swallowed by the undigesting reason, and from the time that I learnt that a Father meant a real Father, a Son a real Son, and a Holy Spirit a real Spirit, who was really

Letter on the Trinity

good and holy, I have been able to draw all sorts of practical lessons from it in the pulpit, and ground all my morality, and a great deal of my natural philosophy upon it, and shall do so more. The procession of the Spirit from the Father and the Son, for instance, is most practically important to me. If the Spirit proceeds only from the Father, the whole theorem of the Trinity, as well as its practical results, fall to pieces to my mind. I don't mean that good men in the Greek Church are not better than I. On the contrary, I believe that every good man therein believes in the procession from both Father and Son, whether he thinks that he does or not. But in this case, as in others, one has extreme difficulty in remembering, and still more in making others understand, that a man may believe the facts which the doctrine connotes without believing the doctrine, just as he may believe that a horse is a horse, for every practical purpose, though he may have been mistaught to call it a cow. It is this slavery to formulæ — this mistaking of words for conceptions, and then, again of conceptions for the facts, which seems our present curse; and how much of it do we not owe to the Calvinists, who laid again on our necks the yoke of conceptions which we were bursting at the Reformation, because neither we nor our fathers could bear it? It was this which made me reject Mansel and Hamilton's 'The Absolute' and 'The Infinite.' I am taking a regular course of metaphysic, as a tonic after the long debauchery of fiction-writing. I say to you, once for all, Have patience with me, and I will pay thee — not all, but a little, and I know you will not take me by the throat. If you did, you would break my heart; which could be much more easily broken than people think. If a man is intensely in earnest after truth, be it what it may, and also intensely disgusted with his own laziness, worldliness, and sensuality, his heart is not difficult to break. . . .

"You say, 'The *Articles* were not intended to bind men's thoughts or consciences!' Now, I can't help feeling that when they assert a proposition, *e.g.*, the Trinity, they assert that that and nothing else on that matter is true, and so bind thought; and that they require me to swear that I believe it so, and so bind my conscience. In the case where they condemn an error, it seems to me quite different. There they proscribe *one* form of thought, and leave all others open by implication, binding neither thought nor conscience. Thus the Tract XC. argument was quite fair — *if its author could have used it fairly*. The Romish doctrine of Purgatory is false; but denying that does not forbid me to believe other doctrines of Purgatory to be true, and to speculate freely on the future state. So that what you say applies clearly (to me) to the cases in which the Articles deny. It applies also to all cases in which the Articles do not affirm, *e.g.*, endless torture. Also to all in which it uses words without defining them, *e. g.*, the Article on Predestination, which I sign in what I conceive to be the literal sense not only of it, but of the corresponding passage in St. Paul, without believing one word of the Calvinistic theory, or that St. Paul was speaking of the future state at all. For myself, I can sign the Articles in their literal sense *toto corde*, and subscription is no bondage to me. But all I demand is, that, in signing the Articles, I shall be understood to sign them and nothing more; that I do not sign anything beyond the words, and demand the right to put my construction on the words, answerable only . . . to God and my conscience. *In practice*, Gorham and Pusey both do this, and nothing else, whenever it suits them. I demand that I shall have just the same liberty as they, and no more. But the world at large uses a very powerful, though worthless, argument. Lord * * * answered, when I asked him why the Articles had not defined inspiration, 'Because they never expected that men would arise heretics enough to deny it!' I had to reply — and I think convinced him — that that line of thought would destroy all worth in formula, by making signing mean, 'I sign the XXXIX. Articles, and as many more as the Church has forgotten to, or may have need to, put in.' But the mob, whose superstitions are the very cosmogony of their creed, would think that argument conclusive, and say, — of course, you are expected to believe, over and above, such things as endless torture, verbal dictation, &c., which are more of the essence of Christianity than the creeds themselves, or the Being of a God.

"Meanwhile, each would make a reservation — the 'Evangelical' of the Calvinist School would say in his heart — of course (though I dare n't say so) every man is expected to believe conversion, even though not mentioned; and the Romanist, of course, every man must believe in the Pope, though not mentioned; and the reigning superstition, not the formulæ actually signed, becomes the test of faith. But how we are to better this by doing away with subscription, I don't see yet. As long as the Articles stand, and as long as they are interpreted by *lawyers only*, who will ask sternly, 'Is it in the bond?' and nothing else, I see hope for freedom and safety. If subscription was done away, every man would either teach what was right in his own eyes — which would be somewhat confusing — or he would have to be controlled by a body, not of written words, but of thinking men. From whom may my Lord deliver me!"

"I feel," he said, "a capacity of drifting to sea in me which makes me cling nervously to any little anchor, like subscription. I feel glad of aught that says to me, 'You must teach this and nothing else; you must not run riot in your own dreams!'. . ."

These words show how exercised his own mind was at times, but it may be a comfort to other troubled souls to know of the calm assured faith with which at the last, when standing on the very threshold of the next world, he faced death, and was heard repeating again and again, "It is all right — all under rule." Perhaps his dearly loved George Fox's words best express the habitual attitude of his heart and mind for thirty years. "And I saw that there was an Ocean of Darkness and Death: but an infinite Ocean of Light and Love flowed over the Ocean of Darkness: and in that I saw the infinite Love of God."

"Never, I fancy," said one who knew him well, "at any time did the great and terrible battle of faith and doubt wholly cease within him. Probably few escape the stress of that conflict now-a-days; but I think he knew more about it than most of us. For his reverence for what is called 'consistency' was very limited, and his mind was always busy with the workings of those life-problems which had left their mark upon his brow, and wrought into his very manner a restless energy which foretold a shortened career. Nevertheless there is no doubt but that the victory remained with faith."

To REV. F. D. MAURICE. — "Many thanks for your letter. I am very sorry I differ from you about Savonarola. It seems to me that his protest for the kingdom of God and against sin was little worth, and came to nought, just because it was from the merely negative inhuman monks' standpoint of the 13th century; that he would at best have got the world back to St. Bernard's time, to begin all over again, and end just where Savonarola had found them. Centuries of teaching such as

Wesley and Oxford 207

his had ended in leaving Italy a hell on earth; new medicine was needed, which no monk could give. A similar case, it seems to me, is that of the poor Port-Royalists. They tried to habilitate the monk-ideal of righteousness. They were civilized off the face of the earth, as was poor Savonarola, by men worse than themselves, but more humane, with wider (though shallower) notions of what man and the universe meant."

To REV. J. MONTAGU, *Nov.* 30, 1865. — " I shall be delighted to do all I can, but I fear I am a very Esau now with the Press, going my own way, and joining no literary clique, without which one must submit to hatred and abuse. . . . If —— will send her books to 'Fraser's Magazine,' I will do what I can to get them fair play and a bit of courtesy into the bargain. But really, I have no influence; and as for 'living in the literary world,' it is just what I don't and won't. Not the writing merely, but what a man writes, make him an object of interest to me. . . . So you are leading a hum-drum life — happy man! Free from ambition, disappointment, fears, shame, foolish exaltation, vanity and vexation of spirit. Had I not a boy going to Cambridge, I would never write another word, but live between my microscope and my roses. God bless you. . . . "

To DR. RIGG, *December* 16, 1865. — " I shall be very glad to see Wesley's Journals or anything which explains him to me. He has long seemed to me a true son of Oxford; possibly the precursor of the late great Oxford movement. Had he been born fifty years ago, and under the influences which he himself originated (*qu. e. imposs.*) he would have been a great high churchman, the fellow but the superior of Newman and Pusey. It is these thoughts which make a man liberal — when one considers how man is the creature of circumstances, and we have nought but what we have received. Only to escape atheism and despair, let us remember that the Creator and Ordainer of the circumstances is not chance or nature, but the Father of Our Lord Jesus Christ and of us."

To MR. DIXON (cork-cutter). — "You and your friend's free kindness could not have devised a present more to my taste than 'Bewick's Autobiography.' I have read it through, and am equally delighted and astonished at it. Brought up as I was on 'Bewick's Birds,' and owing much of my early inspirations, such as they were, to his love of natural scenery as well as his love of ornithology, I always held him to be a great genius in his own line, but I was not prepared to find him so remarkable a man in other respects — his temperance and thrift, his simple virtue, his sound and wide views on all matters political and social, astonish me as do the prophecies, if I can so call them — and none more than those on social and economic reform which have since been carried out — salmon preservation amongst the rest. Delightful are the sketches of simple, sturdy, north country life in the last century. A noble breed of men they must have been, and we will hope that the race is not worn out; they cannot be, and need not be, just what their fathers were:

'The old order changeth, yielding place to new,
And God fulfils Himself in many ways,
Lest one good custom should corrupt the world.'

So says Tennyson — and so you may find it come true; the times in which we live, after all, are better and not worse than Bewick's, and you may find it easier, not more difficult, to live a life like Bewick's now, than one hundred years ago. As for regretting the good old-fashioned life, we must recollect that it too had its bad side. For one thing it would be impossible now for the country

Visit of Queen Emma

to be plunged into such a war as Pitt's, or preyed upon by such a swarm of placemen as it was in Bewick's time, simply because whatever the hand-workers have lost, they have gained in intelligence, in weight, in power of expression, and of action."

In the autumn Queen Emma of the Sandwich Islands came on a visit of two days to Eversley Rectory. King Kamehameha, her husband, had read Mr. Kingsley's books, and she was anxious to know him, and to combine with her visit to Eversley one to the Wellington College, of which she had heard much, and where, it was said, if her little son had lived, he would have been sent for his education. "It is so strange to me," she said, "to be staying with you and to see Mr. Kingsley. My husband read your husband's 'Water-Babies' to our little Prince." It was a great pleasure to Mr. Kingsley to receive Queen Emma, and to take her to the College. After going all over it and seeing the boys at dinner in hall, she asked Dr. Benson for a half-holiday for them, upon which Mr. Ponsonby, then head of the school, called for three cheers for Queen Emma; and as they resounded through the hall she was startled almost to terror, by hearing for the first time how English public school boys can cheer. She went on the playground, and for the first time saw a game of cricket, examined the bats, balls, wickets, and pads, looking into everything with her own peculiar intelligence, and in the evening went over again for choral service in the chapel.

In November, while Mr. Kingsley was preaching before the Court, at Windsor Castle, a telegram came to the Queen to announce the death of Leopold, King of the Belgians. He had been asked to write a few lines in the album of the Crown Princess of Prussia, and with his mind full of this great European event, wrote the following Impromptu, which is printed here by the kind permission of her Imperial Highness.

November 10, 1865.

"A king is dead! Another master mind
Is summoned from the world-wide council hall.
Ah for some seer, to say what lurks behind —
To read the mystic writing on the wall!

"Be still, fond man: nor ask thy fate to know.
Face bravely what each God-sent moment brings.
Above thee rules in love, through weal and woe,
Guiding thy kings and thee, the King of kings.

"C. KINGSLEY."

CHAPTER XXII

1866-1867

AGED 47-48

CAMBRIDGE — DEATH OF DR. WHEWELL — THE AMERICAN PROFESSORSHIP — MONOTONOUS LIFE OF THE COUNTRY LABORING CLASS — PENNY READINGS — LONDON SERMONS — STRANGE CORRESPONDENTS — LETTERS TO MAX MÜLLER — THE JEWS IN CORNWALL — PRUSSIAN WAR — THE METEOR SHOWER — SOCIETY AND EQUALITY — THE HOUSE OF LORDS — "FRASER'S MAGAZINE" — DARWINISM — ST. ANDREWS AND BRITISH ASSOCIATION — STAMMERING.

> "We were weary, and we
> Fearful, and we, in our march,
> Fain to drop down and die.
> Still thou turnedst, and still
> Beckonedst the trembler, and still
> Gavest the weary thy hand !
> If in the paths of the world,
> Stones might have wounded thy feet,
> Toil or dejection have tried
> Thy spirit, of that we saw
> Nothing ! To us thou wert still
> Cheerful and helpful and firm.
> Therefore to thee it was given
> Many to save with thyself ;
> And at the en of thy day,
> O faithful shepherd ! to come
> Bringing thy sheep in thy hand."
>
> MATTHEW ARNOLD.

WHILE the Professor was giving his usual course of lectures in the Lent term of 1866 at Cambridge, a great blow fell upon the University in the death of Dr. Whewell, Master of Trinity, and he writes home:

"I am sorry to say Whewell is beaten by his terrible foe. It is only a question of hours now. The feeling here is deep and solemn. Men say he was the leader in progress and reform, when such were a persecuted minority. He was the regenerator of Trinity; he is connected with every step forward that the University has made for years past. Yes. He was a very great man: and men here feel the awful suddenness of it. He never was better or pleasanter than on the Thursday, when I dined there, and he was asking me for my 'dear wife.' His manner with women was always charming. He was very kind to me, and I was very fond of him.[1]

. . . .

"Whewell is dead! I spoke a few solemn words to the lads before lecture, telling them what a mighty spirit had passed away, what he had been to Cambridge and science, and how his example ought to show them that they were in a place where nothing was required for the most splendid success, but love of knowledge and indomitable energy. They heard me with very deep attention. He is to be buried in the College Chapel, Saturday. . . ."

A proposal had been lately made to found an American professorship in Cambridge. The offer was finally rejected by vote of the Senate, to the great regret of many leading men in the University, among them Professor Kingsley, who, in one of the broad-sheets he printed on the subject for circulation, speaks

". . . of the general importance of the scheme, of the great necessity that our young men should know as

[1] Professor Thompson, another very old friend, was elected to succeed Dr. Whewell as Master, so that Mr. Kingsley still remained a welcome guest at the Lodge of Trinity, to his great pleasure.

much as possible of a country destined to be the greatest in the world. I only ask — If in the second century before the Christian era the Romans had offered to send a lecturer to Athens, that he might tell Greek gentlemen of what manner of men this new Italian power was composed, what were their laws and customs, their intentions, and their notion of their own duty and destiny — would Athens have been wise or foolish in accepting the offer? . . ."

The companionship of his eldest son, then an undergraduate of Trinity, and the appointment of Mr. Maurice to the chair of Moral Philosophy, made his Cambridge residence doubly interesting and delightful to the Professor, and he writes to his wife:

"M. is developing fast. He has just asked me for a copying pass to the Fitzwilliam, where he wants to draw the statues. He has just been regretting that he has read so little, and is craving after natural history and for the first time in his life, he says, after *art*. Ah! what a blessing to see him developing under one's eyes, and to be able to help him at last by teaching him something one's self. It is quite right that the school-masters should have the grounding and disciplining, but the father who can *finish* his boy's education, and teach him something of life besides, ought to be very thankful. . . . I am well, and as busy as a bee, not an hour unemployed. . . ."

" . . . Delightful evening last night; dined at Paget's and then gave a lecture on the Norman Conquest, to the Albert Institute — an admirable institute got up by High Church bachelors and undergraduates for getting hold of shopmen and middle-class lads. That class abounded in the room, and were much delighted, as far as appearances could go, with what I told them of the Conquest and the doughty deeds, and grand old Norse blood of their own ancestors. I thoroughly enjoyed myself. Spoke for one hour and a quarter, and had notes enough to speak two. My morning lecture was a very difficult one — all about the changes in Europe at the Congress of Vienna. But Mr. Maurice said I made it all clear, and highly approved of the *moral.*"

His residences at Cambridge, short as they were, gave him not only the advantage of associating with scholars and men of mark in the University, but of paying visits in the neighborhood to houses where good pictures and charming society refreshed and helped him through the toil of his professorial work — to Wimpole, to Ampthill Park, to Barton Hall, and other country houses, where he and his were always made welcome. His intense enjoyment of all works of art, and his eloquence and insight in their presence, were most inspiriting to those who were with him, and it is much to be regretted that he never finished the series of papers on the National Gallery, begun in 1849. When he went to any London collection, a crowd would soon gather round him, and, riveted by his appearance and kindling eye as he stood before some fine picture, would hang on his every word. He, meanwhile, lost in his subject, would be quite unconscious of the impression he was making. While staying with Lord Wensleydale at Ampthill he first saw the pictures at Woburn Abbey and Haynes Park, which were of deep interest to him.

"Once I went over the picture gallery at Woburn with him," writes Mr. George Howard. "It was a great treat to me, as his talk over the historical portraits was delightful. He then made a remark which has since seemed to me quite a key to the criticism of historical portraits: 'That it was formerly the habit of portrait painters to flatter their sitters by making them as like the reigning king or queen as they could.' . . ."

During his heavy parish work, which was done single-handed the greater part of this year, he was more than ever painfully struck by the monotonous, colorless life of English laboring people, varied only by the yearly benefit-club day, and evenings at the public-house. The absence of all pleasure from their existence weighed heavily on his heart. He felt, too, for the women, who, if respectable, were excluded from even the poor amusements of the men; and for their sake quite as much as for his men and boys, he began a series of penny readings. It was characteristic of his chivalrous spirit that at the first reading, when the school-room was crowded with men and boys, he made an appeal to them for their wives and mothers, speaking of the life of toil they led, and of his anxiety to give them some share of amusement, which they so sorely needed. It was therefore arranged that, while the men and boys paid their pennies, the widows and poor over-burdened mothers should have free admittance. These meetings, at which his parishioners kindly helped him, took place once a fortnight, and though set on foot for the poor, brought all classes pleasantly together during the autumn and winter nights; they had music (the best that could be got), the best poetry, the most heroic stories. Sometimes he would give simple lectures on health; accounts of his own travels; and, when his eldest son went abroad, letters of his written expressly for the penny readings at home, were read. Village concerts, too, were got up by his daughter and son, in which friends from London helped for his sake; at which the sight of a well-lighted and decorated room to cottagers who saw nothing at home from one year's end to another but the darkness visible of a farthing dip candle, was a pleasure in itself; and the parents were gratified at seeing their sons in Sunday garments step up on the platform to help in choruses and part songs, while the young men gained in self-respect and refinement, by the share they took in the preparation as well as the performances. "It was to him most curious," he used to say, "to watch the effect of music upon seemingly unimpressionable people, in whom one would expect to find no appreciation for refined sound;" but yet who would walk a long distance on a dark wet night to the village school-room, and sit for two hours in rapt attention, "showing their enjoyment, not by noisy applause but by the kindling face and eye, and the low hum of approbation, that hinted at a deep musical under-current below that rugged exterior." Penny readings and concerts are common now, but in his own neighborhood the Rector of Eversley took the lead in inaugurating these pleasant gatherings. In addition to the penny readings he opened an evening reading-room for the men, for which books, bagatelle-boards, and various games were provided. He made it a self-governed club, and sanctioned the managers having in a cask of good beer, each glass to be paid for on the spot, in hopes it would prevent their going to the public-houses on their way home. The men drew up their own rules under his eye; and for a winter or two it succeeded, but the scattered population made difficulties, and the attraction of seven public-houses in a parish of only 800 inhabitants, after a time was too strong for the young men — the reading-room languished, and eventually was shut up.

His literary work this year consisted in two lectures on Science and Superstition[1] at the Royal Institution, and an article in the Fine Arts Review. "Hereward," which had been coming out in "Good Words," was published as a book. He preached for the first time in one of the great Nave services at Westminster Abbey, also on "Civilized Barbarism," for the Bishop of London's Fund; to the boys of Wellington College; to the Queen at Clifden and Windsor; and at Whitehall, perhaps the boldest of his sermons, on "The Shaking of the Heavens and the Earth;"[2] in which he spoke of the great revolutions in modern science and modern thought, in Ethics and Theology, and of the spirit in which new truth should be approached by those who believe in that living, ruling, guiding Christ who Himself sends new truth, who shakes the heavens and the earth now as He did at the Reformation, who is shaking now the "mediæval conception of the physical world — of heaven and hell" — of "moral

---

[1] Since republished in "Health and Education."
[2] These sermons have since appeared in a volume, "The Water of Life."

retribution"—of "dogmatic propositions," of "endless punishment," &c. His London congregations were enormous, and when he preached for a hospital it was striking to see the medical students standing the whole length of the service, watching him with rapt attention. In the little church at Eversley during the summer months, many distinguished men might be observed.

His correspondence was, as usual, of a varied and singular character. One day there came a long letter from a London newspaper reporter, who, in return for some kindly, cheering words, revealed the inner life of Bohemia with wonderful vividness, and ended, "I have written you a very long and tedious letter, Mr. Kingsley, and were I writing to an ordinary man, I should be mad to address him at this length and in this vein. But *you* understand things, and I am almost certain that you will understand me and my long-windedness. Thank you again. Think gently of Bohemia and its free lances." Another, from Brighton, signed "A Chartist and Cabman," thanking him for "Alton Locke." Again, "One who can never forget you," who had accidentally read "Alton Locke" "in a time of overwhelming misery — You were the means of saving me from ruin and destruction, to which I was fast drifting." From South Australia, a barrister writes, thanking him for his "Sermons for the Times," "Pentateuch," and "Good News," which had presented life and its duties to him in a new light, and which he and other laymen appointed by the Bishop read aloud in remote places, where they had no ordained clergyman.

Mr. Impey, superintendent of Wesleyan missions in South Africa, after thanking him for spiritual help, adds:

"I am only saying what thousands elsewhere could reiterate that in the far-off corners of the world, in the regions of heathen darkness, and of the very shadow of death, and to men whose lot has been cast on the very verge, or beyond it, of civilized life, your books have, under God's blessing, conveyed light and peace and comfort."

"The debt I owe you," writes a newspaper compositor, from Leeds, "of which you know nothing, is this, that under God's blessing you have been the means of preventing me from becoming perhaps one of the dregs and scum of idle scoundrelism, and of raising me to a position from which I can estimate, faintly it may be, what is due from man to his own manhood, and to his fellow man and to God. Before I read 'Alton Locke' I was idle and dissolute. . . ."

Letters came from China, India and from the other side of the Rocky Mountains — all telling the same tale. One or two found their way to "Charles Kingsley, England," many without any signature, neither written from egotism nor from the desire of getting an autograph in return — simple outpourings of loving hearts. Here is one:

"CHARLES KINGSLEY, — My dear friend, permit me to engage your kind attention for a little. I often remember you and 'the kindness of God,' which you showed towards me some years ago. You found me in the way near Hartly Row, a poor, homeless, friendless, penniless stranger. God sent you as an angel of mercy to me, a very unworthy creature. You were, indeed, like the good

Samaritan to me. You took me to the Lamb Inn, and there, for your sake, I was very hospitably cared for. On the walls of a room in that inn I wrote a prayer, which came from the very depths of my heart. It was for you, that the Father of the fatherless would make you most glad with His countenance for ever. That prayer I have often breathed since then. I was not aware, till afterwards, that you were the author of so many books, and a person of so great note. I rejoice in your honorable fame."

Such letters, and many a strange communication, cheered him in his work, and deepened his knowledge of and sympathies with human nature in its varied aspects. He little thought they were treasured up, to give others some small insight into his great work, by one who feels it is no treachery to disclose them now, or to mention what he never alluded to in his lifetime!

In the summer while staying with Lord Hardwicke at Sidney Lodge, he went with him to a banquet given at Southampton to ex-Governor Eyre, where his presence was severely commented on by the press.

"You are kind enough," he writes to Mr. Dixon, "to compliment me for following Carlyle's advice about one 'sadly tried.' I *have* followed the sage of Chelsea's teaching, about my noble friend, ex-Governor Eyre of Jamaica. I have been cursed for it, as if I had been a dog, who had never stood up for the working-man when all the world was hounding him (the working-man) down in 1848-9, and imperilled my own prospects in life in behalf of freedom and justice. Now, men insult me because I stand up for a man whom I believe ill-used, calumniated, and hunted to death by fanatics. If you mean Mr. Eyre in what you say, you

To Max Müller

indeed will give me pleasure, because I shall see that one more 'man of the people' has common sense to appreciate a brave and good man, doing his best under terrible difficulties."

November 20, 1866. "If you knew the continual labor in which I live, you would forgive my omitting to answer a letter at once. Your letter did interest me and deeply. I felt pleased and proud to find one more man who had the true ambition. Not the mere political ambition, laudable as well as lawful in a free Englishman, but which he can share with scamps, and spouters, and self-seekers, but the true ambition which cries after *wisdom* rather than riches, and knows what Solomon meant when he spoke of her in his proverbs : the ambition to know what is beautiful, good, and true, that he may go and do likewise. Ah! that more men in all ranks would choose the part which you have chosen. Then they would look on the inequalities — I do *not* mean the injustices — but the necessary inequalities of position in this world as slight matters, while they toiled after the divine equality of virtue and wisdom which is open to all men in a free land, and try to take their place among 'the *aristocracy* of God.' Your record of your sight of our dear and lost Prince Consort touched me deeply. As for the uselessness of the monument (in Hyde Park), I do not quite agree. I think it is good to have in a land great beacons of that kind, which attract the attention, and impress the imagination of the most brutal and careless. This ought to be done, and not to leave the other undone."

To Prof. Max Müller, *Nov.* 16, 1866. — "Dearest Max, — Story, bless you, I have none to tell you, save that in Cornwall these same old stories, of Jews' tin and Jews' houses, got from the miners, filled my young brains with unhistoric nonsense, like Mara-zion, the bitterness of Zion; which town the old folk, I can't tell why, call Market Jew still."

". . . What you say about metamorphic language is most true (even in my little experience). You do not mention 'Jews' tin.' This is lumps of smelted tin (if I recollect right) with a coating of hydrated oxide of tin, which is caused by lying in water and bog. Jews' tin is found inside Jews' houses, or in the diluvium of old stream works. May this not be merely, according to your etymology, 'house tin,' the tin found in the houses? Ah! that I had legs as an antelope and time as a butterfly, I would take you to lonely places and show you old ruined houses, and pit workings, and stream workings, and cromlechs, and stone circles, and real British villages, the old kraal of flat granite slabs, and inside it the circular huts of ditto, about ten feet diameter, the stones leaning inward, probably thatched with heather, which now, by decomposing into peat soil, has buried the whole half-way up, and bridges of single granite blocks, polished by the feet of ages. And our 'portion should be among the smooth stones of the brook,' and we would pour out to them 'our drink offering' as we talked over old nature-worship, and lost ourselves and our toil in the abysses of the ages. But that will not be yet.

". . . My dear Max, what great things have happened for Germany, and what great men your Prussians have shown themselves. Much as I was wroth with them about Schleswig-Holstein, I can only see in this last campaign a great necessary move for the physical safety of every North German household, and the honor of every North German woman. To allow the possibility of a second 1807-1812 to remain, when it could be averted by any amount of fighting, were sin and shame, and had I been a Prussian I would have gone down to Sadowa as a sacred duty to wife and child and fatherland."

The Meteor Shower

The great meteor shower of November, 1866, was naturally of intense and, as he said himself, awful interest to him. In trembling excitement he paced up and down the church-yard, where he had a greater sweep of horizon than elsewhere, long before the time arrived; and when the great spectacle began called his wife and children out of their beds to watch with him. He preached on the subject in his own church and at the Chapel Royal, where, after speaking of the seemingly pitiless laws of Nature "as we miscall them," he bursts forth:

"Horrible, I say, and increasingly horrible, not merely to the sentimentalist, but to the man of sound reason and of sound conscience, must the scientific aspect of nature become, if a mere abstraction called law is to be the sole ruler of the universe; if — to quote the famous words of the German sage — 'If, instead of the Divine Eye, there must glare on us an empty, black, bottomless eye-socket;' and the stars and the galaxies of heaven, in spite of all their present seeming regularity, are but an 'everlasting storm which no man guides.' . . . But did the thought occur to none of us, how morally ghastly, in spite of all its physical beauty, was that grand sight, unless we were sure that behind it all there was a Living God? That He had appointed the path, and the time, and the destiny, and the use of every atom of that matter of which science could only tell us that it was rushing without a purpose, for ever through the homeless void. . . . In one word, the question is not whether there be a God, but whether there be a Living God, who is in any true and practical sense Master of the universe over which He presides; a King who is actually ruling His kingdom, or an epicurean deity who lets his kingdom rule itself? Is there a Living God in the universe, or is there none? That is the greatest of all questions. Has our Lord Jesus Christ answered it, or has He not? . . ."[1]

To PROFESSOR ADAMS. — "The seeming generation of these magnificent objects, out of a point of nonentity and void, was the most beautiful and striking sky phenomenon which I ever witnessed. Yet the actual facts of their course are far more wonderful and awful than even that appearance. I tried to picture to myself the thought and feelings of a mediæval observer, however rational or cool-headed he might have been, in presence of that star shower; and when I thought of the terror with which he had a right to regard it, and the fantastic explanation which he had a right to put upon it, I thanked you astronomers for having 'delivered us by science from one more object of dread.'"

TO PROFESSOR LORIMER OF EDINBURGH

EVERSLEY: *December* 17, 1866. — "I write to express my great pleasure in your book on 'The Constitutionalism of the Future.' The views which you put forth are just those to which I have been led by twenty years of thought and observation; its manner, I wish I could copy. In it, clearness and method are not merely ornamented, but strengthened by a vein of humor, which is a sure sign of mastery of the subject, and of that faculty which no education can give, called genius. I wish that in the writings of our mutual friend, Mr. Mill, I could see some touch of that same humor. Mr. —— 's party have let loose that spirit of envy, which is the counterfeit of your righteous idea of equality relative, and tempts men to demand that impossible equality absolute, which must end in making the money lenders the only privileged class. To men possessed

[1] "The Meteor Shower," "Water of Life and Other Sermons."

Society and Equality 225

by envy, your truly scientific, as well as truly religious method, of looking for the facts of God's world, and trying to represent them in laws, will be the plot of a concealed aristocrat. Mr. Mill seems to me to look on man too much as the creature of circumstances. This it is, which makes him disparage, if not totally deny, the congenital differences of character in individuals, and still more in races. He has, if I mistake not, openly denounced the doctrine of difference and superiority in race. And it is this mistake (as it seems to me) which has led him and others into that theory that the suffrage ought to be educational and formative, which you have so ably combated.

"Of course if it is assumed that all men are born into the world equals, and that their inequality, in intellect or morals, is chargeable entirely to circumstance, that inequality must be regarded as a wrong done by society to the less favored. Society therefore has no right to punish them by withholding the suffrage, for an inferiority which she herself has created; she is bound to treat them as if they were actually what they would have been but for her, and if they misuse their rights, she must pay the penalty of her previous neglect and cruelty. This seems to me to be the revolutionary doctrine of 1793 — 1848, which convulsed Europe; and from its logic and morality there is no escape as long as human beings are asserted to be congenitally equal, and circumstances the only cause of subsequent inequality. I held that doctrine strongly myself in past years, and was cured of it, in spite of its seeming justice and charity, by the harsh school of facts. Nearly a quarter of a century spent in educating my parishioners, and experience with my own and others' children, in fact that schooling of facts brought home to the heart, — have taught me that there are congenital differences and hereditary tendencies which defy all education from circumstances, whether for good or evil. Society may pity those who are born fools or knaves, but she cannot, for her own sake, allow them power if she can help it. And therefore in the case of the suffrage, she must demand some practical guarantee that the man on whom it is bestowed is not dangerously knavish or foolish. I have seen, also, that the differences of race are so great, that certain races, *e.g.* the Irish Celts, seem quite unfit for self-government, and almost for the self-administration of justice involved in trial by jury, because they regard freedom and law, not as means for preserving what is just and right, but merely as weapons to be used for their own private interests and passions. They take the letter of freedom which killeth, without any conception of its spirit which giveth life. Nay, I go further, and fear much that no Roman Catholic country will ever be fit for free constitutional government, and for this simple reason. De Tocqueville and his school (of whom I speak with great respect) say that the cause of failure of free institutions in the Romance countries has been, the absence of the primary training in municipal self-government. That I doubt not. But what has been the cause of that want? — the previous want of training in self-government of the individual himself. And as long as the system of education for all classes in the Romance countries is one of tutelage and espionage (proceeding from the priestly notions concerning sin), so long will neither rich nor poor have any power of self-government. Any one who knows the difference between a French *lycée* and an English public school ought to see what I mean, and see one main cause of the failure of all attempts at self-government in France. May I without boring you go on to another subject, which seems to me just now of great importance? I think the giving intellect and civilization its due weight, by means of plurality of votes, as you so well advise, practically hopeless just now.

The House of Lords 227

But is there no body or influence in the state which may secure them their due weight nevertheless? I think that there is, namely, the House of Lords. You seem to regard, as the majority do, the Peers, as standing alone in the state, and representing only themselves. I, on the contrary, look at them as representing every silver fork in Great Britain. What I mean is this. A person or body may be truly representative without being elected by those whom they represent. You will of course allow this. Now the House of Lords seems to me to represent all heritable property, real or personal, and also all heritable products of moral civilization, such as hereditary independence, chivalry, &c. They represent, in one word, the hereditary principle. This, no House of Commons, no elective body, can represent. It can only represent the temporary wants and opinions of the many, and that portion of their capital which is temporarily invested in trade, &c. It cannot represent the hereditary instinct which binds man and the state to the past and future generations. If you watch the current of American feeling and society you will see full proof of this. If the family bond should break up there, soon the bond will break up which makes a nation responsible in honor for the deeds of its ancestors, and therefore regardful of the obligation of international treaties. Now a body is required which represents the past and the future, and all material or spiritual which has been inherited from the past or bequeathed to the future. And this body must itself be an hereditary one.

" 1. That such a body must be non-elected, to keep it safe from the changes of temporary popular opinion. An elective upper chamber is a monster which is certain to become a den of demagogues and money-lenders. 2. That it must be hereditary, because it is impossible for men to represent that which they are not themselves. The Peers are the incarnation of the hereditary principle. I look on them therefore as what they are in fact, not a caste, not even a class, but a certain number of specimens of a class chosen out by the accident (and a very fair choice, because it prevents quarrels and popular intrigues) of being eldest sons. I look on them as the representatives, not only of every younger brother, &c., of their own kin, and of every family which has ever intermarried, or hopes to intermarry with them (though that would include the great majority of well-educated Britons), but as the representatives of every man who has saved up enough to buy a silver fork, a picture, a Yankee clock, or anything, in fact, which he wishes to hand to his children. I hold that while Mr. Bright may, if he likes, claim to be represented merely by the House of Commons, his plate and house is represented by the House of Lords, and that if the House of Lords were abolished, Mr. Bright's children would discover that fact by the introduction of laws which would injure the value of all heritable property, would tax (under the name of luxuries) the products of art and civilization, would try to drive capital into those trades which afforded most employment for *un*-skilled labor, and supplied most the temporary necessities of the back and belly, and would tend to tax the rich for the sake of the poor, with very ugly results to civilization. This picture may seem overdrawn. I answer, this is already the tendency in the United States. The next fifty years will prove whether that tendency can be conquered or not in a pure democracy, such as they have now for the first time become; since they have exterminated their Southern hereditary aristocracy, and their Northern hereditary aristocracy, the Puritan gentlemen of old families, have retired in disgust from public life.

"Pray excuse the length of this letter. But your

book awoke such an interest in me — a solitary country thinker — that I could not resist the temptation of pouring out to you some of the results of many years of practical observation of, and pondering on, facts."

In 1867 he gave three Lectures at the Royal Institution on the *Ancien Régime*, and worked hard at the ice problems of the Bagshot Sands in the district round Eversley, at his theory of raised beaches, and in correspondence on Darwinism. He also undertook for a few months the editorship of "Fraser's Magazine" for Mr. Froude. He seized upon this opportunity to get some papers on science into its pages, in which various friends helped him, while he himself contributed one of his most lovely idylls, "A Charm of Birds." — (Prose Idylls.)

"Could you give me anything, however short?" he writes to Professor Newton. "You must tell me instantly where I can get most information about our birds of passage. Especially I want to know why the three phyllopneustes build dome-shaped nests? With what other birds are they embryologically connected? Also, is the hyppolais a warbler embryologically, or is he a yellow finch connected with serins and canaries, who has taken to singing? Can you tell me where I can find any Darwinite lore about the development of birds? Can you tell me anything about anything? For, as you won't write me an article for this month, I must write one myself."

To REV. J. LL. DAVIES. — *May* 23, 1867. — "I will surely be with you, please God, on Sunday. . . . I am writing a sermon on the Wheat and the Tares, entreating general toleration of all parties, and bringing it to bear on the Bishop of London's Fund question. I presume that you will not object to this line of preaching . . . but if you do, let me know, and I will try something else. The older I grow, the more tolerant I get, and believe that Wisdom is justified of all her children, and poor dear old Folly of some of hers likewise. . . ."

He was selected by Lord Spencer to preach to the Volunteers at the Wimbledon meeting this year. In September he was refreshed by a visit to Scotland, which included some days of the British Association at St. Andrews, and with M. Van de Weyer at Abergeldie Castle; while there he was collecting facts for his book on the Hermits.

To his Wife. — St. Andrews : " I am looking out on a glassy sea, with the sea-birds sailing about close under the window. I could wish to be at home seeing you all go to church. Yesterday was a day of infinite bustle. The University and City received the British Association and feasted them. Everything was very well done, except putting me down for a speech against my express entreaty. However, I only spoke five minutes. After this early dinner a reception *soirée* of all the ladies of Fifeshire, 'East Neuk.' We escaped early. I hate being made a lion of. I sat at dinner between dear old Philips and Geikie, with Grant Duff next, who has asked me to come on to him if I have time, and kill his salmon. Hurrah ! To-day to church at one, and dine at Principal Tulloch's after, to meet Stanley, who is in great force in his beloved St. Andrews, which he called, in a very charming speech last night, his second university. Jowett comes to-morrow with a reading party. Blackwood (of the Magazine), who lives close by, has been most civil to me ... wanting me to come and stay with him, &c.; he has told me much that is curious about De Quincey, Hogg, Wilson, &c. He and B. and T. have been trying hard to make me preach in Boyd's Church; but I talked it over with —— last night, and I was glad to find that he thought with me, that it is quite legal, but that there was no need for a sudden and uncalled-for row with the Puseyites. I am most careful about all that. Nothing can be more pleasant than my stay here has been. But the racket of the meeting is terrible; the talking continual, and running into Dundee, by two trains, with the steamer at Broughty Ferry, between, is too much; so I have taken up my hat, and am off to Tillypronie to-morrow; with the Provost of Dundee, and worse, the dear Red Lion Club crying to me to stop and dine. These dear Scots folk — I should like to live always among them; they are so full of vigorous life and heart. I am very well, but longing for the heather. Tell Maurice golf is the queen of games, if cricket is the king: and the golfing gentlemen as fine fellows as ever I saw. Kiss all the darlings for me, Grenville especially."

"Best of all," said Dean Stanley in a letter from Dundee, speaking of the banquet, "was Kingsley's speech, comparing the literature of science to camp followers[1] picking up scraps from the army, plundering, begging, borrowing, and stealing, and giving what they got to the bairns and children that ran after them, ending with a very delicate and well-timed serious turn of 'the voice of God revealed in facts.'"

From Abergeldie Castle he writes to his wife, who was starting their youngest boy to his first school:

[1] The term used by Mr. Kingsley was "The Jackals of Science."

"I am quite unhappy to-day thinking of your parting with the dear boy, for I can understand, though my man's coarser nature cannot feel as intensely, the pang to you of parting with a bit of yourself. More and more am I sure, and physiologists are becoming more sure also, that the *mother* is the more important [parent], and in the case of the *boy* everything; the child *is* the mother, and her rights, opinions, feelings, even fancies about him, ought to be first regarded. You will write to me all about his starting; but I have no fear of his being anything but happy. . . ."

TO HIS YOUNGEST DAUGHTER. — "MY MARY, — This is the real castle where I am, and in the bottom of that tower a real witch was locked up before she was burnt on Craig-na-Ban, overhead. At the back of the house, under my window, which is in the top of the tower, the Dee is roaring, and the salmons are *not* leaping, and a darling water-ouzel, with a white breast, is diving after caddises. And as soon as I have had luncheon I am going to fish with two dear little girls, who catch lots of trout with a fly; and a real gilly in a kilt, who, when he and I caught a salmon two days ago, celebrated the event by putting on his Prince of Wales's tartan and uniform, taking an enormous bagpipe, and booming like an elephantine bumble-bee all round the dinner-table, and then all about the house. It is very pleasant — like a dream — real stags in the forest looking at you, and real grouse, and blackcock, and real princesses walking about; but I long to be home again with you all, and that is truth. Love to Rose, and tell her to write to me to Aboyne. Your affectious pater,

"C. K."

TO MR. T. DIXON. — "I am much surprised to hear of alms-houses paying rates. The whole Poor-Law Question has got into the hands of the small shopkeepers, as far as I can see, altogether. But as for shifting the burden of rates and taxes, — the true place to shift it, it seems to me, is on to the large shopkeepers and employers of labor, who rapidly grow rich, and therefore could endure a little more taxation. As for putting it on the land — you cannot be aware that land does not now pay more than 2½ or 3 per cent. to buy, so that the possession of it is a *luxury*, which only the rich can afford. This is owing to the heavy burdens which lie already on the (generally) exhausted and poor soil of England; and its effect is, that the land is drifting into too few hands. That happens by no privilege or injustice, but simply by supply and demand, there being so very few purchasers for the luxury of being a landowner. This is a serious evil, and a growing one. But I do not think that much shifting of taxes is needed — what is needed, is not squandering them when they are raised — and if there is that waste it must be the fault of the House of Commons, and nobody else. If we do not put good men into Parliament, we must be punished for our own folly. God grant the working men in their elections may choose honest and virtuous men (I don't care what their opinions are), leaving them as much *un*-pledged and free as possible, and trusting to their conscience and honor to do what is right."

To L. T., Esq. — " As for stammering, I have seldom known a worse case than my own. I believe it to be perfectly curable, by the most simple and truly scientific rules — if persevered in. The great obstacles to cure are — 1. Youth, which prevents attention and force of will. 2. In after life, nervous debility of any kind. But with the cure of stammering, nervous debility decreases, owing to the more regular respiration, and therefore more perfect oxygenation of the blood, and so the health improves with the speech. Try a simple experiment, it is an old and notorious method. Before beginning to speak, take two or three deep breaths, and always breathe at a stop, so as to prevent doing what all old stammerers do, speaking with an empty lung. Take a pair of very light dumb-bells and exercise your chest with them, taking care to *in*-spire deeply when you raise them over your head, and when (consequently) the ribs are raised, and the lungs expanded. Do this slowly and quietly, and I think you will find, though it will not cure you, yet it will relieve and literally *comfort* your breathing enough to give you confidence in my hints."

CHAPTER XXIII

1868

AGED 49

ATTACKS OF THE PRESS — LECTURES ON SIXTEENTH CENTURY — LETTERS ON EMIGRATION — NEWMAN'S DREAM OF ST. GERONTIUS — MILITARY EDUCATION — SANDHURST — COMTISM — ON CRIME AND ITS PUNISHMENT — PARTING WITH HIS SON — LETTER FROM REV. WILLIAM HARRISON — THEOLOGICAL VIEWS — THE BOOK LOVER — KINGSLEY'S TOLERANCE

> " Life, I repeat, is energy of love,
> Divine or human; exercised in pain,
> In strife, and tribulation, and ordained
> If so approved and sanctified, to pass
> Through shades and silent rest, to endless joy."
> WORDSWORTH.

> " I never saw in any man such fearlessness in the path of duty. The one question with him was, 'Is it right?' No dread of consequences, and consequences often bitterly felt by him, and wounding his sensitive nature, ever prevented him from doing that to which conscience prompted. His sense of right amounted to chivalry." — *Life of* PROFESSOR FORBES.

THE professorial lectures this year were on the 16th century, and were crowded, as usual; but some severe attacks on his teaching in two leading newspapers in the preceding autumn (though in each case they might be traced to some personal animosity), had inclined him, for his own honor, and for that of his University, to resign his post. Before doing this, he consulted some of the Cambridge authorities, on whose friendship and impartiality he could rely;

and on their advice he decided to retain the Professorship, though the work was too heavy for him, for at least another year. "Dry-as-dust is invaluable in his way, but he cannot create an interest in his subject where it does not exist," wrote one distinguished member of the University, who strongly dissuaded him from resigning, not knowing who might be his successor. Writing to his wife from Cambridge at this time he says:

"I have been very unhappy about your unhappiness about me, and cannot bear to think of your having a pang on my account. But you must remember that these battles and this abuse, painful as they may be, are what every man has to go through who attains any mark, or does any good in the world. Think how far more obloquy was gone through by Buckland, Milman, Maurice, Hare, Stanley, Robertson, Arnold; they have all had to fight their fight. But they conquered, and so shall I, please God, in spite of my mistakes. . . . In the meantime I will keep out of war, and *do the duty that lies nearest me*, that all may be well. So pray comfort yourself and think cheerfully and hopefully of the future, which after all is not so very dark, if one looks at it fairly. . . . I have got well through my lecture on Paracelsus. I should think there were a hundred men there, and the Public Orator and Wright. Then I heard a noble lecture from Mr. Maurice."

His calmness and magnanimity under attacks of the press, especially when made by literary men, were always remarkable; and no truer words were ever spoken than those by Mr. Matthew Arnold on hearing of his death:

"I find myself full of the thought of something in which he seemed to me unique. I think he was the most generous man I have ever known; the most forward to praise what he thought good, the most willing to admire, the most free from all thought of himself in praising and in admiring, and the most incapable of being made ill-natured, or even indifferent, by having to support ill-natured attacks himself. Among men of letters I know nothing so rare as this; it will always keep his memory surrounded, in my mind, with a freshness and an honor peculiarly his own. . . . His fine talents and achievements in literature will now have full justice done to them again; the injustice which he and they had in some quarters to experience will be no longer busy."

Happily he was well and vigorous this year, and had so much work on hand in his parish and with his pen, that he had not time to be depressed by attacks from without. In preparation for one lecture in his proposed course for 1869, he read through nearly the whole of Comte's works. He began his little history of the Hermits, and a series of papers for children on Natural Science, called, "Madam How and Lady Why;" and answered countless letters.

To MR. T. DIXON. —*January* 17, 1868. — "I send you a letter about the land question, which you can use as you like. I think if you will go over it with any neighboring farmer, you will find it pretty right; and if he will alter prices from my south country estimates to your north country ones, it will be, I think, valuable to quiet the minds of many who think they could do better than now, if the land was in their hands, being ignorant that agriculture is the least paying trade (in England) that a man can follow *owing to the general exhaustion of all the good soils.* I have not so much hope of Home Colonization in England as I had; but if it could be applied to Ireland, it might do well. But *emigration* is the thing. . . . I am pleased with what you say of your father. Give me the man who, like the old middle-aged master workers, is not ashamed to teach his men by doing their work with them. *That* spirit is dying now in manufacturers and shopkeepers. Really, the country squires, who are many of them good practical farmers, and do not think it below them to use their own hands at hard labor, are the only examples left. My father would have put his hand to a spade or an axe with any man, and so could I pretty well, too, when I was in my prime, and my eldest son is now working with his own hands at farming, previous to emigrating to South America, where he will do the drudgery of his own cattle-pens and sheep-folds; and if I were twenty-four and unmarried, I would go out there too, and work like an Englishman, and live by the sweat of my brow."

January 25, 1868. — " I cannot but think that you might find worthy capitalists round you who would advance money for a scheme even temporary, for employing the poor fellows on breaking up waste land. But if they are not accustomed to it they will find it terrible work. I have handled spade and fork myself at it many an hour, and *know*. Our lads here can do it, because the one set of muscles get hardened to it from youth; but only the strong ones can make much wages at it. Ah, that the advice which I gave twenty years ago had been taken, and that the trades' unions would have organized an emigration committee for each trade, and chosen by ballot a certain number to emigrate every year, on funds furnished by the society; then things might have been different. But they had not confidence enough in each other, and were unwilling to sacrifice a portion of their earnings to set some of their number up in affluence and comfort; and so, penny wise and pound foolish, have spent tens of thousands in doing nothing, where they might have spent thousands in doing permanent good."

To REV. SIR W. E. COPE, *May* 2, 1868. — "I have read Newman's 'Dream of Gerontius' with awe and admiration. However utterly I may differ from the *entourage* in which Dr. Newman's present creed surrounds the central idea, I must feel that that central idea is as true as it is noble, and it, as I suppose, is this: The longing of the soul to behold Deity, converted by the mere act of sight, into a self-abasement and self-annihilation so utter, that the soul is ready, even glad, to be hurled back to any depth, to endure any pain, from the moment that it becomes aware of God's actual perfection and its own utter impurity and meanness.

"How poor my words are in expressing in prose what Dr. N. has expressed in poetry, I am well aware. But I am thankful to any man, who under any parabolic, or even questionably true forms, will teach that to a generation which is losing more and more the sense of reverence, and beginning confessedly to hate excellence for its own sake, as the Greek ostracized Aristides, because he was tired of hearing him called the Just. As for the mocking of the fiends, I did not feel with the Bishop of Oxford that it indicated any possibility of unbelief, but rather showed merely that Dr. N. had looked fairly at the other side of a great question, and dare say the worst which can be said on it, which he would not have dared to do, had he not made up his mind. Jean Paul Richter says somewhere, that no man believes his own creed thoroughly till he can afford to jest about it, a daring paradox, which seems to be fulfilled in Dr. N. But there was much in Gerontius, as in the rest of the book [Verses on various occasions], which shocked and pained me much, and which will continue so to do."

TO CAPTAIN ——,

(Who consulted him about Military Education.)

EVERSLEY: *June* 12, 1868. — " . . . What Sandhurst wants is discipline and public spirit. The former can be got. The latter not till a great war, which will make the officer again necessary and valuable in the eyes of the people. . . ."

" . . . What should be done with Sandhurst is: 1. Either to make it a mere finishing college, for one year, for young men who have already been through public schools, and have there learnt self-government, by having got into the fifth or sixth forms, and to treat such young men with the full liberty and confidence which they have at the universities. This would be the best plan; but failing that, Sandhurst should be turned into a thorough public school, taking lads in at 13 or 14, or even 12, and conducting their whole education till they enter the army. In either case, all the teachers and other officers should be military men, who should not be shelved by becoming Sandhurst professors, but have their time there, which should not be more than five years, counted to them as if they were with their regiments, and all such teachers should have gone through the Staff College. Only those lads who passed through Sandhurst with honor should go into the army by direct commission. Those who did not should be turned into the world (as from other public schools), and not be allowed to enter by purchase, as having already proved themselves incompetent. Much as I dislike any professional education, whether for the church or the army, or any other business, I think that this plan would be far better than the present. The chaplain, if he is to have any moral influence, should be always a young man, a scholar, a gentleman, and an athletic genial man — such as can be found by dozens at the universities. And his post should be only for five or seven years, never a permanent and shelving one. . . ."

To REV. F. D. MAURICE, *Sept.* 10, 1868. — " I have been reading with great delight your 'Lectures on Conscience.' I feel more and more that the root of the matter is in your view; and I am very glad to see that Rolleston of Oxford, in an address he has just sent me, gives in his unqualified adhesion to the doctrine that the I is the man, and has nothing to do with physiology at all. The present tendency of physiologists to deny psychology and metaphysic, for the sake of making man a function of his own brain, which is done by a psychology and a metaphysic of their own inventing, though they call it by a different name, must be combated, or we shall all drift together into some sort of Comtism. . . . . I am hard at work at Comte. A great deal of what he says is by no means new to me meanwhile, so that I am not dazzled by it, though at times it is difficult not to be cowed by his self-sufficient glibness and cheerfully naïve sophistry. But I cannot but hope that my love for natural science, and practice in inductive processes, may be of use to me in forming a fair estimate of him on his own ground. As far as I have gone, I suspect more and more that he is not an inductive (the only true positive) philosopher, but a mere systematizer and classifier. As for the 'laws' on which he determines the 'evolution' of the middle age and sixteenth century, they seem to me a set of mere maxims worthy of Polonius. His great discovery of the three stages of the human mind I don't believe at all, even though fetichism were the first stage, which is not proved. I hope to come up to Cambridge to lecture the whole of the Lent Term on these matters. My notion is, to take your 'Kingdom of Christ,' Carlyle's 'French Revolution,' and Bunsen's 'God in History,' and show the men how you all three hold one view (under differences), and Comte and all who are on his side an absolutely different one. Whether God will give me understanding to do this is another question; but I shall think of nothing else between now and then. . . . ."

October 23.—"I want much to have serious talk with you about Comte and his school. My heart is very full of it, as well as my head. The very air seems full of Comtism. Certainly the press is; and how to make head against the growing unbelief in any God worth calling a God is more than I can see. Bunsen's Life has at once elevated and humiliated me. . ."

To SIR HENRY TAYLOR, *Dec.* 26, 1868.—"I have to thank you for your able pamphlet 'On Crime and its Punishment.' As against any just and rational treatment of crime, two influences are at work now. 1. The effeminacy of the middle class, which never having in its life felt bodily pain (unless it has the toothache) looks on such pain as the worst of all evils. My experience of the shop-keeping class (from which juries are taken) will hardly coincide with yours. You seem to think them a hardier and less dainty class than our own. I find that even in the prime of youth they shrink from (and are often unable to bear, from physical neglect of training) fatigue, danger, pain, which would be considered as sport by an average public schoolboy. I think that Mill and those of his school are aware of this,

Parting with his Son

and look on it with disfavor and dread, as an instinct of that 'military class' whom they would (whether justly or not) destroy; and that from the 'extreme left' of thought you would have heavy opposition on this ground, and also because,

"2. The tendency of their speculations is more and more to the theory that man is not a responsible person, but a result of all the circumstances of his existence; and that therefore if any thing or person is responsible for a crime, it is the whole circumambient universe. Doubtless, men who utterly believed this might be as Draconic towards human beings as towards wasps and snakes, exterminating the bad as failures of nature, not as criminals. But the average folk, who only half believe this theory, supplement it by a half belief in the human responsibility of a criminal, a confusion which issues in this: The man is not responsible for his faults. They are to be imputed to circumstance. But he is responsible for, and therefore to be valued solely by, his virtues. They are to be imputed to himself. An ethical theorem, which you may find largely illustrated in Dickens's books, at least as regards the lower and middle classes. Hence the tendency of the half-educated masses in England will be (unless under panic) toward an irrational and sentimental leniency."

He parted in the summer with his eldest beloved son, who, inheriting his father's thirst for travel and passionate longing to see the prairies and tropic forests of the New World, decided to go out to the estate of a cousin in South America for farming and exploring. It was the first break-up of the family circle, and the prospect of the first Christmas at Eversley without his boy inspired the lines which begin:

"How will it dawn, the coming Christmas Day?
. . . .
. . . How to those —
New patriarchs of the new-found under-world,
Who stand, like Jacob, on the virgin lawns,
And count their flocks' increase? To them that day
Shall dawn in glory, and solstitial blaze
Of full midsummer sun: to them, that morn,
Gay flowers beneath their feet, gay birds aloft.
Shall tell of nought but summer; but to them,
Ere yet, unwarned by carol or by chime,
They spring into the saddle, thrills may come
From that great heart of Christendom which beats
Round all the worlds;
. . . for here or there,
Summer or winter, 't will be Christmas Day."[1]

His parish cares were now shared by the Rev. William Harrison, who soon became his intimate companion and friend, and for six years carried out all his plans in church and parish, winning the love and reverence of the people of Eversley, and lifting a heavy burden from his Rector's mind. Mr. Harrison followed him to Westminster as minor canon, and was with him in his last failing months, and on his death-bed. His own words describe the impression Mr. Kingsley made on him during the last seven years of his life on earth.

"Soon after I entered upon my duties as curate at Eversley, in May, 1868, old parishioners, who could recall the days prior to Mr. Kingsley's residence among them, began to tell me of the many great reforms he had effected in the parish in the years during which he had worked there. I do not think that the majority of his people ever fully understood that their rector's words

[1] "Christmas Day." (Poems, p. 353.)

were eagerly listened for in the outside world, and that his name was known far and wide. For these things never affected his manner towards them. They loved him emphatically for himself: for what he was, and had been to them. They loved him because he was always the same — earnest, laborious, tender-hearted; chivalrous to every woman; gentle to every child; true to every man; ready for, and vigorous in, every good work; stern only towards vice and selfishness; the first to rejoice in the success of the strong and healthy, and the first to hasten to the bedside of the sick and dying.

"He knew his people intimately: their proper callings, tastes, failings, and virtues. He was interested, as a matter of fact, and not from the mere desire to please, in the occupations of everyone, and had the right word for each and all. Men at once felt at ease with him, because there was such unmistakable ring of sincerity, such evident understanding of their wants, and such real acquaintance and sympathy with what they were thinking and doing, in all that he said. The poor could tell him freely what they felt and what they wanted, seeing at once that he knew more about them than men of his social standing generally know. At the same time there was a natural stateliness in his bearing which precluded the possibility of undue familiarity in any one towards him. He is too frequently misunderstood to have been a mere clerical 'Tom Thurnall;' a character which he has drawn with great skill, and with which certainly he had many points of sympathy. That he was unfettered by conventional modes of thought and speech, and exhibited at moments a certain element of fierceness, with a detestation of all cant and unmanliness, cannot be denied. But there was, when I knew him, a lofty courtesy and abiding seriousness about him, in his very look and appearance, and in all he said and did, which marked him out from other men, and secured to him at all times the respectful attention and reverence alike of friends and strangers. 'I am nothing,' he once said to me, 'if not a Priest.'

"I think that the tenderness of his nature has never been sufficiently dwelt upon. In his warm and manful love for physical strength, and for capability of any kind, his imaginative forbearance toward dulness and weakness has, as it seems to me, been sometimes lost sight of. Indeed, even towards wrongdoing and sin, although terribly stern in their presence, he was merciful in an unusual degree. He would often say, after sternly rebuking some grave offender, 'Poor fellow! I daresay if I had been in his place I should have done much worse.'

"It is almost needless to say that every natural object, from the stones beneath his feet, to the clouds above his head, possessed a peculiar and never-failing interest for him. As he strode through the heather, across his well-beloved moors, he would dilate on all he saw and heard in his vigorous and poetic way. Nature appealed to him from many diverse sides. For not only would his mind busy itself with the more scientific and abstruse thoughts which a landscape might suggest, but he could find all an artist's contentment and pleasure in the mere beauty of its forms and colors. He had retained the freshness of boyhood; and approached and noted everything with delight. It was refreshing to see how much enjoyment he could extract from things which most men would never perceive or notice; with what untiring and reverent perseverance he would seek to know their *raison d'être*; and with what a glow and glory his fruitful imagination clothed everything.

"He certainly possessed the power of investing natural objects at the right moment with his own thought, either for joy or pathos, in a most striking manner. Thus I recollect on one occasion (amongst the Welsh mountains) the eagerness with which he knelt down by the side of a tinkling waterfall, and said in a whisper of delight, 'Listen to the fairy bells!' And thus, again, I recall with tender sorrow an incident that occurred in one of the last walks he ever took, on those dark winter days which preceded his own illness, and when a great and overwhelming sorrow was hanging over him. We were passing along one of the Eversley lanes. Suddenly we came on a large tree, newly cut down, lying by the roadside. He stopped, and looked at it for a moment or so, and then, bursting into tears, exclaimed, 'I have known that tree ever since I came into the parish!'

"Doubtless there is more or less truth in the assertion that Mr. Kingsley was a Broad Churchman. But assuredly in no party sense; and the only time I ever heard him approach to anything like an exact definition of his position, he described himself as 'an old-fashioned High Churchman.' It was his pride to belong to the Church of England, '*as by law established;*'—he was never tired of quoting the words, nor of referring to the Prayer Book on all disputed points. I have never known any one speak more emphatically and constantly of the value of the Creeds, and the efficacy of the Sacraments, to which he alluded in almost every sermon I heard him preach. The two most distinctive features of his religious teaching were, I think, that the world is God's world, and not the devil's, and that manliness is entirely compatible with godliness. Yet, whilst his name will indissolubly be associated with the latter doctrine, it must not be supposed that he was lacking in gentleness and delicate sympathy. There was in him a vein of almost feminine tenderness, which I fancy increased as life advanced, and which enabled him to speak with a peculiar power of consolation to the sad and suffering, both in private and from the pulpit.

With Puritanism he had little sympathy: with Ritualism none. The former was to his rich poetic imagination and warm chivalrous nature ludicrously defective as a theory of life. The latter was, in his opinion, too nearly allied in spirit to Romanism ever to gain his support or sanction in any way; and of Rome he was the most uncompromising opponent I have ever known. None of the great parties in the Church — it is an important fact — could lay claim to him exclusively. Intrepid fearlessness in the statement of his opinions; a dislike to be involved in the strife of tongues; unexpected points of sympathy with all the different sections of the Church; a certain ideal of his own, both with regard to personal holiness and church regimen; — these things always left him a free lance in the ecclesiastical field.

"The opinion may be taken for what it is worth, but it certainly is my opinion, that whilst Mr. Kingsley's convictions, during his career as a clergyman, remained substantially the same, as may be proved by a careful comparison of his later with his earlier writings, his belief in revealed truth deepened and increased, and his respect for the constituted order of things in Church and State grew more and more assured.

"Surely if ever room could be haunted by happy ghosts it would be his study at Eversley, peopled as it must ever be with the bright creations of his brain. There every book on the many crowded shelves looked at him with almost human friendly eyes. And of books what were there not? — from huge folios of St. Augustine[1] to the last treatise on fly-fishing. And of what would he not talk? — classic myth and mediæval romance, magic and modern science, metaphysics and poetry, West Indian scenery and parish schools, politics and fairyland, &c., &c. — and of all with vivid sympathy,

[1] Once the property of John Sterling, and given to Mr. Kingsley by Thos. Carlyle.

The Book Lover 249

keen flashes of humor, and oftentimes with much pathos and profound knowledge. As he spoke he would constantly verify his words. The book wanted — he always knew exactly where, as he said, it 'lived' — was pulled down with eager hands; and he, flinging himself back with lighted pipe into his hammock, would read, with almost boylike zest, the passage he sought for and quickly found. It was very impressive to observe how intensely he realized the words he read. I have seen him overcome with emotion as he turned the well-thumbed pages of his Homer, or perused the tragic story of Sir Humphrey Gilbert in his beloved Hakluyt. Nor did the work of the study even at such moments shut him in entirely, or make him forgetful of what was going on outside. 'It's very pleasant,' he would say, opening the door which led on to the lawn, and making a rush into the darkness, 'to see what is going on out here.' On one such occasion, a wild autumnal night, after the thrilling recital of a Cornish shipwreck he had once witnessed, and the memory of which the turbulence of the night had conjured up, he suddenly cried, 'Come out! come out!' We followed him into the garden, to be met by a rush of warm driving rain before a southwesterly gale, which roared through the branches of the neighboring poplars. There he stood, unconscious of personal discomfort, for a moment silent and absorbed in thought, and then exclaimed in tones of intense enjoyment, 'What a night! Drenching! This is a night on which you young men can't think or talk too much poetry.'

"Nevertheless, with this appreciation of nature in her wilder moods, he possessed all a poet's love for her calmness. Indeed I think that anything that was savage in aspect was deeply alien to his mind. . . . Order and cultivation were of supreme value in his eyes; and, from a point of artistic beauty, I believe he would have preferred an English homestead to an Indian jungle.

Nay, even town scenes had a very great charm for him; and one bright summer day, after his return from America, whilst walking in Kensington Gardens, he declared that he considered they were as beautiful as anything he had seen in the New World. Looking at some photographs of bleak and barren mountain ranges, he said to a young painter who was admiring their grandeur: 'Yes; paint them, and send the picture to the Academy, and call it, "The Abomination of Desolation"!' I once ventured to ask him whether his scientific knowledge had not dulled the splendor and dissipated much of the mystery that fill the world for the poet's heart. A very sad and tender look came over his face, and for a little while he was silent. Then he said, speaking slowly: 'Yes, yes; I know what you mean; it is so. But there are times — rare moments — when nature looks out at me again with the old bride-look of earlier days.'

"I would speak of his chivalry — for I can call it nothing else — in daily life; a chivalry which clothed the most ordinary and commonplace duties with freshness and pleasantness. I soon discovered that an unswerving resolution at all times, and under all circumstances, to spare himself no trouble, and to sustain life at a lofty level, was the motive power of this chivalry: — and those who conscientiously set themselves to this task best know the innumerable difficulties that beset it. No fatigue was too great to make him forget the courtesy of less wearied moments; no business too engrossing to deprive him of his readiness to show kindness and sympathy. To school himself to this code of unfaltering, high, and noble living was truly one of the great works of his life; for the fulfilment of which he subjected himself to a rigorous self-discipline — a self-discipline so constant that to many people, even of noble temperament, it might appear Quixotic. He would have liked that word applied to him. There was much in him of that knightly character which is heroic even to a fault; and which, from time to time, provokes the shafts of malice and ridicule from lesser men. That the persistent fortitude by which he gained and sustained this temper was one of the root-principles of his life was touchingly illustrated to me one day, when, seeing him quit his work to busy himself in some trivial matter for me, I asked him not to trouble about it then and there, and he, turning on me, said with unusual warmth, 'Trouble! Don't talk to me of that, or you will make me angry. I never allow myself to think about it.'

"I would speak of him as a friend. His ideal of friendship was very full and noble, tenderer, perhaps, than most men's. He took his friends as he found them, and loved them for what they really were, rather than for what he fancied or wished them to be. In this, as in other aspects of his nature, the beautiful boy-likeness was conspicuous. To the last he was ready to meet and to make new friends, to love and to be beloved with the freshness of youth. If there was anything at all admirable in a person he was sure to see and appreciate it. It was not that he was wanting in the critical faculty; nothing escaped his notice; speech, manner, dress, features, bearing, all were observed, but in the most kindly spirit, the good points alone were dwelt and commented upon. 'People are better than we fancy, and have more in them than we fancy;' so he has said in one of his sermons, and so I have heard him say again and again in his daily life. And here I must speak, with the deepest gratitude and love, of the friendship he bestowed on me, unwavering, helpful, exalting, tender, truthful. The memories of that friendship are too many and too sacred for me to dilate upon. Its sweetness and worth have made life a new thing to me, but cannot well be expressed in words."

CHAPTER XXIV

1869-1870

AGED 50-51

WORK OF THE YEAR — RESIGNATION OF PROFESSORSHIP — WOMEN'S SUFFRAGE QUESTION — LETTERS TO MR. MAURICE AND JOHN STUART MILL — CANONRY OF CHESTER — SOCIAL SCIENCE MEETING AT BRISTOL — WEST INDIAN VOYAGE — TROPIC SCENES — RETURN HOME — EVERSLEY A CHANGED PLACE — FLYING COLUMNS — HEATH FIRES — FIRST RESIDENCE AT CHESTER — BOTANICAL CLASS — FIELD LECTURES — HUMAN SOOT — MEDICAL EDUCATION OF WOMEN — FRANCO-PRUSSIAN WAR — WALLACE ON NATURAL SELECTION.

> "But let my due feet never fail
> To walk the studious cloister's pale,
> And love the high-embow'ed roof
> With antique pillars massy proof,
> And storied windows richly dight
> Casting a dim religious light:
> There let the pealing organ blow
> To the full-voiced choir below
> In service high and anthems clear,
> As may with sweetness, through mine ear
> Dissolve me into ecstasies
> And bring all Heaven before mine eyes."
>
> MILTON.

THE year 1869, which closed his professorial work at Cambridge, saw the beginning of a new chapter of his life as Canon of Chester. It was a year of severe intellectual work and great activity; but the resignation of the professorship relieved his mind from a heavy load of

Work of the Year 253

responsibility, and the prospect of a voyage to the West Indies, on the invitation of Sir Arthur Gordon, then Governor of Trinidad, fulfilling one of the dreams of his life, helped to carry him through his work. He lectured on Natural Science to the boys at Wellington and Clifton Colleges, at various industrial and mechanics' institutions in the diocese, and to ladies at Winchester, on health and ventilation ("The Two Breaths"), and on "Thrift," in which last he treated not only of thrift in the household, but of the highest thrift — thrift of all those faculties which connect us with the unseen and spiritual world — thrift of the immortal spirit — "thrift of the heart, thrift of the emotions," as contrasted with "a waste the most deplorable and ruinous of all" for women, the reading of sensation novels — "that worst form of intemperance, intellectual and moral."[1] He was elected President of the Education Section of the Social Science Congress at Bristol. He finished his children's book, "Madam How and Lady Why," and wrote an article on "Women and Politics." His parish prospered; the penny readings and entertainments for the laborers became more popular. He gave his last course of lectures at Cambridge, "in preparing which," he said, "I worked eight or nine months hard last year, and was half-witted by the time they were delivered." Of these, an undergraduate writes, "Your last series, and especially the grand concluding one on Comte, have made an impression just at the moment when it was needed."

[1] "Health and Education."

He left Cambridge with feelings of deep gratitude to men of all classes in the University, and for the experience of the last nine years, and dissatisfied only with his own work. His pupils felt differently.

"Allow me," writes one of them, "to testify to Canon Kingsley's great influence over the young men at Cambridge. It was not only the crowded room and breathless attention that told the interest, but many of us now, at the interval of fifteen years of busy life in our positions as clergymen, in dealing at home and at Missions with men of thought and mind, can trace back, as I can, their first impressions of true manly Christianity to his stirring words. . . ."

"The very name of 'Kingsley's Lecture,'" writes another, "impelled one to the lecture-room. There was a strange fascination about him which no young man could resist. There was no lecture-room half so full, and there was none half so quiet — one could hear a pin fall."

To REV. F. MAURICE. — *Jan.* 16, 1869. — "It was a real pleasure to me to hear you had read my clumsy little papers ('Madam How and Lady Why'). I wished to teach children — my own especially — that the knowledge of nature ought to make them reverence and trust God more, and not less (as our new lights inform us). They are meant more as prolegomena to natural theology, than as really scientific papers, though the facts in them are (I believe) true enough. But I know very little about these matters, and cannot keep myself '*au courant*' of new discoveries, save somewhat in geology, and even in that I am no mineralogist, and palæontologist. Science is grown too vast for any one head. . . .

"R. and I now mean to sail, if God permits (for one must say that very seriously in such a case), by the April mail. Ah! that you were coming too, and could be made to forget everything for a while, save flowers and skies and the mere sensation of warmth, the finest medicine in the world! What you say about not basing morality on psychology I am most thankful for. I seem to get a vista of a great truth far away. Far away enough from me, Heaven knows. But this I know: that I want to re-consider many things, and must have time to do it; that I should like to devote the next twenty years to silence, thought, and, above all, prayer, without which no spirit can breathe."

To J. STUART MILL, ESQ. — "I have had the honor of receiving 'from the author' your book on the 'Subjection of Women.' I shall only say, in thanking you for it, that it seems to me unanswerable and exhaustive, and certain, from its moderation as well as from its boldness, to do good service in this good cause. It has been a deep pleasure to me to find you, in many passages in which you treat of what marriage ought to be, and what marriage is, corroborating opinions which have been for more than twenty-five years the guides and safeguards of my own best life. I shall continue to labor, according to my small ability, in the direction which you point out; and all the more hopefully because your book has cleared and arranged much in my mind which was confused and doubtful. . . ."

" . . . I wish much to speak to you on the whole question of woman. In five-and-twenty years my ruling idea has been that which my friend Huxley has lately set forth as common to him and Comte; that 'the reconstruction of society on a scientific basis is not only possible, but the only political object much worth striving for.' One of the first questions naturally was, What does science — in plain English, nature and fact (which I take to be the acted will of God) — say about woman, and her relation to man? And I have arrived at certain conclusions thereon, which (in the face of British narrowness) I have found it wisest to keep to myself. That I should even have found out what I seem to know without the guidance of a woman, and that woman my wife, I dare not assert : but many years of wedded happiness have seemed to show me that our common conclusions were accordant with the laws of things, sufficiently to bring their own blessing with them. I beg you therefore to do me the honor of looking on me, though (I trust) a Christian and a clergyman, as completely emancipated from those prejudices which have been engrained into the public mind by the traditions of the monastic or canon law about women, and open to any teaching which has for its purpose the doing woman justice in every respect. As for speaking at the meeting, my doing so will depend very much on whether there will be, or will not be, newspaper reporters in the room. I feel a chivalrous dislike of letting this subject be lowered in print, and of seeing pearls cast before swine — with the usual result. . . ."

A visit to Mr. Mill at Blackheath, during which he attended the first woman's suffrage meeting in London, was one of great interest to Mr. Kingsley.

"When I look at his cold, clear-cut face," he remarked of Mr. Mill to Dr. Carpenter, "I think there is a whole hell beneath him, of which he knows nothing, and so there may be a whole heaven above him. . . ."

In August Mr. Gladstone writes to him:

"I have much pleasure in proposing to you that you should accept the Canonry of Chester, vacated by the appointment of Dr. Moberly to the See of Salisbury.

Canonry of Chester 257

. . . I know that the act will be very agreeable to her Majesty. The cathedral of Chester is under an energetic Dean, and nave services are now carried on in it with excellent effect."

Many were the congratulations he received. The answer to one of them is characteristic:

"You never were more right than when you said that I should not like to be a bishop. . . . And even a deanery I shrink from; because it would take me away from Eversley; the home to which I was ordained, where I came when I was married, and which I intend shall be my last home; for go where I will in this hard-working world, I shall take care to get my last sleep in Eversley churchyard."

In October he went to Bristol to the Social Science Congress, as President of the educational section. His address, which made a profound sensation at the time, was printed, and about 100,000 copies distributed by the education League. He had this year joined the League with several other clergymen, who, like himself, nearly despaired of a Government scheme for compulsory education, in which alone they saw hope for the masses; but he subsequently withdrew, and gave his warm allegiance to Mr. Forster's Act. He had long deplored the religious disputes which formed the chief hindrance to a National Education Act, and in a sermon in London some years before had spoken thus of them:

"Let me remind you very solemnly, that the present dearth of education in these realms is owing mainly to our unhappy religious dissensions; that it is the disputes, not of unbelievers, but of Christians, which have made it impossible for our government to fulfil one of the first rights, one of the first duties, of any government in a civilized country; namely, to command, and to compel every child in the realm to receive a proper education. Strange and sad that it should be, yet so it is. We have been letting, we are letting still, year by year, thousands sink and drown in the slough of heathendom and brutality, while we are debating learnedly whether a raft, or a boat, or a life-buoy, is the legitimate instrument for saving them; and future historians will record with sorrow and wonder a fact which will be patent to them, though the dust of controversy hides it from our eyes — even the fact that the hinderers of education in these realms were to be found, not among the so-called skeptics, not among the so-called infidels; but among those who believed that God came down from heaven, and became man, and died on the cross, for every savage child in London. Thus Compulsory Government Education is, by our own choice and determination, impossible." — *Discipline and other Sermons.*

". . . It is the duty of the State, I hold, to educate all alike in those matters which are common to them as citizens; that is, in all secular matters, and in all matters also which concern their duties to each other as defined by law. Those higher duties which the law cannot command or enforce, they must learn elsewhere; and the clergy of all denominations will find work enough, and noble work enough, in teaching them. We shall have always work enough in such times as these in teaching what no secular education can ever teach; in diffusing common honesty, the knowledge of right and wrong, and the old-fashioned fear of God as the punisher of those who do ill, and the rewarder of those who do well. . . ." — *Speech at Bristol.*

West Indian Voyage

On the 2nd of December he and his daughter embarked at Southampton for the West Indies.

"At last I, too, was crossing the Atlantic. At last the dream of forty years, please God, would be fulfilled, and I should see the West Indies and the Spanish Main. From childhood I had studied their natural history, their charts, their romances, and alas! their tragedies; and now at last I was about to compare books with facts, and judge for myself of the reported wonders of the earthly paradise. . . ."

MAIL STEAMER SHANNON: *December*, 1869. — "Latitude 25°, longitude 50°, *i.e.*, in the Doldrums or Calves of Cancer, past the Gulf-weed, and among the flying-fish. . . . We are having the most charming passage which even old hands remember at this time of year, and the steamer is full of delightful and instructive people, so that I am learning something every day. We have already invitations to Barbadoes, to Jamaica, to Cuba, Granada, Tobago — so that we might spend months in the West Indies; but I shall be home, please God, by the mail I promised. I have done duty, and preached twice, and I hope not in vain. I go up with your prayer-book every morning on the paddle-box on deck, before any passengers are up, so that I have a quiet gracious time — up at six, and breakfast at nine. . . . It all seems at times like a dream, then as if one had been always on board; then I want to show or tell you something, and forget for the moment you are three thousand miles off, in frost, perhaps, and snow, while we are in rich showery midsummer, with such sunrises and sunsets. . . ."

It would be a twice told tale to those who have read his "At Last" to do more than glance at his account of the voyage and its new experiences, the historic memories which the sight of the Azores woke up of Sir Walter Raleigh, Sir Richard Grenville, and many of England's forgotten worthies; and of all he felt at finding himself on the track of the "old sea heroes," Drake and Hawkins, Carlile and Cavendish, Cumberland, Preston, Frobisher, and Duddely, Keymis and Widdon — and of the first specimen of the Gulf-weed which brought back "the memorable day when Columbus's ship plunged her bows into the tangled ocean meadow, and the sailors were ready to mutiny, fearing hidden shoals, ignorant that they had four miles of blue water beneath their keel," — and of the awe which the poet and the man of science must needs feel at that first sight of the "Sargasso sea, and of the theories connected with it — not wholly impossible — of a sunken Atlantic continent — and of his enjoyment of the glorious cloudland, and the sudden sunsets when

> 'The sun's rim dips, the stars rush out,
> At one stride comes the dark;'

to be succeeded after balmy nights by the magnificent pageant of tropic sunlight" — and of the first sight of the New World, and the look out for Virgin Gorda, one of those numberless islands which Columbus discovered on St. Ursula's day; and of the arrival at St. Thomas, with its scarlet and purple roofs piled up among orange trees, and the first glimpse of a tropic hill-side. "Oh! for a boat to get into that paradise!" and how the boat was got; and how he leapt out on a sandy beach — and then the revelation of tropic vegetation, and the unmistakable cocoa-nut trees, and the tall aloes, and the gray-blue Cerei, and the bright deep green of a patch of Guinea grass; — and the astonishment which swallowed up all other emotions at the wonderful wealth of life — and the "effort, at first in vain, to fix our eyes on some one dominant or typical form, while every form was clamoring as it were to be looked at, and a fresh Dryad gazed out of every bush, and with wooing eyes asked to be wooed — and the drooping boughs of the shoregrape with its dark velvet leaves and crimson midrib, and the fragrant Frangipane, and the first cocoa-nut, and the mangrove swamp, and then the shells — the old friends never seen till now but in cabinets at home, earnests that all was not a dream; the prickly pinna, the great strombi, with the outer shell broken away, disclosing the rosy cameo within and looking on the rough beach pitifully tender and flesh-like; and the lumps of coral, all to be actually picked up and handled — and the first tropic orchid, and the first wild pines clinging parasitic on the boughs of strange trees, or nestling among the angular shoots of the columnar cereus;" and the huge green calabashes, the playthings of his childhood, alive and growing; and how "up and down the sand we wandered collecting shells, till we rowed back to the ship over white sand where grew the short manati grass, and where the bottom was stony, we could see huge prickly sea urchins, huger brainstone corals, round and gray, and above, sailing over our heads, flocks of brown and gray pelicans, to show us where we were — and met the fleet of negro boats laden with bunches of plantains, yams, green oranges, sugar canes;" and then the steaming down the islands, and the sight of the Lesser Antilles, the beauty and grandeur of which exceeded all his boyish dreams; and St. Kitts with its great hill, which took in Columbus's imagination the form of the giant St. Christopher bearing on his shoulder the infant Christ — and how "from the ship we beheld with wonder and delight the pride of the West Indies, the Cabbage Palms — well named by botanists the Oreodoxa, the glory of the mountains — gray pillars, smooth and cylindrical as those of a Doric temple, each carrying a flat head of darkest green;" and how Guadaloupe, Dominica, and Martinique were passed, and St. Vincent and its *souffrière* gazed on with awe and reverence — and the beautiful St. Lucia with its wonderful Pitons, and through the Grenadines to Granada, the last of the Antilles, as now the steamer ran dead south for seventy miles, and on St. Thomas's Day, at early dawn,

"We became aware of the blue mountains of North Trinidad a-head of us; to the west the island of the Dragon's Mouth, and westward again, a cloud among the clouds — the last spur of the Cordilleras of the Spanish Main. There was South America at last; and as a witness that this, too, was no dream, the blue waters of the Windward Isles changed suddenly into foul bottle-green. The waters of the Orinoco, waters from the peaks of the Andes far away, were staining the sea around us. With thoughts full of three great names, connected as long as civilized men shall remain, with those waters — Columbus, Raleigh, Humboldt — we steamed on . . . and then saw before us . . . to the eastward, the northern hills of Trinidad, forest clad down to the water: to the south a long line of coast, generally level with the water's edge, green with mangroves or dotted with cocoa palms. That was the Gulf of Paria and Trinidad beyond...."

Christmas found him the guest of his kind friend Sir Arthur Gordon, Governor of Trinidad, at the Cottage, Port of Spain, the earthly paradise which he had reached at last, and where he could revel in his Palm worship.

".... Those groo groo palms, a sight never to be forgotten — to have once seen palms breaking through, and as it were defying the soft rounded forms of the broad-leaved vegetation by the stern force of their simple lines; the immovable pillar-stem, looking the more immovable beneath the toss, the lash, and flicker of the long leaves, as they awake out of their sunlit sleep, and rage impotently for a while before the mountain gusts, to fall to sleep again. Like a Greek statue in a luxurious drawing-room, sharpcut, cold, virginal, showing, by the mere grandeur of form, the voluptuousness of mere color, however rich and harmonious; so stands the palm tree, to be worshipped rather than to be loved...." — *At Last.*

"THE COTTAGE, TRINIDAD, *January* 23, 1870.

".... You may conceive the delight with which I got your letter, and M——'s, and to think that the telegram should have arrived on Christmas Day! ... I have not been so well this seven years. I have been riding this week six to eight hours a day, through primeval forests, mud, roots, gullies, and thickets. ... As for what I have seen, no tongue can tell. We have got many curiosities, and lots of snakes. I have only seen one alligator, about five to six feet long, and only marks of deer and capo. But I have seen one of the mud volcanoes; and as for scenery, for vastness and richness mingled, I never saw its like. Oh that I could transport you to the Monserrat hills for one hour. . . . The woods are now vermilion with *bois immortel;* in a fortnight they will be golden with *poui* (all huge trees). I have seen a tree which for size beats all I ever dreamed of, a sandbox, forty-four feet round and seventy-five feet (we got down a liana and measured it) to the first fork, which did not seem half up the tree. But with too many of these giants, you can get no good view, their heads being lost in the green world above. But I have seen single trees left in parks over one hundred and twenty feet, with vast flat heads, which are gardens of orchids, &c., and tons of lianas hanging down from them, and the spurs of their roots like walls of board as high as a man. On Tuesday we start again for the north coast, then a short dash to the east, and then home. I have resisted all solicitations and invitations, and poor F. H—— being ill, gives me a plain reason for keeping my promise to you. Besides, I have seen enough already to last me my life. I keep saying, I cannot *not* have been in the tropics. And as I ride, I jog myself, and say, You stupid fellow, wake up. Do you see that? and that? Do you know where you are? And my other self answers, Don't bother. I have seen so much, I can't take in any more, and I don't care about it all. So I am in a state of intellectual repletion, indigestion, and shall take full twelvemonths to assimilate and arrange the mass of new impressions. I assure you I am very careful. I had to lie off a mangrove swamp in burning sun, very tired, after having ridden four hours, and been shoved over the mud in a canoe among the calling crabs, by three niggers, and I did not feel it the least, though the mud stank, and the wind was off shore, because before I got into the canoe, I took a good dose of quinine, which I always carry. Moreover, there are here wonderful angostura bitters (the same which cured Humboldt of his fever) which people take here before dinner, or when wet, tired, or chilly, and their effect is magical. They are tonic, not alcoholic. I have kept a great number of notes, and must make more. But this week I have travelled too fast, and have had no luggage, save at my saddle-bow. It is a glorious life in the forest, and I should like six months of it without stopping, if it did not rain.

January 24. — "A charming fellow has arrived, Mr. D. V——, governor of St. Lucia, who has seen and done unspeakable things among Indians and wild animals. I am learning a great deal from him, as I do from every one. . . . How strange a thing is man. I longed to get here. I have been more than satisfied with being here, and now I long to get back again. I long to find us running past those glorious Windward Islands, and away from St. Thomas to the cold north-east. But — this will be a possession — 'a thing of beauty is a joy for ever,' and this will make me young again. . . . I had the most delightful of days at the Pitch Lake with Admiral Wellesley, and he wanted to carry me off in the 'Royal Alfred' to Granada, &c., which would have been glorious. He is a noble man, and all his officers adore him. Give my love to William Harrison, and tell him how deeply obliged to him I am for taking care of everything in the parish while I am away. Remember me to every one in the parish. . . . I have nothing more to say just now, save that the Botanic Gardens are a perpetual treasure, because they are full of most rare trees and fruits from all the tropics, India, South Sea Islands, &c. I have learned more botany than I expected."

Seven weeks of intense enjoyment, spent in the society of the friend to whom he owed this unique episode in his life, and of scenery, the memories of which were fresh as ever on his death-bed, passed only too quickly. And early in February he took leave of lovely Trinidad, refreshed in brain, strengthened in health, enriched with beautiful memories, and in the possession of a friendship which was true to the last. Sir Arthur Gordon little thought that in five years he should be standing by Charles Kingsley's grave at Eversley, on the eve of setting sail for his new seat of government in the Fiji Islands.

The voyage home was successful, and when, towards the end of February, the Land's End was visible, regrets for the lovely western paradise were all swallowed up in bright thoughts of "the cold northern home as we ran northwards for the Needles. We had done it, and within the three months, as we promised. As the king in the old play says, 'What has been, has been, and I've had my hour.' At least we had seen it, and we could not unsee it. We could not *not* have been in the tropics."

He now settled down with renewed vigor to parish work; finding, to his great joy, his beloved son Maurice returned from South America for a short holiday before starting off afresh for Colorado. The parish benefited by their respective travels at penny readings and in their visits to the cottages. The Rector loved to give his people the results of his own and his children's new experiences in life; for Eversley, too, had advanced a step in intelligent sympathy with the great world outside. It was the same Eversley, and yet different to what it had been when he first came there twenty-eight years before. His own personal influence, and the influence of new circumstances, had told upon it. It was no

Heath Fires

longer the secluded spot it had been in his curate days, or even at a later period when he loved to dwell on its "monotony" as "so pleasant in itself, morally pleasant and morally useful." The monotony was broken occasionally by very startling incidents — the neighborhood of Aldershot bringing flying columns to the Flats and Bramshill Park. Engineering parties camped out and wells were sunk on the newly-enclosed glebe land, as for an advancing army; artillery wagons rumbled past the quiet Rectory, and bugle calls were heard at all hours by the Rector and his people. Now and then, too, the monotony was broken by quite another excitement, when a great heath fire broke out on the Flats, and committed havoc among the firs at Bramshill Park.

"At such a time," says a friend, "the Rector was all activity. On one occasion the fire began during the time of divine service. A messenger posted down in hot haste, to call the men out of church; and Mr. Kingsley, leaving his curate to finish the service, rushed to the scene of action, taking a flying leap, in surplice, hood, and stole, over the churchyard palings. The fire was an extensive one; but he, armed with a bill-hook, and now divested of everything ecclesiastical, was everywhere, organizing bands of beaters, and, begirt with smoke and flame, resisting the advance of the fire at every advantageous point. For many nights subsequently watchers were placed in the woods; and at a late hour (between 11 P.M. and 2 A.M.) Mr. Kingsley would sally forth and go the rounds, carefully inspecting the country as he went, cheering the watchers with kind hearty words of encouragement — himself intensely interested in the general picturesqueness of the event, and excited by the feeling that the alarm might be given at any moment, and the firs which he loved so dearly be wrapped in flame."

He was now invited to be President of the Devonshire Scientific Society for 1871, and he writes to Mr. Pengelley:

"Many thanks. I accept joyfully the honor which is offered me, and the date thereof. I only feel a dread at so great a pleasure, so far off, and at what may happen meanwhile ; for 'life is uncertain,' say folks. 'Life is certain,' say I, because God is educating us thereby. But this process of education is so far above our sight, that it looks often uncertain and utterly lawless. Wherefore fools (with M. Comte) conceive there is no living God, because they cannot condense His formulas into their small smelling-bottles. My eldest son, who has learnt his trade well at Cirencester and in the River Plata, is just going off to try his own manhood in Colorado, United States. You will understand, therefore, that it is somewhat important to me just now, whether the world be ruled by a just and wise God, or by $(x + \eta + \zeta) = 0$. It is also an important question to me whether what is said to have happened to-morrow (Good Friday) be true or false. But I am old-fashioned and superstitious, and unworthy of the year 1870."

On the 1st of May he took possession of "The Residence" in Abbey Square, Chester, for three months. Dean Howson, under whom he worked so happily, and whose after-friendship he truly prized, received him with a kindness, all the more generous because of the strong prejudice he had once felt against him before they met.

"I had read 'Alton Locke,' on its first appearance, and had thought it very unjust to the University of which

Residence at Chester

both he and I were members . . . and I must confess that when a letter came to me from him to tell me that he had been appointed a Canon of Chester, I was full of fear. There seemed to me an incongruity in the appointment. I fancied that there was no natural affinity between the author of 'Alton Locke' and cathedral life. Here I soon found that I had made a mistake. . . . To describe Canon Kingsley's work and usefulness in Chester, I must note the extraordinary enthusiasm with which he entered upon his connection with the place. Chester has certainly a very great charm for any one who is fond of the picturesque aspects of history; and upon him it told immediately. . . . With this enthusiasm I must note his old-fashioned courtesy, loyalty, and respect for official position. I suppose his political and social views would have been termed 'liberal;' but his liberalism was not at all of the conventional type. I should have described him as a mixture of the Radical and the Tory, the aspect of character which is denoted by the latter word being, to my apprehension, quite as conspicuous as that which is denoted by the former. Certainly he was very different from the traditional Whig. I have spoken of his respect for official position. I believe that to have caused inconvenience to me, to have done what I did not like, to have impeded me in my efforts to be useful, would have given him the utmost pain. That he was far my superior in ability and knowledge made no difference. I happened to be Dean, and he happened to be Canon; and this was quite enough. . . . I record this, that I may express my gratitude; but I note it also as a mark of character. . . ."

It was a happy and important circumstance to Mr. Kingsley that Chester was the first cathedral with which he was connected. Choral services had hitherto had little attraction for him: the slovenliness which in bygone years characterized them having shocked him from the æsthetic and still more from the religious point of view. Had this been the case at Chester it would have been a serious drawback to the happiness of his cathedral life there. But there all was in harmony with his ideal of Christian worship. And it filled the new Canon's heart with thankfulness that the lot had fallen to him in a cathedral, where the dignity of the services, the reverence of all who conducted them, from its Visitor, Bishop Jacobson, much beloved, down to the little chorister boys — impressed him deeply; where not only the Dean but all the officials worked earnestly to one end; and he could say with truth, as day by day he entered the venerable cloisters, "How amiable are Thy dwellings, O Lord, Thou God of hosts. My soul hath a desire and longing to enter into the courts of the Lord, for one day in Thy courts is better than a thousand." The early morning prayers were his great refreshment, and seemed to hallow the day to him; and many peaceful moments did he spend in the old chapter-house, in reading and prayer, before the clergy and choir assembled for worship, at eight o'clock, A.M. He found the Sunday services, including the vast nave congregation in the evening, exciting and exhausting; but through all, he experienced an abiding satisfaction of soul, a sense of the fitness of things, which was quite unexpected to himself and to those who had known his previous habit of life and feeling. Without ever professing to understand music, he had loved it, as a man of his genius and fine organization necessarily must, but at Chester his love deepened daily, and he soon

Residence at Chester

learned to look out eagerly for particular anthems and services.

A few days after arriving he took the chair at a meeting of the Archæological Society, and on being asked whether he belonged to the old Cheshire branch of the Kingsley family, he said that:

"His own feeling in coming to Chester was that he was coming home, for although he was landless, his ancestors had not been. He confessed to a feeling of pride in his connection with Cheshire, and to the mention of his name in the old Tarporley hunting song:

' In right of his bugle and greyhounds to seize
Waif, pannage, agistment, and wind-fallen trees;
His knaves through our forest Ralph Kingsley dispersed,
Bow-bearer-in-chief to Earl Randall the First.

' This Horn [1] the Grand Forester wore at his side
Whene'er his liege lord chose a-hunting to ride —
By Sir Ralph and his heirs for a century blown,
It passed from their lips to the mouth of a Done.'

He was glad to come to a county where many of his kin had lived. He was by no means an ambitious man, as the world called a man ambitious — he had no higher ambition than to live and die Canon of Chester. All he wanted was time to do his work and write his books; and if in anything set on foot in this ancient city — any movement connected with literary and scientific societies or mechanics' institutes — he might be able to help in his humble way, he was at the service of the good citizens of Chester. He did not wish to thrust himself forward, to originate anything grand, or to be in anybody's

---

[1] This bugle-horn, which is still in the family coat-of-arms, was the one which his ancestors, as Grand Foresters, had the right to carry.

way; but if they could find him reasonable work, as he was a rather overworked man, he would be happy to do it, without any regard to creed, politics, or rank in any way whatsoever. He thanked the gentlemen who had said so much in his favor, and hoped he should not forfeit the good opinion they had somewhat hastily formed of him."

"I am very happy here," he writes to Mr. Froude. "I have daily service, which is very steadying and elevating. Plenty of work in the place. I have started a botanical class for middle-class young men, which seems to go well; an opportunity of preaching to shrewd, able Northern men, who can understand and respond; and time to work at physical science — the only thing I care for much now — for it is the way of God who made all; while, —

> 'All the windy ways of men
> Are but dust which rises up
> And is lightly laid again.'"

Besides the daily services, which were an occupation in themselves, and the preparation of his sermons, he was anxious to get some regular week-day work that would bring the cathedral and the town in close contact. As usual his heart turned to the young men, whose time on long spring and summer evenings might be turned to account, and he offered to start a little class on physical science, expecting to have perhaps at most sixteen to twenty young shopmen and clerks. Botany was the chosen subject, and in a small room belonging to the city library, he began — the blackboard and a bit of white chalk being, as usual, of important help to the lectures, which he illustrated throughout. The class soon increased so much in numbers that they had to migrate to a larger room — a walk and a field lecture was proposed once a week — and the Canon and his party of sixty men sometimes puzzled people who watched them from the walls, as they went across country. This was the beginning of the Chester Natural History Society, which now numbers between five and six hundred members, with president, secretary, monthly meeting report, regular summer excursions, and winter courses of lectures.

During his first residence he preached a sermon for the Kirkdale Ragged Schools in Liverpool, where the condition of the masses affected him deeply, the Dean being anxious that the work of the chapter should extend beyond the cathedral city. "I remember," says a clergyman who heard him on that occasion, "that marvellous sermon on 'Human Soot.'[1] It made me more than ever know the magnificent mental calibre of the man. Canon Kingsley was one of a few, and they giants."

"What is your relation," he asks, "to the children in your streets — ragged, dirty, profligate, perishing? I do not blame the people of Liverpool, in our present imperfect state of civilization, for the existence among them of brutal, ignorant, degraded, helpless people. It is no one's fault, just because it is every one's fault — the fault of the system: but it is not the will of God, and therefore the existence of such an evil is proof patent and sufficient that we have not yet discovered the whole will of God about this matter; that we have not yet mastered the laws of true political economy which (like all other natural laws) are the will of God revealed in facts. Our processes are hasty,

---

[1] Published in "All Saints' Day and other Sermons."

imperfect, barbaric; and their result is vast and rapid production, but also waste, refuse, in the shape of a dangerous class. We know well how, in some manufactures, a certain amount of waste is profitable — that it pays better to let certain substances run to refuse, than to use every product of the manufacture — as in a steam-mill every atom of soot is so much wasted fuel; but it pays better not to consume the whole fuel and to let the soot escape. So it is in our present social system: it pays better. Capital is accumulated more rapidly by wasting a certain amount of human life, human health, human intellect, human morals, by producing and throwing away a regular percentage of human soot — of that thinking and acting dirt which lies about, and, alas! breeds and perpetuates itself in foul alleys and low public-houses, and all and any of the dark places of the earth. But as in the case of the manufactures, the Nemesis comes swift and sure. . . .

"I can yet conceive a time when, by improved chemical science, every foul vapor which now escapes from the chimney of a manufactory, polluting the air, destroying the vegetation, shall be seized, utilized, converted into some profitable substance, till the Black County shall be black no longer, and the streams once more run crystal clear, the trees be once more luxuriant, and the desert which man has created in his haste and greed, shall, in literal fact, once more blossom as the rose. And just so can I conceive a time when, by a higher civilization, founded on political economy, more truly scientific because more truly according to the will of God, our human refuse shall be utilized like our material refuse, when man as man, even down to the weakest and most ignorant, shall be found to be (as he really is) so valuable that it will be worth while to preserve his health, to the level of his capabilities, *to save him alive*, body,

Human Soot

intellect, and character, at any cost; because men will see that a man is, after all, the most precious and useful thing in the earth, and that no cost spent on the development of human beings can possibly be thrown away...... For God asks no impossibilities of a human being. But as things are, one has only to go into the streets of this or any great city to see how we, with all our boast of civilization, are as yet but one step removed from barbarism. Is that a hard word? Only there *are* the barbarians around us, at every street corner — grown barbarians, it may be now, all but past saving — but bringing into the world young barbarians, whom we may yet save, for God wishes us to save them. . . . Do not deceive yourselves about the little dirty offensive children in the street. If they be offensive to you; they are not to Him who made them. 'Take heed that ye despise not one of these little ones, for I say unto you, their angels do always behold the face of your Father which is in Heaven.' . . ."

To the Rev. J. Pulliblank, who asked him for a sermon for St. Mary's schools, he replies: —

". . . It is due to myself to ask you to tell your Vicar that I shall preach for any self-supporting Church of England schools with all the more pleasure, because I advocate 'secular education' as necessary only where the Church has not done her work; and desire to make up, as a Churchman, somewhat of those '*lâches*' of hers (one must use a French word sometimes, because one does not, alas! know English well enough), which have caused this education cry and league. My dear young gentleman, in whom I have seen high and truly liberal instincts, believe a stauncher conservative (though a radical) than most men are, when I say, It is all our own fault. We parsons of the Church of England have had three hundred years of the most splendid opportunity, with the freest and justest Government in the world to back us by establishment. And what have we done? Not ill. But not well. We have 'tolerably well' written against us in the Chancery of Heaven, when, with such opportunities as we have had since good Queen Bess's time, we ought to have had a great 'Optime' scored against us. Now, in the 'Day of the Lord' the revolutionary shaking of all things which shall sift them as wheat, to see what has worth, and what has not, judgment is going to begin at the house of God; and we parsons, who have only half-done our work (God knows we have not been altogether sluggards), shall have an evil time of it, perhaps, for a generation or two. But what of shopkeepers, manufacturers, merchants? Even of lazy honest old squires and peers, whom the former abuse and envy, though they are not a whit better, if not actually worse? Is it not written, If judgment begin at the house of God, where shall the unrighteous and the sinner appear?

"Where you are [Liverpool], therefore, remember that you are in the very centre of the barbaric mercantile system of England, whose rule is, 'They that make haste to be rich,' instead of 'piercing themselves through with many sorrows,' do their best as wise and prudent citizens. Remember that *that* is a lie; and without offending any one (and the most solemn truths can be spoken without offence, for men in England are very kind-hearted and reasonable), tell them so, and fight against the sins of a commercial city. Till they are cured, education, falsely so called, will do no good, and no harm either."

Among the letters this year, are two on "Woman's Rights;" significant of his latest views on this question. The proceedings of some of its advocates had shocked him so, that

Education of Women

he refused to attend any of their meetings, and the only branch of the subject to which he willingly gave his influence latterly was the medical education of women, which he had held for years (long before the question of "Women's Suffrage" was mooted) to be one of deep importance, and which to the last had his entire sympathy. Mr. John Stuart Mill, hearing that he had withdrawn more or less from the movement, wrote to Mrs. Peter Taylor to ask his reasons, which Mr. Kingsley thus gives:—

CHESTER: *May* 27, 1870.—"I have the honor of acknowledging your letter respecting the Women's Suffrage Question. If I, as one who has the movement at heart more intensely than I choose to tell any one, and also as one who is not unacquainted with the general public opinion of England, might dare to give advice, it would be, not in the direction of increased activity, but in that of increased passivity. Foolish persons have 'set up the British Lion's back,' with just fears and suspicions. Right-minded, but inexperienced persons have set up his back with unjust (though pardonable) fears and suspicions. I do not hesitate to say, that a great deal which has been said and done by women, and those who wish to support women's rights, during the last six months, has thrown back our cause ... We shall not win by petitions. The House of Commons cares nothing for them. It knows too well how they can be got up, and takes for granted that we shall get up ours in the same way. By pamphleteering we shall not win. Pamphlets are now too common. They melt on the debauched and distracted sensorium of the public, like snow on water. By quiet, modest, silent, private influence, we shall win. 'Neither strive nor cry, nor let your voice be heard in the streets,' was good advice of old, and is still. I have seen many a movement succeed by it. I have seen many a movement tried by the other method, of striving and crying, and making a noise in the street. But I have never seen one succeed thereby, and never shall. I do not hesitate to say, that unless this movement is kept down to that tone of grace, and modesty, and dignity which would make it acceptable to the mass of cultivated and experienced, and therefore justly powerful, Englishmen and Englishwomen, it will fail only by the fault of its supporters. I warn you of a most serious danger. I have found that when the question has been put in its true, practical, rational light, to men and women who had the greatest horror of it from prejudice, their consciences and reasons gave way at once, and they were ready to submit and agree. But I have found, alas! that within a week, some one or other had said or done something premature, or even objectionable, which threw back the process of conversion. This is the true cause of our seemingly unexpected failure. And I entreat you to control, instead of exciting, just now, those over whom you have influence. . . ."

"MY DEAR MR. MILL, — As you have done me the unexpected honor of asking my opinion on an important matter, I can only answer you with that frankness which is inspired by confidence and respect. 1. I do not think that ladies speaking can have had, or can have, any adverse influence. . . . My fear is, not so much that women should speak, as *who* the women are who speak. . . . There exist, in all ranks of the English, and in none more than in the highest rank, women brave, prudent, pure, wise, tried by experience and sorrow, highly cultivated and thoughtful too, whose influence is immense, and is always exercised for good, as

Education of Women 279

far as they see their way. And unless we can get these, of all ranks, and in each rank, down to the very lowest, to be 'the leaders of fashion,' for good, instead of evil, we shall not succeed. I am pained, in a very large acquaintance of all ranks, to find the better rather than the worse women against us — while foolish women, of no sound or coherent opinions, and of often questionable morals . . . are inclined to patronize us in the most noisy and demonstrative way. I am aware of the physical and psychical significance of this fact. I know, and have long foreseen, that what our new idea has to beware of, lest it should be swamped thereby, is hysteria, male and female. Christianity was swamped by it from at least the third to the sixteenth century, and if we wish to save ourselves from the same terrible abyss, and to — I quote my dear friend Huxley's words, with full agreement, though giving them a broader sense than he would as yet — 'to reconstruct society according to science,' we must steer clear of the hysteric element, which I define as the fancy and emotions unduly excited by suppressed sexual excitement. It is all the more necessary to do this, if we intend to attack 'social evils,' *i.e.*, sexual questions, by the help of woman raised to her proper place. That you mean to do so I take for granted. That I do, I hope you take for granted. If not, I should be glad some day to have the honor of talking over with you this whole matter, on which I have long thought, and on which I have arrived at conclusions which I keep to myself as yet, and only utter as Greek, φωνᾶντα συνετοῖσι, the principle of which is, that there will never be a good world for woman, till the last monk, and therewith the last remnant of the monastic idea of, and legislation for, woman, *i.e.*, the canon law, is civilized off the earth.

"Meanwhile, all the most pure and high-minded

women in England, and in Europe, have been brought up under the shadow of the canon law, have accepted it, with their usual divine self-sacrifice, as their destiny by law of God and nature; and consider their own womanhood outraged, when it, their tyrant, is meddled with. It is to them, therefore, if we wish (as I do) for a social revolution, that we must address ourselves mildly, privately, modestly, rationally. Public meetings drive them away, for their experiences, difficulties, wrongs, are too sacred to be detailed even before women of whom they are not sure, much more before men, most of all before a press, which will report, and next morning cynically comment on, the secrets of their hearts. A free press — with all its innumerable advantages — is the great barrier (I say it to you deliberately) to the moving in this matter of that great mass of matrons for whom, in the long run, the movement is set on foot; and by whom alone it can be carried out. At least, so it seems to me, who fight, not for the maiden so much as for the matron, because, if the mother be benefited, the child is benefited in her. And therefore I deprecate the interference in this movement of unmarried women. . . . But I see with pain this movement backed up by men and women who, unknown themselves to the English nation, and knowing nothing of it, and its actual opinions and habits for good or evil, in a word, sectarians (whether they know it or not), seem ready to scramble back into a society which they have in some cases forfeited, by mixing themselves up with questions which it is not for such as they to speak of, either in the study or the forum. I object, also, to the question of woman's right to vote or to labor, and above all, to woman's right to practise as physicians and surgeons, being mixed up with social, *i.e.*, sexual questions. Of woman's

Education of Women

right to be a medical practitioner, I hold that it is perhaps the most important social question hanging over us. I believe that if once women can be allowed to practise as freely as men, the whole question of the relation of the sexes, according to natural laws, and, therefore, according to what I believe to be the will and mind of God, the author of nature [will be made clear]. . . . But for that very reason, I am the more anxious that women should not meddle with these sexual questions, first, before they have acquired a sound, and also a general, scientific physiological training, which shall free them from sentiment, and confine them to physical laws and facts, on these matters. Second, before they have so accustomed the public to their ministrations, as to show them that they are the equals of men in scientific knowledge and practical ability (as they are); and more, that they know, as women, a hundred woman's secrets, which no one but a woman can know truly, and which it is a disgrace to modern civilization that a man should have the right of trying to interpret. Therefore I deprecate, most earnestly, all the meddling, however pure-minded, humane, &c., which women have brought to bear on certain questions during the last six months. I do not say that they are wrong. Heaven forbid! But I do say, that by so doing they are retarding, it may be for generations, the cause which they are trying to serve. And I do say (for I have seen it) that they are thereby mixing themselves up with the fanatical of both sexes; with the vain and ambitious, and worst of all, with the prurient. Prurience, sir, by which I mean lust, which, unable to satisfy itself in act, satisfies itself by contemplation, usually of a negative and seemingly virtuous and Pharisaic character, vilifying, like St. Jerome in his cell at Bethlehem, that which he dare not do, and

which is, after all, only another form of hysteria —
that is the evil which we have to guard against, and
we shall not do so, unless we keep about this whole
movement a tone of modesty, delicacy, lofty purity,
which (whatever it knows, and perhaps it knows all)
will not, and dare not, talk aloud about it. That tone
will not be kept, if we allow the matrons, and after
them the maidens (by whom I mean women still under
the influence of their fathers and mothers), or women
having by their own property a recognized social
position, to be turned out of sight in this movement
by 'emancipated' women.

"I know that the line is very difficult to draw. I
see how we must be tempted to include, nay, to welcome
as our best advocates, women who are smarting under
social wrongs, who can speak on behalf of freedom
with an earnestness like that of the escaped slave. But I
feel that we must resist that temptation; that our
strength lies not in the abnormal, but in the normal
type of womanhood. And I must say, that any sound
reformation of the relations between woman and man,
must proceed from women who have fulfilled well their
relations as they now exist, imperfect and unjust as they
are. That only those who have worked well in harness,
will be able to work well out of harness; and that only
those that have been (as tens of thousands of women
are every day) rulers over a few things, will be fit to be
rulers over many things; and I hold this — in justice to
myself I must say it — not merely on grounds 'theological' so called, but on grounds without which the
'theological' weigh with me very little — grounds material and physiological — on that *voluntatem Dei in
rebus revelatam*, to which I try, humbly though confusedly, to submit all my conclusions.

"Meanwhile, I shall do that which I have been
doing for years past. Try to teach a noble freedom, to

those whom I see most willing, faithful, conscientious in their slavery, through the path of self-sacrifice; and to influence their masters likewise, to see in that self-sacrifice something far more divine than their own self-assertion. To show them that wherever man and wife are really happy together, it is by ignoring and despising, not by asserting, the subordination of woman to man, which they hold in theory. To set forth in every book I write (as I have done for twenty-five years) woman as the teacher, the natural and therefore divine guide, purifier, inspirer of the man. And so, perhaps, I may be as useful to the cause of chivalry, dear equally to you and me, as if I attended many meetings, and spoke, or caused to be spoken many speeches."

His correspondence this year was voluminous, principally on botanical problems connected with his West Indian experiences, and on the Franco-Prussian war, but want of space admits of only a small selection.

". . . As for the war, I dare not give an opinion on it. It is the most important event since the Revolution of 1793, and we are too near it yet to judge of it fairly. My belief is, that it will work good for generations to come. But at what an awful price! . . ."

TO PROFESSOR MAX MÜLLER.

"Accept my loving congratulations, my dear Max, to you and your people. The day which dear Bunsen used to pray, with tears in his eyes, might not come till the German people were ready, has come, and the German people are ready. Verily God is just, and rules too; whatever the press may think to the contrary. My only fear is, lest the Germans should think of Paris, which cannot concern them, and turn their eyes away from that which does concern them, the re-taking Elsass (which is their own), and leaving the Frenchman no foot of the Rhine-bank. To make the Rhine a word not to be mentioned by the French henceforth, ought to be the one object of wise Germans, and that alone. In any case, with love to dear G——, I am yours, full of delight and hope for Germany."

TO SIR CHARLES BUNBURY. — "And now a few words on this awful war. I confess to you, that were I a German, I should feel it my duty to my country to send my last son, my last shilling, and after all, my own self to the war, to get that done which must be done, done so that it will never need doing again. I trust that I should be able to put vengeance out of my heart — to forget all that Germany has suffered for two hundred years past, from that vain, greedy, restless nation ; all even which she suffered, women as well as men, in the late French war : though the Germans do not forget it, and some of them, for their mothers' or aunts' sakes, ought not. But the average German has a right to say : — Property, life, freedom, has been insecure in Germany for two hundred years, because she has been divided. The French kings have always tried to keep her divided, that they might make her the puppet of their ambition. Since the French Revolution, the French people (all of them who think and act, viz., the army and the educated classes) have been doing the same. They shall do so no longer. We will make it impossible for her to interfere in the internal affairs of Germany. We will make it an offence on her part — after Alfred de Musset's brutal song — to mention the very name of the Rhine. As for the present war, it was inevitable, soon or late. The French longed for it. They wanted to revenge 1813-15, ignoring the fact that Germany was then avenging — and very gently — 1807. Bunsen used to say to me — I have seen the tears in his eyes as he said it — that the

Franco-Prussian War

war must come; that he only prayed God that it might not come till Germany was prepared, and had recovered from the catastrophes of the great French war. It has come, and Germany is prepared — and would that the old man were alive, to see the 'battle of Armageddon,' as he called it, fought, not as he feared on German, but on French soil. It must have come. The Germans would have been wrong to begin it; but when the French began, they would have been 'niddering' forever not to have accepted it. If a man persists for years in brandishing his fist in your face, telling you that he will thrash you some day, and that you dare not fight him — a wise man will, like Germany, hold his tongue till he is actually struck; but he will, like Germany, take care to be ready for what *will* come. As for Prussia's being prepared for war being a sort of sin on her part — a proof that she intended to attack France, such an argument only proves the gross ignorance of history, especially of German history, which I remark in average Englishmen. Gross ignorance, too, or willing oblivion of all that the French have been threatening for years past, about 'rectifying their frontier.' The Germans had fair warning from the French that the blow would be struck some day. And now that it is struck, to turn the other cheek in meekness may be very 'Christian' toward a man's self; but most unchristian, base, and selfish, towards his women, his children, and his descendants yet unborn. There can be no doubt that the French programme of this war was, to disunite Germany once more, and so make her weak, and at the mercy of France. And a German who was aware of that — as all sensible Germans must have been aware — had to think not of the text which forbids us to avenge private injuries, but of that which says, 'They that take the sword shall perish by the sword;' not of the bodily agony and desolation of the war, but of Him who said, 'Fear not them that can kill the body,' and after that have nothing left to do; but fear him — the demon of selfishness, laziness, anarchy, which ends in slavery, which can kill both body and soul in the hell of moral and political degradation. As for this being a 'dynastic war,' as certain foolish workingmen are saying — who have got still in their heads the worn-out theory that only kings ever go to war — it is untrue. It is not dynastic on the part of Germany. It is the rising of a people from the highest to the lowest, who mean to be a people, in a deeper sense than any republican democrat, French or English, ever understood that word. It is not dynastic on the part of France. The French Emperor undertook it to save his own dynasty; but he would never have done so, if he had not been of opinion (and who knows the French as well as he?) that it would not be a dynastic war, but a popular one. Else, how could it save his throne? What could it do but hasten his fall, by contravening the feelings of his people? But it did not contravene them. Look back at the papers, and you will find that Paris and the army (which between them, alas! constitute now the French people) received the news of war with a delirium of insolent joy. They were mistaken, and have received Trulla's answer to Hudibras:

> 'And mounting on his trunk astride,
> Quoth she, "I told you this would come
> Of all your vaporing vile scum."'

The Emperor was mistaken . . . in spite of all his cunning. He fancied that after deceiving the French people — after governing them by men who were chosen because they could, and dared deceive, that these minions of his, chosen for their untruthfulness, would be true, forsooth, to him alone; that they would exhibit, unknown, in a secret government, virtues of honesty,

On Natural Selection 287

economy, fidelity, patriotism, which they were forbidden to exercise in public, where their only function was, to nail up the hand of the weather-glass, in order to insure fine weather; as they are doing to this day in every telegram. So he is justly punished, and God's judgments are, as always, righteous and true. . . .

September 5.— "Since Waterloo, there has been no such event in Europe. I await with awe and pity the Parisian news of the next few days. As for the Emperor, while others were bowing down to him, I never shrank from expressing my utter contempt of him. His policy is now judged, and he with it, by fact, which is the 'voice of God revealed in things,' as Bacon says; and I at least, instead of joining the crowd of curs who worry where they lately fawned, shall never more say a harsh word against him. Let the condemned die in peace if possible, and he will not, I hear, live many months— perhaps not many days. Why should he wish to live? This very surrender may be the not undignified farewell to life of one who knows himself at his last."

TO ALFRED WALLACE, ESQ , F.L.S.

"*October* 22, 1870.— I have read your 'Essay on Natural Selection' with equal delight and profit. . . . The facts, of course, are true, as all yours are sure to be; but I have never been able to get rid of the belief, that every grain of sand washed down by a river — by the merest natural laws — is designedly put in the exact place where it will be needed some time or other; or that the ugliest beast (though I confess the puzzle here is stranger), and the most devilish, has been created because it is beautiful and useful to some being or other. In fact, I believe not only in 'special providences,' but in the whole universe as one infinite complexity of special providences. I only ask you to extend to all nature the truth you have so gallantly asserted for man — 'That the laws of organic development have been occasionally used for a special end, just as man uses them for his special ends.' Page 370. Omit 'occasionally,' and say 'always,' and you will complete your book and its use. In any case, it will be a contribution equally to science and to natural theology."

CHAPTER XXV

1871

AGED 52

LECTURE AT SION COLLEGE — CORRESPONDENCE — IDEAL FEU-
DALISM — SCIENTIFIC AGRICULTURE — WORDS OF CONDO-
LENCE — EXPEDITIONS OF THE CHESTER NATURAL SCIENCE
SOCIETY — LECTURES ON TOWN GEOLOGY — A LUMP OF
COAL — THE RACE WEEK AT CHESTER — LETTERS ON
BETTING — CAMP AT BRAMSHILL — PRINCE OF WALES'S
ILLNESS — SERMON ON LOYALTY AND SANITARY SCIENCE
— LECTURES AT BIDEFORD, WOOLWICH, AND WINCHESTER.

"To conclude, therefore, let no man, out of a weak conceit of sobriety, or an ill-applied moderation, think or maintain that a man can search too far, or be too well studied in the book of God's word, or in the book of God's works, divinity or philosophy, but rather let men endeavor at endless progress or proficiency in both."

BACON, ADVANCEMENT OF LEARNING.

"Who art thou that complainest of thy life of toil? Complain not! Look up, my wearied brother. To thee Heaven, though severe, is not unkind. Heaven is kind, as a noble mother, as that Spartan mother, saying when she gave her son his shield, 'With it, my son, or upon it!' Thou, too, shalt return home in honor. Doubt it not, — if in the battle thou keep thy shield."

CARLYLE.

IN January he gave a lecture on "The Theology of the Future,"[1] at Sion College; which made a profound impression, and brought hope and comfort to many. In it he asserted his own belief in final causes, and urged on the clergy

[1] This lecture, or rather part of it, is incorporated into the preface of his "Westminster Sermons," published in 1874.

the necessity of facing the scientific facts of the day, and accepting the great work of reconciling science and the creeds.

"I wish to speak," he says, "not on natural religion, but on natural theology. By the first I understand what can be learnt from the physical universe of man's duty to God and his neighbor; by the latter I understand what can be learned concerning God Himself. Of natural religion I shall say nothing. I do not even affirm that a natural religion is possible; but I do very earnestly believe that a natural theology is possible; and I earnestly believe also that it is most important that natural theology should, in every age, keep pace with doctrinal or ecclesiastical theology. . . ."

He goes on to speak of Bishop Butler, Berkeley, and Paley, as three of our greatest natural theologians, and of the important fact, that the clergy of the Church of England, since the foundation of the Royal Society in the seventeenth century, have done more for sound physical science than the clergy of any other denomination; and expresses his conviction that if our orthodox thinkers for the last hundred years had followed steadily in the same steps, we should not now be deploring the wide and, as some think, widening gulf between science and Christianity. He very strongly recommends to the younger clergy "Herder's Outlines of the Philosophy of the History of Man" as a book, in spite of certain defects, full of sound and precious wisdom. He presses the study of Darwin's Fertilization of Orchids (whether his main theory be true or not) as a most valuable addition to natural theology. He speaks of certain popular hymns of the present day as proofs of an unhealthy view of the natural world, with a savor hanging about them of the old monastic theory of the earth being the devil's planet instead of God's, giving characteristic instances, and contrasting their keynote with that of the 104th, 147th, and 148th Psalms, and the noble *Benedicite Omnia Opera* of our Prayerbook. He contrasts the Scriptural doctrine about the earth being cursed with the popular fancies on the same point. He speaks of the 139th Psalm as a "marvellous essay on natural theology," and of its pointing to the important study of embryology, which is now occupying the attention of Owen, Huxley, and Darwin. Then he goes on to "Race," and "the painful and tremendous facts" which it involves, which must all be faced; believing that here, too, Science and Scripture will not ultimately be found at variance. Then, after an eloquent protest against the "child-dream of a dead universe governed by an absent God," which Carlyle and even Goethe have "treated with noble scorn," he speaks of that "nameless, invisible, imponderable, yet seeming omnipresent thing which scientific men are finding below all phenomena which the scalpel and the microscope can show" — the life which shapes and makes — that "unknown and truly miraculous element in nature, the mystery of which forever engrossing, as it does, the noblest minded of our students of science, is yet forever escaping them while they cannot escape it." He calls on the clergy to have courage to tell them — what will sanctify, while it need never hamper, their investigations — that this perpetual and omnipresent miracle is no other than the Breath of God — The Spirit who is The Lord, and the Giver of Life. "Let us only wait," he says — "let us observe — let us have patience and faith. Nominalism, and that 'sensationalism' which has sprung from Nominalism, are running fast to seed; Comtism seems to me its supreme effort, after which the whirligig of Time may bring round its revenges; and Realism, and we who hold the Realist creeds, may have our turn. . . ."

"I sometimes dream," he adds, " of a day when it will be considered necessary that every candidate for ordination should be required to have passed creditably in at least one branch of physical science, if it be only to teach him the method of sound scientific thought. And if it be said that the doctrine of evolution, by doing away with the theory of creation, does away with that of final causes — let us answer boldly, Not in the least. We might accept what Mr. Darwin and Professor Huxley have written on physical science, and yet preserve our natural theology on exactly the same basis as that on which Butler and Paley left it. That we should have to develop it, I do not deny. That we should have to relinquish it, I do. . . ."

The correspondence of this year shows that his West Indian experiences and his Chester life acted as a fresh stimulus to his accustomed rapid thinking on every sort of subject. He was much occupied with the distribution of plants — with the existence of a Palæo-tropic belt of land round the world — a Palæo-tropic civilization of an immensely remote epoch — with raised beaches — and sunken forests, &c., &c., besides the questions of the day, social, sanitary, political. His lectures were more brilliant than ever. And but for his power of sleeping at any moment and for any length of time, the brain could not have held out even so long against the amount of intensity which he carried into his varied work. For some years past he had been in the habit of sleeping profoundly for two hours before dinner.

To SIR C. BUNBURY, *Feb.* 7, 1871.— "I received your most pleasant letter at Sandringham, whence I had hoped to have come to Barton, even if only for an hour or two; but I had to run all the way home yesterday.

"I do not think I undervalue, or have overlooked, any difficulties in the supposed junction of the South American and African lands; but I find just as great difficulties in the other theory of Oliver's, of a junction between the sunken 'Lemuria' of the Indian Ocean with South America *viâ* Polynesia. Not that I deny it. I rather hold to a past belt of land all round the tropics, at an immensely remote epoch; for when I see a Ravenala (Urania) in Guiana, and another in Madagascar (with none between either way), common sense makes me suspect the former has travelled from Madagascar to Guiana, or *vice versâ;* but at what an antiquity! Before the Andes rose, before humming birds existed, &c. —— When, on the other hand, I see the jaguar, ocelot, and other spotted cats in South America, I cannot but suspect them of having come from Africa, the home of the leopard; and if it is answered that the leopard and spotted cats are also Indian, and may have come across the Pacific, I must demur, from the fact, that not only no cats, but no mammals at all are left in Polynesia : a very serious difficulty. . . .

To PROFESSOR MAX MÜLLER. — " About St. Michael's Mount, I believe that the present general form of the Mount is owing entirely to rain-wash and tide-wash. There was land between it and Marazion, and beyond it to S. and S. W. a whole continent, in fact, for ages, during which the flora and much of the fauna was the same as at present. But —

"Since the Mount assumed its (general) present form and size, there was a period during which oak, &c., forests formed all along the lowlands close to the sea. Then a subsidence (as between the Mount and the shore, and a dozen other places,) put those forests far below low-tide mark; then an elevation which carried them up again close to low-tide mark, and lifted the beaches, which had been formed behind them, high and dry. How deep the forests sank I cannot tell. The last 'sob' of the earth lifted the beaches above them fifteen or twenty feet. As for time, I know nought of it. I always count by hundreds of thousands of years, and believe man to be of any antiquity which he may be proved to be of. . . ."

To DR. RIGG. — " I return your proofs of the Lecture on Pantheism. I think them excellent and true; but I think you speak in too hard a tone of the Germans. Be sure that they will be needed to be revived — all of them which can live and should live — if we are to be delivered out of the Positivist Materialism of the day. I could have wished, but it is too late, that you had defined Pantheism, not only from Theism and Atheism but from Positivism. It is Positivism — of a loose maundering kind — which is really growing among young men. When Huxley proclaims himself a disciple of Kant and Berkeley, they think in their hearts, then he is a retrograde dreamer — 'almost as bad as that fool of a Christian, Kingsley.'

" But I warn you that your words will be of little use. The desire to get rid of a personal God is based on grounds which the many do not talk of, and which you do not touch. They say, boldly enough among themselves,

Ideal Feudalism 295

and sometimes to me as civilly as they can, 'We will have nothing to do with God, as long as He is one who sends the many to Tartarus, the few to Olympus. We will have nothing to do with a future state, as long as it is said to contain a Tartarus, and that an endless and irremediable one. The Olympus is beautiful, possible, but unprovable. The Tartarus is horrible to our moral sense, and shall be exterminated from the human mind.' . . ."

To SIR CHARLES BUNBURY. — "As to '*La petite Culture*,'. . . I hold that there should be large farms and small farms; and the proportion of one to the other should be left very much to the demands of the markets, and the experience of which culture is the most profitable on a given estate. Here the landlord could exercise a discretion, and say to the large farmer, 'You shall not absorb more land into a great farm; there are portions which would do better if cultivated on a more special system;' or to the small farmer, 'You shall not subdivide my land into 10 to 40 acre holdings, because you will be compelled, from the lightness of the soil, merely to do (and do badly) with it what the large farmer is doing well, and with less outlay per acre.' . . .

"But this I do hold. That each tenant should be an hereditary tenant as much as possible: *glebæ adscriptus*. His landlord should have no power of ejection as long as the farm was properly cultivated, and as long as a fair rent — to be fixed by a court of arbitrators — was duly paid by him and his son after him. I would, if I could, restore the feudal system, the highest form of civilization — in ideal, not in practice — which Europe has seen yet. I would bind the tenant to the landlord, the landlord to the lord-lieutenant, and him and all to the Crown, by more than the old '*Trinoda Necessitas*' of military service, roads and bridges. I would add to them the duty of public education, of agricultural drainage on a large scale, and of sanitary reform or sanitary police. . . . In a word, I would make every man, as in the Middle Age, responsible to some superior who represented to him the Crown. . . .

" . . . I quite agree with you that my semi-feudal ideal has become impossible. But still, it is an ideal; and one which will probably ' realize ' itself in some more highly civilized country hereafter. . . .

"And this brings in another and a painful thought. Are we not tending to that anarchy of irreverence which France is now paying for in tears and blood? The anarchy which is brought on by being governed by the Press, *i.e.*, by men who, having failed in regular labor of any kind, establish themselves as anonymous critics of all who labor, under an irresponsibility and an immunity which no despot ever enjoyed? Professing to speak the mind of the people, they live by pandering to its no-mind, *i.e.*, its merest fancies and prejudices. I see a possibility of all government becoming as impossible in England as it has been for two generations at least in France.

"But as an old supporter of the ballot (with the cynical reservation that it will do practically, *i.e.*, morally, neither good nor harm) I shall be glad to see the Ballot Bill carried, and an old grievance (even if a fancied one) removed."

To MISS CRAWFORD. — "As a practical agriculturist, I have interested myself much for twenty-five years in the small farm question. The least extent of English soil on which a man and his family can live comfortably, *i.e.*, as well as an average day-laborer, is four acres. To do so he must have capital to start with of at least £10 per acre, equal to £40. Besides, he must have a house, barn, manure-reservoir, &c., ready made. He must be a powerful man, as he must use hand-labor (not plough)

Scientific Agriculture 297

almost entirely. He must also be a practical agriculturist and stock-raiser. Even then is a question whether he will succeed if he grows merely food. He ought to grow flax, or hemp, or both; and know how to prepare the former, at least, for the market — as in Belgium; and this is an art in itself. The French and German peasants, who own or rent little farms, have long hereditary skill in agriculture, which the English artisan has not. The crops which they raise per acre are miserably small compared to those on a large English farm. I speak from the sight of my own eyes; and that an immediate result of breaking up the present farms into little allotments would be to diminish the food-producing powers of this realm at least one half. For a single fact, the small farmer could never fat a single bullock; and English beef would disappear from the market, its place being taken (as in France and Germany) by veal — the calves being killed to save the expense of rearing. The foreign peasant in the north lives far worse than a good English laborer. Meat he never tastes, or white bread. Black rye bread and pottage is his staple food, and his wife, from early field-work, becomes a haggard old woman at twenty-five. God forbid that I should ever see in England such wives and mothers as are common on the Continent. Moreover, in France his land is mortgaged, usually heavily, to the attorney in the next town. Arguments drawn from the peasantry of warmer climates, *e.g.*, the S.E. of France, well known to Mr. J. S. Mill, will not hold good here, or in North France. In the S.E. a man grows *maize* as well as wheat, and has his mulberries for silk, his vines, his almonds, his olives, all bringing him in a good profit over and above his food-producing land. Flax and hemp would be the only non-eatable crops here; and they (as has been shown by repeated failures of experiment) are not in sufficient demand to command a high profit. Since I took up scientific agriculture twenty-five years ago, in order to see if (as I hoped) some such scheme would not cure many social ills, I have gradually, but steadily, given up the hope. The only chance of deliverance from the present system which I see, and which may God send, is this : That science should discover some valuable raw article of manufacture, which can be grown freely on English soil, and which will require careful hand labor — like the vine, mulberry,[1] tea, coffee, cocoa, &c. Then, indeed, would the small farmer have a chance *if he had saved money to start with in the meantime.* As it is, were I a land-owner I should certainly try this experiment. I should let some four to five acre lots to the very ablest laborers at the usual low farmer's rent, on the condition that they used spade and fork, not plough, and give them all fair play, with the right of buying the land gradually from me if they saved money, which I fear they would not do. But if a town artisan came to ask me for a similar bit of land, I would say, 'Come in, my good fellow, and eat and drink with me, and go your way back to your own trade. For if you settled down on this bit of land, you would be either in the workhouse or the grave in twelve months, and the land a wilderness.' And if he were a sensible man I would make him see that I was right. The peasant on the Continent, nowhere more than in France, is, and must be, the slave of the government and of the clergy; because there is no strong land-owning class to stand between the poor man and the government officials who combine to oppress him. A French peasant grows up in barbarism and superstition. . . . No

[1] For many years he had given much time and thought to agriculture, he had tried experiments in growing maize, the white mulberry for silk culture, &c ; and had planned the cultivation of flax and cranberries on his own glebe See " Agricultural Crisis " in his Miscellanies.

Words of Condolence 299

gentleman — and worse, no lady — speaks to him or his from the cradle to the grave; and his civilization is impossible. . . . "

The next letters will show with what a tender awe and with how few words he dared to approach the sorrows of his friends. He felt dumb, he said, in the presence of bereavement.

To MISS ———: *May,* 1871. — " We were shocked at the news, and all felt deeply for you. And now, what shall I say? I am not going to tell you impertinent commonplaces as to how to bear sorrow. I believe that the wisest plan is sometimes not to try to bear it — as long as one is not crippled for one's every day duties — but to give way to sorrow utterly and freely. Perhaps sorrow is sent that we *may* give way to it, and in drinking the cup to the dregs, find some medicine in it itself, which we should not find if we began doctoring ourselves, or letting others doctor us. If we say simply, I am wretched — I ought to be wretched; then we shall perhaps hear a voice, ' Who made thee wretched but God? Then what can He mean but thy good?' And if the heart answers impatiently ' My good? I don't want it, I want my love;' perhaps the voice may answer, 'Then thou shalt have both in time.' . . . "

To MRS. ——— ———. — " I write to you because I know that every expression of human sympathy brings some little comfort, if it be only to remind such as you that you are not alone in the world, but that your loss draws towards you all the more those who love or even esteem you. I know nothing can make up for such a loss as yours. But you will still have love on earth all round you; and *his* love is not dead. It lives still in the next world for you, and perhaps with you. For, why should not those who are gone, if they are gone to the Lord, be actually nearer us, not further from us, in the heavenly world, praying for us, and it may be influencing and guiding us in a hundred ways, of which we, in our prison-house of mortality, cannot dream? Yes! Do not be afraid to believe that he is near you, and you near him, and both of you near God, who died on the cross for you. That is all I can say. But what comfort there is in it, if one can give up one's heart to believe it! May God bless you, and give you strength and faith to bear and to believe."

To —— ——, Esq.—" . . . One thing you know as well as I, and it is the only thing of which I can remind you, that in such a world as this, with such ugly possibilities hanging over us all—there is but one anchor which will hold, and that is utter trust in God. Keep that, and we may both get to our graves yet, without *misery* though not without *sorrow*."

The work at Chester this year assumed larger proportions, for the successful botanical class of 1870 had been the nucleus of the Scientific Society in 1871, and he followed it up this year by one for geology; these geological lectures were still more fully attended; not only the number of members increased, but each member was allowed to bring a lady friend. Consequently, in preparation for walks and field lectures, he had to go over the ground himself a day or two before, to judge of its capabilities for geology and botany, and also to arrange for a place of rest and refreshment for the class. In these researches he was accompanied by some member of the Cathedral body, always ready with loyal and intelligent help. Expeditions now were taken to more distant spots; the railway authorities had to be consulted about trains — they, too, gave most willing assistance; and, at the appointed place and hour, a happy party, numbering sometimes from sixty to a hundred, would find the Canon and his daughters waiting for them on the platform of the railway, he with geological hammer in hand, botany box slung over his shoulder, eager as any of his class for the day's holiday, while feeling the responsibility of providing teaching and amusement for so many, who each and all hung upon his words. Those were bright afternoons, all classes mingling together; people who had lived next door to each other in Chester for years perhaps without exchanging a word, now met upon equal and friendly terms, in pursuit of one ennobling object, and travelled in second class carriages together without distinction of rank or position, to return at the end of the long summer evening to their old city, refreshed and inspirited, — with nosegays of wild flowers, geological specimens, and happy thoughts of God's earth and of their fellow-creatures. Perhaps the moral gain of these field lectures was as valuable as their scientific results, uniting Cathedral and town as they did in closer bonds. In order to give importance to the Society, he wrote to Sir Charles Lyell, Sir Philip Egerton, Dr. Hooker, Professors Huxley, Tyndall, Hughes, &c., to beg permission to enrol their names as honorary members.

The room hitherto used at the City Library had now to be given up, and by the Dean's kindness the King's School was used as lecture-room. A preliminary lecture on the subject of physical science was given and followed by six, which will long be remembered in Chester; on The

Soil of the Field, The Pebbles in the Street, The Stones in the Wall, The Coal in the Fire, The Lime in the Mortar, The Slates on the Roof.[1] The blackboard was in constant use. Many of those who were present at the lecture on coal must recall the look of inspiration with which his burning words were accompanied, and the poetry he threw into his theme, as he went through the various transformations of the coal, till it reached the diamond; and with what kindling eyes he lifted a lump of coal off the table and held it up to his breathless listeners:

"A diamond, nothing less!—We may consider the coal upon the fire as a middle term of a series, of which the first is live wood, and the last diamond; and indulge safely in the fancy, that every diamond in the world has probably, at some remote epoch, formed part of a growing plant. A strange transformation, which will look to us more strange, more poetical, the more steadily we look at it. The coal on the fire, the table at which I stand, what are they made of? Gas and sunbeams, with a small percentage of ash, or earthy salts, which need hardly be taken into account.

"Gas and sunbeams! Strange, but true. The life of the growing plant—and what that life is who can tell?—laid hold of the gases in the air and in the soil, of the carbonic acid, the atmospheric air, the water, for that too is gas. It drank them in through its rootlets; it breathed them in through its leaf-pores, that it might distil them into sap, and bud, and leaf, and wood. But it had to take in another element, without which the distillation and the shaping could never have taken place. It had to drink in the sunbeams, and absorbed

[1] These lectures, published in 1872 as "Town Geology," were dedicated to the members of his class.

A Lump of Coal

them, buried them in itself—no longer as light and heat, but as invisible chemical force, locked up for ages in that woody fibre.

"So it is. Lord Lytton told us, in a beautiful song, how 'The wind and the beam loved the rose.' But Nature's poetry is more beautiful than man's. The wind and the beam love the rose — or rather the rose takes the wind and the beam, and builds up out of them, by her own inner life, her exquisite texture, hue and fragrance. What next? The rose dies; the timber tree dies — decays down into vegetable fiber, is buried, and turned to coal: but the plant cannot altogether undo its own work. Even in death and decay it cannot set free the sunbeams imprisoned in its tissue. The sun-force must stay, shut up age after age, invisible, but strong; working at its own prison-cells, transmuting them, or making them capable of being transmuted by man, into the manifold products of coal, coke, petroleum, mineral pitch, gases, coal-tar, benzole, delicate aniline dyes, and what not, till its day of deliverance comes. Man digs it, throws it on the fire, a black dead-seeming lump. A corner, an atom of it, warms till it reaches the igniting point; the temperature at which it is able to combine with oxygen. And then, like a dormant live thing, awaking after ages to the sense of its own powers, its own needs, the whole lump is seized, atom after atom, with an infectious hunger for that oxygen which it lost centuries since in the bottom of the earth. It drinks the oxygen in at every pore; and burns. And so the spell of ages is broken. The sun-force bursts its prison-cells, and blazes with the free atmosphere as light and heat once more, returning in a moment into the same forms in which it entered the growing leaf a thousand centuries since. Strange it all is, yet true. But of nature, as of the heart of man, the old saying stands — that truth is stranger than fiction."

No man ever had a more appreciative audience — intelligent, enthusiastic, affectionate. "They spring to touch," he would say, "at every point," and never did he receive such a warm grasp of the hand as from men of all ranks in the beloved old city. The Chester residence was one of the dearest episodes of his life, and after he was transferred to Westminster he could never speak of it without tears in his eyes.

It so happened that the first week of his annual three months in Chester, being always in May, was the race week, which for the time being turned the streets of the venerable old town into a sort of pandemonium; and the temptations of the young men in the middle and lower classes from betting and bad company, with the usual ending of a suicide, and the ruin of many, weighed heavily on his heart, as on that of the Dean and many of the residents. Most of the respectable tradesmen deplored the effect of the race-week, not only on the higher ground of morality, but because the stagnation of all trade except in the public-houses, and the losses to the working-classes which resulted from it were so serious. The Dean started a series of short papers on "Chester Races and their Attendant Evils" and gave Mr. Kingsley the subject of Betting, upon which he wrote this characteristic letter "To the Young Men of Chester:"[1]

"MY DEAR YOUNG MEN, — The human race may, for practical purposes, be divided into three parts: 1. Honest men: who mean to do right; and do it. 2. Knaves:

[1] This letter was published later in a tract form by Messrs. C. Kegan Paul & Co.

On Betting

who mean to do wrong; and do it. 3. Fools: who mean to do whichever of the two is the pleasanter. And these last may be divided again into —

"Black fools: who would rather do wrong; but dare not; unless it is the fashion.

"White fools: who would rather do right; but dare not; unless it is the fashion.

"Now the honest men do not need my advice; and the knaves will not take it; neither, I fear, will the black fools. They will agree, in their secret hearts, most of them, that every word I say is true. But they do not wish it to be true; and therefore they will tell every one that it is not true, and try to wriggle out from under it by far-fetched excuses, and go back next races, 'like the dog to his vomit, and the sow to her wallowing in the mire,' and bet and gamble boldly, because then that will be the fashion. But of the white fools I have hope. For they are not half bad fellows: some of them, indeed, are very near being very good fellows, and would like so much to do anything which is right and proper — only it takes so much trouble; and perhaps it might look rather odd now and then. Now let me ask them — and really I have so much liking for them, that I fear at times I must be one of them myself — in all friendliness and courtesy — Why do you bet and gamble at the races? Consider well what your answer will be. Certainly it will not be that you do so to avoid trouble, which you so much dislike in general. For you must confess at once that it is more trouble to bet, more anxiety, and often more grief and sorrow, than it is not to bet, but to leave the matter alone. And while you are preparing your reasons, I will give you two at least of mine, for leaving the matter alone. The first reason (which seems to me the strongest reason which can be given against any matter whatsoever) is this — that betting, and gambling of every kind, is in itself wrong and immoral. I do not say that every man who bets is an immoral man. Far from it: many really honest men bet; but that is because they have not considered what they are doing. Betting is wrong: because it is wrong to take your neighbor's money without giving him anything in return. Earn from him what you will, and as much as you can. All labor, even the lowest drudgery, is honorable; but betting is not laboring nor earning: it is getting money, without earning it, and more, it is getting money, or trying to get it, out of your neighbor's ignorance. If you and he bet on any event, you think that your horse will win: he thinks that his will; in plain English, you think that you know more about the matter than he: you try to take advantage of his ignorance, and so to conjure money out of his pocket into yours — a very noble and friendly attitude in which to stand to your neighbor, truly. That is the plain English of it: and look at it upwards, downwards, sideways, inside out, you will never make anything out of betting, save this — that it is taking advantage of your neighbor's supposed ignorance. But says some one, 'That is all fair, he is trying to do as much by me.' Just so: and that again is a very noble and friendly attitude for two men who have no spite against each other; a state of mutual distrust and unmercifulness, looking each selfishly to his own gain, regardless of the interest of the other. I say, regardless. You know whatever you lose, he will expect you to pay, however much it may inconvenience you; while if he loses you expect him to pay, however much it may inconvenience him. Thus betting is founded on selfishness; and the consequence is, that men who live by betting are, and cannot help being, the most selfish of men, and (I should think) among the most unhappy and pitiable; for if a man who is given up to selfishness, distrust, and cunning, who is tempted every hour to treachery and falsehood, without the possibility of one noble or purifying feeling throughout his whole day's work, or the consciousness that he has done the slightest good to a human being — not even as much good as an old woman at a stall has by selling a penny-worth of apples — if that man is not a pitiable object, I do not know what is.

"But some will say, 'It is not the money I care for, but the amusement.' Excuse me: but if so, why do you bet for money? That question I have asked again and again, and have never got an answer. Why do you bet for money, and not counters, or pins, or pebbles? Why, but because you want the money, to buy with it money's worth?

"Of course, I know well enough that plenty of bets pass on every race, which are practically quite harmless. A dozen of kid gloves to a lady — when you know that she will expect you to pay her, while you are bound not to ask her to pay you — he would be a very strait-laced person who could see any great harm in that; any more than in a rubber of sixpenny whist. And yet it would be better for many a young man, for some of the finest fellows of all, men of eager temper, high spirit, delicate honor, if they would make up their mind never to bet, even a shilling; never to play cards, except for love. For gambling, like drinking, grows upon some men, and upon the very finest natures too. And remember, that in betting and gambling, the more honorable man you are, the worst chance you have; gambling is almost the only thing in the world, in which the bad man is the stronger by very virtue of his badness, the good man the weaker by very virtue of his goodness. The man who will not cheat is no match for the man who will. The honorable man who will pay his debts, is no match for the dishonorable man who will not. No match indeed: not even in that last sad catastrophe, which I have seen too often: when the honorable man, throwing good money after bad to recover his losses, grows desperate, tries his hand just once at foul play, and sells his soul — for nothing. For when he borrows the knave's tools, he cannot use them; he is ashamed of himself, hesitating, clumsy; is found out — as I have known such found out: and then — if he does not put a pistol to his own head, and blow his brains out, it is not because he does not long, poor wretch! to do so.

"I hold, then, that betting is itself more or less wrong and immoral. But I hold, too, that betting, in three cases out of four, is altogether foolish; so foolish that I cannot understand why the very young men who are fondest of it, should be the very men who are proudest of being considered shrewd, knowing, men of the world, and what not. They stake their money on this horse and on that. Now judging of a horse's capabilities is an art, and a very delicate and difficult art, depending first on natural talent, and next on experience, such as not one man in a thousand has. But how many betting young men know anything about a horse, save that he has four legs? How many of them know at sight whether a horse is sound or not? Whether he can stay or not? Whether he is going in good form or not? Whether he is doing his best or not? Probably five out of six of them could not sit on a race-horse without falling off; and then such a youth pretends to himself that he is a judge of the capabilities of a noble brute, who is a much better judge of the young gentleman's capabilities, and would prove himself so within five minutes after he had got into the saddle.

"'But they know what the horse has done already.' Yes; but not what the horse might have done. They do not know — no one can, who is not in the secrets of the turf — what the horse's engagements really are; whether he has not been kept back in view of those engagements; whether he will not be kept back

On Betting

again; whether he has not been used to make play for another horse; and — in one word — whether he is meant to win. 'But they have special information: they have heard sporting men on whom they can rely, report to them this and the other wonderful secret.' Of all the various follies into which vanity, and the wish to seem knowing, and to keep sporting company, lead young men — and mere boys often — this I think is about the most absurd. A young lad hangs about the bar of a sporting public-house, spending his money in drink, in hopes of over-hearing what the initiated Mr. This may say to the initiated Mr. That — and goes off with his hearsay, silly fellow! forgetting that Mr. This probably said it out loud to Mr. That in order that he might overhear; that if they have any special information, they will keep it to themselves, because it is their stock-in-trade whereby they live, and they are not going to be foolish enough to give it away to him. Mr. This and That may not be dishonest men; but they hold that in betting, as in love and war, all is fair; they want to make their books, not to make his; and though they very likely tell him a great deal which is to their own advantage, they are neither simple enough, nor generous enough, to tell him much that is to his advantage; or to prevent him from making the usual greenhorn's book by which he stands sure to lose five pounds, and likely to lose fifty.

"'Ah, but the young gentleman has sent his money on commission to a prophet in the newspaper, in whom he has the highest confidence; he has prophesied the winner two or three times at least; and a friend of his sent him money to lay on, and got back ever so much; and he has a wonderful Greek name, Lynceus, or Polyphemus, or Typhlops, or something, and so he must know.' Ah! fool, fool. You know how often the great Polyphemus prophesied the winner, but you do not know how often he did not. Hits count of course; but misses are hushed up. And as for your friend getting money back, if Polyphemus let no one win, his trade would stop. The question is, not whether one foolish lad won by him, but whether five-and-twenty foolish lads did not lose by him. He has his book to make, as well as you, and he wants your money to pay his own debts with if he loses. He has his bread to earn, and he wants your money to earn it with; and as for sending him money, you may as well throw a sovereign down a coal-pit and expect it to come up again with a ton of coals on its back. If any young man will not believe me, because I am a parson, let him read, in the last chapter or two of 'Sponge's Sporting Tour,' what was thought of the Enoch Wriggles and Infallible Joes, by a better sportsman and a wiser man than any Chester betting young gentleman is likely to be.

"'Ah, but the young gentleman has a private friend. He knows a boy in Mr. So-and-So, or Lord the Other's stables, and he has put him up to a thing or two. He is with the horse day and night; feeds him; knows the jockey who will ride him.' Does he then? What a noble and trustworthy source of information! One on the strength of which it would be really worth a lad's while to disobey his father, make his mother miserable, and then rob his master's till, so sure must he be to realize a grand haul of money! A needy little stable-boy, even a comfortable big groom, who either tells you what he does not know, and so lies, or tells you what he does know, and so is probably a traitor; and who in any case, for the sake of boasting and showing off his own importance, or of getting half-a-crown and a glass of brandy-and-water, will tell you anything which comes uppermost. I had almost said he is a fool if he does not. If you are fool enough to buy his facts, his cheapest and easiest plan must be to invent sham facts,

On Betting

and sell them you, while he keeps the real facts for his own use. For he too has his little book to make up; and like every one who bets, must take care of himself first, with his hand against every man, and every man's hand against him.

"I could say much more, and uglier things still. But to what I have said, I must stand. This used to be the private history of small bettings at races thirty years ago; and from all I hear, things have not grown better, but worse, since that time. But even then, before I took Holy Orders, before even I thought seriously at all, things were so bad that I found myself forced to turn my back on race-courses, not because I did not love to see the horses run – in that old English pleasure, taken simply and alone, I can fully sympathize — but because I found that 'hey tempted me to betting, and that betting tempted me to company, and to passions, unworthy not merely of a scholar and a gentleman, but of an honest and rational bargeman or collier. And I have seen what comes too often of keeping that company, of indulging those passions. I have known men possessed of many virtues, and surrounded with every blessing which God could give, bring bitter shame and ruin, not only on themselves, but on those they loved, because they were too weak to shake off the one passion of betting and gambling. And I have known men mixed up in the wicked ways of the world, and too often yielding to them, and falling into much wrong doing, who have somehow steered through at last, and escaped ruin, and settled down into a respectable and useful old age, simply because they had strength enough to say — 'Whatever else I may or may not do, bet and gamble I will not.' And I very seriously advise my good friends the White Fools to make the same resolution, and to keep it.   Your very good friend,

"*February* 1, 1871.   C. KINGSLEY."

Charles Kingsley

The following letter was written many years before, to his eldest son when a school-boy, on his telling his father he had put into a lottery for the Derby without thinking it any harm:

"MY DEAREST BOY,— There is a matter which gave me much uneasiness when you mentioned it. You said you had put into some lottery for the Derby, and had hedged to make safe. Now all this is bad, bad, nothing but bad. Of all habits gambling is the one I hate most and have avoided most. Of all habits it grows most on eager minds. Success and loss alike make it grow. Of all habits, however much civilized men may give way to it, it is one of the most intrinsically *savage*. Historically it has been the peace excitement of the lowest brutes in human form for ages past. Morally it is unchivalrous and unchristian. 1. It gains money by the lowest and most unjust means, for it takes money out of your neighbor's pocket without giving him anything in return. 2. It tempts you to use what you fancy your superior knowledge of a horse's merits — or anything else — to your neighbor's harm. If you know better than your neighbor you are bound to give him your advice. Instead, you conceal your knowledge to win from his ignorance; hence come all sorts of concealments, dodges, deceits — I say the devil is the only father of it. I hope you have not won. I should not be sorry for you to lose. If you have won I should not congratulate you. If you wish to please me, you will give back to its lawful owners the money you have won. If you are a loser in gross thereby, I will gladly reimburse your losses this time. As you had put in, you could not in honor draw back till after the event. Now you can give back your money, saying you understand that Mr. B. and your father disapprove of such things, and so gain a very great moral influence. Recollect always that

On Betting

the stock argument is worthless. It is this: 'My friend would win from me if he could, *therefore* I have an equal right to win from him.' Nonsense. The same argument would prove that I have a right to maim or kill a man if only I give him leave to maim or kill me if he can and will.

"I have spoken my mind once and for all on a matter on which I have held the same views for more than twenty years, and trust in God you will not forget my words in after life. I have seen many a good fellow ruined by finding himself one day short of money, and trying to get a little by play [1] or betting — and then the Lord have mercy on his simple soul, for simple it will not remain long. Mind, I am not the least *angry* with you. Betting is the way of the world. So are all the seven deadly sins under certain rules and pretty names, but to the devil they lead if indulged in, in spite of the wise world and its ways. YOUR LOVING FATHER."

In addition to his course of lectures in the King's School, he gave one, by urgent request, at Crewe, to the men connected with the railway works, on "The Aristocracy of the Future." Also one on "Primeval Man" in Chester. This year he succeeded Mr. Froude, his "friend, and more than friend," as he calls him in his address, as President of the Devonshire Literary and Scientific Association at Bideford:

"It is not," he said, "without solemn memories that I find myself here, revisiting the scenes which have in-

[1] So strong was his feeling about gambling, that, though to rest his brain, he always played dominoes, backgammon, patience, whist, or some other game of cards, with his children in the evening for an hour or two, he would never allow play for money in his own house.

spired me for more than forty years with all that Nature can teach of her purest and noblest—scenes which first taught me to sympathize with and then to learn from the genius of Wordsworth, and to find in him, while watching the contact between his soul and Nature, not merely a great poet but a great philosopher. And after forty years, thanks to that magnificent patience—tardiness if you will—of Nature, which my dear and honored friend Sir Charles Lyell, first in our later centuries, has seized as the true basis for all geological thought—thanks, I say, to Nature's tardiness, I find all the beloved natural objects, at least to my hasty glance, unchanged. With a sigh of relief, I find still unabolished the Torridge and the Hubbastone, and Tapeley, and Instow, and the Bar, and the Burrows, and the beloved old Braunton Marshes and Sandhills, and doubt not that the raised beach under Santon is as safe as it has been any time this 20,000 years, and that not an ounce of rock has been worn off the Morte stone since I first steamed past it as a boy. We abolish many things, good and evil, wisely and foolishly in these fast-going times; but, happily for us, we cannot abolish the blue sky, and the green sea, and the white foam, and the everlasting hills, and the rivers which flow out of their bosoms. They will abolish themselves when their work is done, but not before. And we, who, with all our boasted scientific mastery over nature, are, from a merely mechanical and carnal point of view, no more than a race of minute parasitic animals burrowing in the fair Earth's skin, had better, instead of boasting of our empire over Nature, take care lest we do not become parasites too troublesome to Nature, by creating, in our haste and greed, too many great black countries through which I have too lately passed, and too many great dirty warrens of houses, miscalled cities, peopled with savages and imps of our own mis-creation; in which case Nature, so far from allowing

us to abolish her, will by her inexorable laws abolish us.
Therefore, I rejoice to see so little abolished here. . . ."

In the course of his address he expresses, with deepest respect for Mr. Darwin, his regret at certain of his speculations on the descent of man, and says at the close:

"The question of the physical 'Origin of Man' I decline to touch here. It is strictly a physiological and anatomical question, not to be discussed in a mixed assembly. It seems, moreover, less important to me than it does to many persons on both sides, whom I revere and love. However physical science may decide the controversy, I say boldly, as a man and as a priest, that its decision will not affect one of my duties here, one of my hopes for hereafter. . . ."

On his return from Chester the quiet parish of Eversley was startled into new life by the formation of a military camp in Bramshill Park and on Hartford Bridge Flats, at the opening of the autumn manœuvres, during which the Prince of Wales camped out with his regiment, the 10th Hussars. The tumult of enthusiasm and pride of the little parish at the Prince's presence and gracious courtesy (which will never be forgotten in Eversley); had scarcely subsided, when the country was electrified by the news of H.R.H.'s being struck down with fever and at the point of death, and rector and parishioners grieved and prayed and wept together. When all danger was over, and the heart of the whole nation rebounded with joy, Mr. Kingsley preached on the day of Thanksgiving at the Chapel Royal, St.

James's, a sermon on Loyalty, in which he presses the subject of Sanitary Reform. The "Times" acknowledged, in strong terms, the eloquent and practical use he made of the occasion.

"But," says the writer, "our immediate purpose in referring to this grand sermon is to be found in its sequel. 'Let our hearts,' said the Canon,[1] 'be bowed as the heart of one man, to say that, so far as we have power, so help us God, no man, woman, or child in Britain, be he prince or be he beggar, shall die henceforth of preventible disease. Let us repent of and amend that scandalous neglect of the well-known laws of health and cleanliness which destroys thousands of lives yearly in this kingdom without need or reason, in defiance alike of science, of humanity, and of our Christian profession. Two hundred thousand persons, I am told, have died of preventible fever since the Prince Consort's death a few years ago. Is not that a national sin to bow our hearts as the heart of one man? Oh, if his Royal Highness's foul and needless disease, by striking at once at the very highest, shall bring home to us the often-told, seldom-heeded fact, that this same disease is striking perpetually at hundreds among the very lowest, whom we leave to sicken and die in dens unfit for men, unfit for dogs — if this illness shall awaken all loyal citizens to demand and to enforce, as a duty to their Sovereign, their country, and their God, a sanitary reform in town and country, immediate, wholesale, imperative — if it shall awaken the ministers of religion to preach *that* — I hardly ought to doubt it — till there is not a fever alley or a malarious ditch left in any British city; then indeed, this fair and precious life will not have been imperilled in vain; and generations yet unborn will bless the memory of a prince who sickened as poor men

[1] "All Saints' Day and other Sermons."

sicken, and all but died as poor men die; that his example and, it may be, hereafter his exertions, might deliver the poor from dirt, disease, and death.'"

In the autumn he was invited to give a lecture at the Woolwich Royal Artillery Institution. His subject was "The Study of Natural History," in which he pressed upon his hearers the importance of the "inductive habit of mind" which, working steadily and by rule from the known to the unknown, is so specially valuable to military men, to whom the advantage of the knowledge of botany —· for instance, when leading an exploring party or engaged in bush warfare — would be great, if only from knowing what plants are poisonous, what are eatable, what would yield vegetable acids as preventives of scurvy, what for medicine or styptics, what timbers are available to resist wet or the attacks of insects, &c., &c. Again, how great the use of "geology and mineralogy and meteorology, in finding limestone, building stone, road metal — in finding water, of what sort and at what depth — and in ascertaining, with a view to malaria, rainfalls, and all those questions which so deeply affect the health of troops, whose lives are too often ignorantly sacrificed in these days by being placed in barracks built in spots purely pestilential." He reminded them of one significant fact, that the greatest captain of the old world was trained by the greatest philosopher of the old world, the father of Natural History; that Aristotle was the tutor of Alexander of Macedon —

"But why? What need for the soldier and the man of science to fraternize just now. This need. The two classes which will have an increasing influence on the fate of the human race for some time will be the men of science and the soldiers. . . . They will be left to rule; because they alone have each in his own sphere learnt to obey. . . . I may be a dreamer: and I may consider, in my turn, as wilder dreamers than myself, certain persons who fancy that their only business in life is to make money, the scientific man's only business to show them how to make money, and the soldier's only business to guard their money for them. Be that as it may, the finest type of civilized man which we are likely to see for some generations to come, will be produced by a combination of the truly military with the truly scientific man. I say, I may be a dreamer: but you at least, as well as my scientific friends, will bear with me; for my dream is to your honor. . . ."

At Christmas he gave a lecture for the Winchester Scientific Society on Bio-geology, which, while rich in facts, was still the very poetry of science; and after a masterly review of the Bio-geology of Hampshire — its plants, reptiles, &c., and glances at the European and Atlantic flora, he wound up, as usual, with theology, which to his mind was taught even by the law of natural selection:

"My friends, whether you will be the happier for it, or for any knowledge of physical science, or for any other knowledge whatsoever, I cannot tell: that lies in the decision of a Higher Power than I; and, indeed, to speak honestly, I do not think that bio-geology or any other branch of physical science is likely, at first at least, to make you happy. Neither is the study of your fellow-men. Neither is religion itself. We were not sent into the world to be happy, but to be right — at least, poor

Lectures

creatures that we are—as right as we can be, and we must be content with being right, and not happy. . . . And we shall be made truly wise if we be made content—content, too, not only with what we can understand, but content with what we do not understand—the habit of mind which theologians call (and rightly) faith in God, true and solid faith which comes often out of sadness, and out of doubt, such as bio-geology may well stir in us at first sight. For our first feeling will be—I know mine was when I began to look into these matters—one somewhat of dread and of horror. Here were all these creatures, animal and vegetable, competing against each other. 'Woe to the weak' seems to be Nature's watchword. The Psalmist says—'The righteous shall inherit the land.' If you go to a tropical forest, or, indeed, if you observe carefully a square acre of any English land, cultivated or uncultivated, you will find that Nature's text at first sight looks a very different one. She seems to say—not the righteous, but the strong, shall inherit the land. Plant, insect, bird, what not—find a weaker plant, insect, bird, than yourself, and kill it. . . . This is Nature's law, and is it not at first sight a fearful law? Internecine competition, ruthless selfishness, so internecine and so ruthless that, as I have wandered in tropic forests where this temper is shown more quickly and fiercely, though not in the least more evilly, than in our slow and cold temperate one, I have said—really these trees and plants are as wicked as so many human beings. Throughout the great republic of the organic world the motto of the majority is and always has been, as far back as we can see, as it is, and always has been, with the majority of human beings—'Every one for himself, and the devil take the hindmost.' Selfish competition, overreaching tyranny, the temper which fawns and clings, and plays the parasite as long as it is down; and, when it has risen, fattens on its patron's blood and life. These, and the other works of the flesh, are the works of average plants and animals as far as they can practise them. At least, so says at first sight the science of bio-geology, till the naturalist, if he be also human and humane, is glad to escape from the confusion and darkness of the universal battle-field of selfishness into the order and light of Christmas-tide. For then there comes to him the light. And are these all the facts? And is this all which the facts mean? That mutual competition is one law of Nature we see too plainly. But is there not, besides that law, a law of mutual help? True, it is, as the wise man has said, that the very hyssop on the wall grows there because all the forces of the universe could not prevent its growing. All honor to the hyssop — a brave plant. It has fought a brave fight, and has its just deserts (as everything in Nature has), and so has won. But did all the powers of the universe combine only to prevent it growing? Is not that a one-sided statement of facts? Did not all the powers of the universe also combine to make it grow, if only it had valor and worth wherewith to grow? Did not the rains feed it, the very mortar in the wall give lime to its roots? Were not electricity, gravitation, and I know not what of chemical and mechanical forces, busy about every cell of the little plant, kindly and patiently ready to help it, if it would only help itself? Surely this is true — true of every organic thing, animal and vegetable, and mineral, too, for aught I know; and so we must soften our sadness at the sight of the universal mutual war by the sight of an equally universal mutual help. But more. It is true — too true if you will — that all things live *on* each other. But is it not, therefore, equally true that all things live *for* each other? That self-sacrifice, and not selfishness, is at the bottom the law of Nature, as it is the law of grace, and the law of bio-geology, as it is the law of all religion and virtue worthy

Lectures

of the name? Is it not true that everything has to help something else to live, whether it knows it or not?— that not a plant or an animal can turn again to its dust without giving food and existence to other plants, other animals? . . . And so, the longer one watches the great struggle for existence, the more charitable, the more hopeful one becomes, as one sees that consciously or unconsciously, the law of Nature is, after all, self-sacrifice. Unconscious in plants and animals — as far as we know — save always those magnificent instances of true self-sacrifice shown by the social insects, by ants (*Termites*), bees, and others, which put to shame by a civilization truly noble — why should I not say divine, for God ordained it — the selfishness and barbarism of man. But be that as it may, in man the law of self-sacrifice — whether unconscious or not in the animals — rises into consciousness just as far as he is a man — and the crowning lesson of bio-geology may be — when we have worked it out — after all, the lesson of Christmas-tide — of the infinite self-sacrifice of God for man. . . ."

And so his keynote, whether at Sion College to the clergy, at Chester to his middle-class pupils, at Woolwich to military men, or to the scientific societies of Devon and Hampshire, was the same, that Science is the Voice of God — her facts, His words — to which as we listen we must each and all reply, "Speak, Lord, for Thy servant heareth."

CHAPTER XXVI

1872

AGED 53

OPENING OF CHESTER CATHEDRAL NAVE — DEATHS OF MR.
MAURICE AND NORMAN McLEOD — CATHEDRAL STALLS
AND LEARNED LEISURE — BISHOP PATTESON — NOTES ON
MODERN HYMNOLOGY — LECTURE AT BIRMINGHAM AND
ITS RESULTS — LECTURES AT CHESTER — CORRESPONDENCE
ON THE ATHANASIAN CREED — ON DISESTABLISHMENT —
A POEM.

"No man can justly blame me for honoring my spiritual mother, the Church of England, in whose womb I was conceived, at whose breast I was nourished, and in whose bosom I hope to die. Bees by the instinct of Nature do love their hives, and birds their nest. But, God is my witness, that, according to my uttermost talent and poor understanding, I have endeavored to set down the naked truth impartially, without either favor or prejudice, the two capital enemies of right judgment. The one of which, like a false mirror, doth represent things fairer and straighter than they are; the other, like the tongue infected with choler, makes the sweetest meats to taste bitter. My desire hath been to have Truth for my chiefest friend, and no enemy but Error."

BISHOP BRAMHALL.

THE year began at Eversley with the usual winter's parish work, night-schools, penny Readings, &c., which were only interrupted for a few days by his going to Chester for the opening of the Cathedral nave.

CHESTER: *January* 24, 1872. — "Service this afternoon magnificent. Cathedral quite full. Anthem, 'Send out Thy Light.' Collection, £105. Cathedral looks lovely, and I have had a most happy day. Every one glad to see me, and inquiries after you all. I do love this place and people, and long to be back here for our spring residence."

Mr. Maurice's death and Dr. Norman McLeod's saddened him, and warned him of the consequences of an overworked brain. Of the former he said in writing to a friend, "You too saw that his work was done. I had seen death in his face for almost two years past, and felt that he needed the great rest of another life, and now he has it;" of the latter, "he is an instance of a man who has worn his brain away, and he is gone, as I am surely going." At the great gathering round Mr. Maurice's grave at Highgate, many eyes were fixed on Charles Kingsley, his much-loved disciple.

"As I think," said one of those present, "of that warrior face of his, like the countenance of one of those old Vikings, whose glories he loved to sing of, with the light of the western sky shed on it, as he stood, strong as he was, with ill-concealed emotion, by the grave of his beloved master, Frederick Maurice, on Easter Monday, 1872, the man's whole aims, character, and work seemed revealed to one in a moment."

Work of all kinds seemed now to redouble; and the mere letters refusing sermons, lectures, church openings, and kind invitations from friends in England and Scotland, who were eager to give him the rest and refreshment which he so sorely needed, gave constant employment to his home secretary. On returning to Chester, he found the Natural Science Society so well established that though he still arranged all the expeditions, he gave fewer lectures; for over-work of brain had brought on a constant lassitude and numbness of the left side, which led him to apprehend coming paralysis, and forced him to confine his work more to preaching and the never-ceasing correspondence. He gave his President's address to the Natural Science Society, then numbering 250 members, on his return from his first sight of the English Lakes, and told them of the feelings which the grave of Wordsworth, that "great poet, great philosopher, great divine," called up in him. After speaking of the grand and sacred physical laws, whether of light, heat, gravitation, &c.,

" they are," he says, " but the dead body, at least, the dead machinery of the universe ; and grander to us and still more sacred is the living soul of the universe, which the microscope and the scalpel can show no man, which the microscope and the scalpel may have tempted him in grim hurry to forget; grander and more sacred than all the machinery of nature is the poetry of nature.

> " ' A presence that disturbs us with the joy
> Of elevated thoughts; a sense of something
> Still more deeply interfused.' "

He quoted the whole passage from Wordsworth's Ode, expressing his gratitude that his own "soul had been steeped from boyhood in that poetry, had learnt from it how to look at and feel with Nature, and had been preserved by Wordsworth's influence from those shallow cynical and materialist views of the universe, which tempt the eager student of science in his exclusive search after the material and the temporary to neglect the spiritual and eternal. . . ."

"... Go forth, my dear friends, with microscope, hammer, dredge, and collecting box; find all you can, learn all you can. God speaks to you through physical facts; but do not forget to take with you at times a volume of good poetry — say 'Wordsworth's Excursion,' above all modern poetry. For so you will have a spiritual tonic, a spiritual corrective, which will keep your heart healthy and childlike, to listen to that other and nobler voice of God which speaks through the æsthetical aspects of nature. ... So, instead of bewailing, like poor Keats, that there was an awful rainbow once in heaven, whose charm was gone now that the laws of refraction had been discovered, you will be ready to say with Wordsworth, however thoroughly you may be acquainted with those laws,

"'My heart leaps up when I behold
A rainbow in the sky;
So was it when my life began,
So is it now I am a man,
So be it when I shall grow old,
Or let me die.'"

And so he toiled on, dreaming of that time of "learned leisure" rather than of "increased activity," for which a Canonry he held should provide; but which did not as yet fall to his lot; and those who watched him most closely and loved him best felt that if rest ever came it would come too late. "Better," however, he said, "to wear out than rust out." He agreed with Dean Goulburn in thinking that the proposed changes in cathedral establishments would involve with increasing work, decreasing scholarship, and writes to him:

February 28, 1872. — "I have long seen a desire, on the part of certain bishops, to acquire, under the name of organization, powers hitherto unknown in the Church of England, to be exercised not directly by themselves, but by nominees and servants of their own, archdeacons and rural deans. That this encroachment, if allowed, would destroy the manly freedom which English rectors have long enjoyed . . . is clear. If, in addition to this, the bishops . . . remodel the cathedral bodies till they become mere working diocesan machines, then 'increased activity' may be obtained; but the Holy Orders of the English Church will have become no fit place for scholars. . . . Meanwhile, if you speak further on this matter, let me beg you to warn the rectors, that, when our liberty as canons goes, theirs will soon follow."

To PROFESSOR MAX MÜLLER. — "I have read your gallant words about Bishop Patteson in the *Times*. I did not know him; but it is at least a comfort to me to read words written in such a tone in this generation. By all means let us have a memorial to him. But where? In a painted window, or a cross here in England? Surely not. But on the very spot where he died. There let the white man, without anger or revenge, put up some simple and grand monolith, if you will; something at least which the dark man cannot make, and which instead of defacing he will rather worship as a memorial to the Melanesian and his children, which they would interpret for themselves. So, indeed, 'he being dead would yet speak.' Think over this."

This spring Dr. Monsell requested Mr. Kingsley and other friends to help him with suggestions for a new Hymnary. Being much over-worked, he had only time to make a few brief notes in the book sent for his remarks, from which the following are selected:

"36. — O Paradise, O Paradise!

Modern Hymnology

"Whence did the author of this hymn learn that 'the world is growing old?' I object much to the use of 'I want to,' instead of 'I long' or desire.

"No. 40. — Hark! hark, my soul, angelic songs are swelling.

"I object to this hymn, as a direct invocation of angels, and as also 'unreal.' People do *not* hear the angels singing over fields and seas.

"No. 61 — For thee, O dear, dear country, our eyes their vigils keep.

"Congregations do *not* lie awake or weep, thinking of heaven. I dread all exaggerated language.
"No. 102 is exaggerated for a whole congregation.

"Lord, in Thy mercy's day,
Holy Jesus, *grant us tears.*

"I object to 'grant us tears.' It savors of the old '*donum lachrymarum*,' which had a special virtue in itself; wherefore witches could never cry.

"No. 124. — Sacred heart of Jesus, heart of God in man.

"Should not this be 'Heart of man in God'? Not by conversion of the Godhead into flesh, but by taking of the manhood into God. A beautiful poem; but not a congregational hymn.

"I shrink from the two Litanies of the Passion and to the Sacred Heart, especially from the former. They are, historically, connected with a creed which we have renounced, and all imitations of which I at least dread; and they are quite alien in tone to any speech of St. Paul or St. John concerning our Lord's person, either in the epistles or the Revelations.

"No. 189, 192. — Save me by the Passion of Thy bleeding feet.
"Sacred Heart of Jesus, pour Love on me while I adore.

"In No. 170 ('Praise to God, immortal praise') I regret the use of 'vine,' 'olive,' and 'fig' in the hymns of a country in which those crops are not cultivated. 'Reality' (as it is now called) in the service of God is very important, if we are to counterbalance the unreality of sensational hymns.

"With regard to hymns 112, 'Long in Darkness did He wait,' and 121, 122, for Good Friday, beginning ' O, Sacred head once Wounded,' and 'Jesus, gentle Sufferer, say.' — I cannot but feel that hymns to Christ, as the ascended and triumphant King of the universe, are more fitting, because more *true* than any which, by a stretch of dramatic imagination, fancy Him still in His humiliation. Let it be always remembered that the Church in the Collects, and we in our name *Good* Friday,' give the keynote for devotion on this day. With regard to the one for Holy Communion, · My love is like the Rose,' I humbly deprecate all hymns adapted from the canticles. The 'Miserere Domine,' No. 196, is a most beautiful poem, though not a congregational hymn; but I do not understand the allusions in the last two verses to our Lord's *fast*.

"Thy fast, Thy fast, O God, Thy fast.

"Christ is not represented as having fasted for man, but as having died for man, and I think words concerning his death would be preferable. For by His death we are forgiven.

"You will forgive my not having put A against '*Hic breve vivitur*' — 'Jerusalem the golden.' 'For thee, oh ! dear, dear country,' and several of that cycle. I may be fastidious; but I cannot approve of them; their very popularity makes their soundness the more suspected by me. In the Church of God I shrink from singing hymns to 'heaven,' just as to angels. We are there to worship God, not heaven, which is a created *thing*."

Lecture at Birmingham 329

These fragments of criticism may seem superfluous: but it would be doing him an injustice to suppress all notice of his strong views on Modern Hymnology, there being no other allusion to the subject except in his preface to the Westminster Sermons. He regretted deeply the adoption of hymns, which he considered combined the faults of Puritanism, Mysticism, and Romanism; he deplored words being put into the mouths of a general congregation which were unreal to them — individual confessions of sin, too solemn to be sung, especially in the part of the service which is set apart for praise; and ardent expressions of a love almost amounting to passion, which if not felt must therefore be an unconscious insult to Him to whom they were addressed. This unfitness shocked him so, that he considered even selections from the discarded old and new version of the Psalms of David in the Prayer-book would be less objectionable than some of the new hymnologies.

In the autumn, being President of the Midland Institute for the year, he went to Birmingham to give his inaugural address. It was on the Science of Health — one of his best and most suggestive lectures, which bore fruit at once, in the noble response made to it. A gentleman of Birmingham (a manufacturer), who had been long wishing to promote scientific knowledge among the working-classes of Birmingham, and deplored the ignorance prevailing on the subject of health, without its having occurred to him that it might be made a distinct object of study, immediately on hearing the address decided to devote the sum of 2,500*l.* to found classes and lectures on Human Physiology and the Science of Health. He believed, with Mr. Kingsley, that if people's interest could only be excited on the subject, physical improvement would be followed by moral and mental improvement, and that hospitals, and even prisons and madhouses, would be relieved of many cases which have their origin in mere ignorance of the laws of health and physiology. A draft scheme of the application of the gift to lectures, open to artisans on the lowest possible scale of payment for admission, etc., was made and submitted to Mr. Kingsley, who replied:

October 31.—" I beg to return the paper which you have sent me, with the expression of my deep satisfaction, and I may say personal gratitude. Your friend will be doing, I believe, solid and lasting good to generations yet unborn, and I trust that his noble example may be followed in every great town of these realms. I think the first title, 'The Teaching of Physiology to the Working Classes,' is the better of the two. But I would define it as 'Human Physiology,' or, better, as 'The Science of Health.' . . . A grant might be given to a mothers' or married women's class, from which men would be excluded. I am solicitous for some such exclusively woman's teaching. . . . An essay, now and then, on the subject, open to all comers of a certain grade, would be most useful, and stir up many minds even more than lectures. It will be necessary to take care that the lectures are really practical lectures on the science and art of health, and not on mere scientific physiology. If not they are likely to become mere lectures on comparative anatomy, or other non-practical, or at least, purely scientific branch. You will have to find, and you will have some trouble in finding, men who really know about

Lectures at Chester

drains and bedrooms, etc., and who are not above talking of them. Let me be so bold as to advise your friend to look at Dr. Edwin Lankester's admirable little 'Practical Physiology,' to see what should be taught, and how. . . ."

The immediate result of this lecture was perhaps the highest earthly reward ever granted to him, *the* blue ribbon of his life, and had he lived to see how the work has been since carried out at Saltley College and elsewhere, his soul would have been satisfied. He may see it now — God knows!

The particulars of a further proposal to found a trust for promoting the teaching the laws of health to teachers in common schools, was submitted to Mr. Kingsley in October, 1874, and he concludes his letter, after pointing to the scheme which he thought would give the whole subject a fixed academical status, with these characteristic words: "Alas! alas! why can we not have a professor of it at Cambridge and another at Oxford, and make every young landowner and student for holy orders attend their lectures?"

Many of his dreams — social, sanatory, and others — equally improbable as they seemed at one time, have been realized; perhaps this may, too, when the day dawns in which man's body — the temple of the Holy Ghost — will be considered as divine as his soul — the workmanship of Him, in whose sight both are equally sacred.

In November he gave a lecture on Heroism, for the Chester City Library and Reading-room, both at that time low in funds. The Duke of Westminster, foremost as usual in giving the lead to all noble thought and noble work in the old city, took the chair. It was intended to be the prologue to a course he hoped to give in his next spring residence, and the next evening, after attending the last Chapter at which he was ever present, he gave a final lecture to the Scientific Society, of which he was still President, on Deep-Sea Dredging.

He was asked this year to join the committee for the defence of the Athanasian Creed, which gave him the opportunity of expressing more forcibly the views he had held for years on the intermediate state and his hopes of the future life. The following are extracts from the correspondence which ensued:

"This seems to me the time for sound Churchmen to use a fresh weapon in defence of the Athanasian Creed, by bringing forward a somewhat neglected Catholic doctrine — that of the intermediate state, or states. Thus, too, I may say in passing, the Church would be shown to be on this — as on other points — more and not less liberal than her dissenting opponents.

. . . .

"I have long held that the maintenance of the Athanasian Creed by the Church of England will exercise a most potent and wholesome influence, not only on the theology, but on the science, both physical and metaphysical, of all English-speaking nations for generations to come. I feel for, though I cannot feel with, the objections of many excellent persons to the so-called damnatory clauses; but I believe that those objections would gradually die out, if there were appended to the Creed, in our Prayer-Book, an explanatory clause, which expressed, or at least allowed, the true and ancient Catholic doctrine concerning the future state."

". . . My rule has been to preach the Athanasian Creed from the pulpit in season and out of season; to ground not merely my whole theological, but my whole ethical teaching, formally and openly on it; to prevent, as far as I could, people from thinking it a dead formula, or even a mere string of intellectual dogmas. And if I were (from my experience) to dare to offer a suggestion, it would be to call on all clergy who value the Creed to preach it continually, and make their congregations feel something at least of its value. But I only speak with hesitation, and am ready to be convinced if I am wrong."

. . . .

"The Athanasian Creed is now construed by the people, in the light of Puritan Eschatology — *i. e.*, of the doctrine which the Puritans (as far as I know) introduced first, namely, that the fate of every man is irrevocably fixed at the moment of death. I need not tell you that this is not the Catholic doctrine; that the Church has held, from a very early age, the belief in an intermediate state. That belief was distorted and abused, in later times, as the Romish doctrine of purgatory. But the denunciation of that doctrine in the Thirty-nine Articles (as Dr. Newman pointed out, if I recollect rightly, in Tract 90) does not denounce any primitive doctrine of purgatory, nay, rather allows it, by the defining adjective 'Romish.' That this Puritan Eschatology is no part of the Creed of the Church of England, is proved by her final rejection of the Article affirming endless punishment. . . .

"Now, it is plain again that men have no right to read the Athanasian Creed in this Puritan sense. In whatsoever age it was composed, it was composed by one who believed in the intermediate state; and there is nothing in its language to hint that he held that there was no hope in that state for the unorthodox whom he denounced; nothing to hint that he held, with the old

Crusaders, that an infidel went straight to hell. So guardedly vague are the expressions of the Creed, as to 'perishing everlastingly,' and 'everlasting salvation,' that it might be believed and used honestly by one who did not hold the 'necessary immortality of the soul,' and therefore thought the final annihilation of the wicked possible.

"The Creed says, and truly, that the knowledge of God, and it alone, is everlasting life. It does not say that that knowledge may not be vouchsafed hereafter to those who have sought honestly for it, in this life, but through unfortunate circumstances, or invincible ignorance, have failed to find it. Provided the search be honestly continued in the unknown realms beyond the grave, the Athanasian Creed does not deny that the seeker, it may be after heavy pains and long wanderings, shall at last discover his Saviour and his God, and discover that for him he had been yearning though he knew it not. It is almost needless for me to point out how such an interpretation of the Athanasian Creed would relieve the consciences of thousands, without (it seems to me) forfeiting our strict honesty, or our claim to Catholic orthodoxy — how it would make the Creed tolerable to thousands to whom (under its Puritan misrepresentation) it is now intolerable; and would render unnecessary that alteration of the so-called 'damnatory clauses,' to which I have consented with much unwillingness, and only as a concession to the invincible ignorance of modern Puritanism.

"I have reason to believe that the English mind (and possibly the Scotch) is specially ripe just now for receiving once more this great Catholic doctrine of the intermediate state, and that by preaching it with all prudence, as well as with all manfulness, we should cut the ground from under our so-called 'Liberal' adversaries' feet. I say — with all prudence. For it is plain that unguarded

The Athanasian Creed

latitude of expression might easily awaken a cry that we were going to introduce 'the Romish doctrine of purgatory,' and to proceed to 'pardons' and 'masses for the dead.' But that if we keep cautiously within the limits permitted by truly Catholic antiquity, we shall set in motion a mighty engine for the Church's help in her need, I, as a student of public opinion, have no doubt whatsoever.

. . . .

"It is not for me, a private clergyman, to lay down the law, as I have been asked to do, what is the Catholic doctrine on this, or any other matter, save as I find it expressed in the formularies of the Church of England, as by law established. Now the Church of England has left this question of the future state, in many points, an open question; the more markedly so, because the Puritan influences of the sixteenth century were pressing her to define and narrow her formularies about it. Those influences, though they failed, thank God, in narrowing her formularies, have actually succeeded till very late years, in narrowing her public opinion about this most important question, among the majority of her members. In the face of that public opinion, I intended to reopen the whole question; to set the clergy searching for themselves, Scripture, Catholic antiquity, and whatsoever of wisest and soundest has been written by our great English divines; to make them think for themselves, and judge for themselves, instead of asking me, or any man, to think and judge for them. For only so will any wider and sounder belief on this, or any other matter, be a real belief of the heart and reason, and not a mere party cry, repeated parrot-like and unintelligently.

"If God should ever give me grace and wit to express clearly my opinion on this matter, I shall do so, after that full research and deliberation which befit so important and awful a subject. But I look to wiser and more learned men than myself to speak better sense upon it than I shall ever speak meanwhile; certain that even though they may differ in details, and even some of them err, they will at least prepare the mind of the Church for the reception of eternal truth. . . ."

. . . .

In his last letter to Thomas Cooper, thanking him for his volume of "Plain Pulpit Talk," he says that, in it,

"I see the thorough right old morality — common to Puritans, old Anglican Churchmen, apostles, and prophets; that you hold right to be infinitely right; and wrong ditto wrong; that you call a spade a spade, and talk to men about the real plagues of their own hearts; as Carlyle says, you 'do not rave against extinct Satans, while quite unaware of the real man-devouring Satan at your elbow.' My dear friend, go on and do that, and whether you call yourself Baptist or Buddhist, I shall welcome you as one who is doing the work of God, and fighting in the battle of the Lord, who makes war in *righteousness*. But more. You are no Buddhist. . . . I happen to be, from reason and science as well as from Scripture and Catholic tradition (I use a word I don't like), I happen to be, I say, an orthodox theologian, and to value orthodoxy more, the more I think, for its own sake. And it was a solid pleasure to me to find you orthodox, and to find you deriving your doctrines concerning right and wrong, and the salvation of men, from orthodox theology.— Pp. 128, 131, is a speech of which no sound divine, either of the Church of England or of the middle age, ought to be ashamed. . . . But, my dear friend, whatever you do, don't advocate disestablishing us. We are the most liberal religious body in these realms. In our pale men can meet who can meet nowhere else. . . . But if we — the one remaining root of union — disestablish and become a sect like the sects, then competition, not Christ, will be God, and we shall bite and devour one another, till atheism and M. Comte are the rulers of modern thought. I am not mad, but speak the words of truth and soberness; and remember (I am sure you will, though orators at public meetings would not) that my plea is quite disinterested. If the Church of England were disestablished and disendowed to-morrow, vested interests would be respected, and I and others living on small incomes till our deaths. I assure you that I have no family livings, or an intention of putting my sons into them. My eldest son — a splendid young fellow — is roughing it successfully and honorably as an engineer anywhere between Denver, U. S., and the city of Mexico. My next and only other son may possibly go to join him. I can give no more solid proof that, while Radical cockneys howl at me as an aristocrat and a renegade, I am none; but a believer in the persons of my own children, that a man's a man for a' that."

While paying a visit in Weybridge this year, he was asked to write some answers to the following questions in a book kept for the autographs of literary men. The answers are genuine and characteristic:

"Favorite character in history? David.
"The character you most dislike? Myself.
"Favorite kind of literature? Physical science.
"Favorite author? Spenser.
"Favorite artist? Leonardo da Vinci.
"Favorite composer? Beethoven.
"Favorite dramatic performance? A pantomime.
"Favorite kind of scenery? Wide flats or open sea.

"Place at home and abroad you most admire? Clovelly.

"Favorite reminiscence? July 6, 1839.

"Favorite occupation? Doing nothing.

"Favorite amusement? Sleeping.

"What do you dislike most? Any sort of work.

"Favorite topics of conversation? Whatever my companion happens to be talking about.

"And those you dislike most? My own thoughts.

"What you like most in woman? Womanliness.

"What you dislike most? Unwomanliness.

"What you like most in man? Modesty.

"What you dislike most? Vanity.

"Your ambition? To die.

"Your ideal? The One ideal.

"Your hobby? Fancying I know anything.

"The virtue you most admire? Truth.

"The vice to which you are most lenient? All except lying.

"Your favorite motto or proverb? 'Be strong.'

"CHARLES KINGSLEY."

His year closed at Eversley with his three children round him, his eldest daughter having returned safe from a long visit to her brother in Colorado, and a perilous journey through Mexico, with him and some American friends who were "prospecting" for the carrying on through the heart of Mexico of the narrow-gauge railway lately built in Colorado. The report made by his son on this survey and the prospects it seemed to hold out for his advancement were a great pride and joy to Mr. Kingsley. It had been a year of hard work, and owing to the increasing infirmities of his mother, who was in her 85th year, and lived with him, he had scarcely left home for more than a few days. The three months now at Chester and the four annual sermons at Windsor, Sandringham, Whitehall, and St. James's made him unwilling to give up his Eversley people for a single Sunday. So that he had no intermission of toil; indeed, since he returned from the West Indies, nearly three years before, he had preached every Sunday once if not twice. Towards winter his mother's dangerous illness and other anxieties weighed heavily on him; they were anxieties which, however, never touched the sacred innermost circle of his home.

"I am blessed in all my children, thank God," he writes, to a friend, who had lost his wife; "and though my beloved one is still with me, and all in all to me, yet I have my sorrows, such as God grant you may never taste."

Once again before clouds thickened, his heart had bubbled up into song, and after the last meet of the fox-hounds in front of Bramshill House at which he was ever present — a sight he dearly loved — he put these verses into his wife's hands:

November 6, 1872.

"THE DELECTABLE DAY.

"The boy on the famous grey pony
   Just bidding good-bye at the door,
Plucking up maiden heart for the fences
   Where his brother won honor of yore.

"The walk to 'the Meet' with fair children
   And woman as gentle as gay, —
Ah! how do we male hogs in armor
   Deserve such companions as they?

"The afternoon's wander to windward,
    To meet the dear boy coming back;
And to catch, down the turns of the valley,
    The last weary chime of the pack.

"The climb homeward by park and by moorland
    And through the fir forests again,
While the southwest wind roars in the gloaming
    Like an ocean of seething champagne.

"And at night the septette of Beethoven,
    And the grandmother by in her chair,
And the foot of all feet on the sofa
    Beating delicate time to the air.

"Ah, God! a poor soul can but thank Thee
    For such a delectable day!
Though the fury, the fool, and the swindler,
    To-morrow again have their way!"

CHAPTER XXVII

1873-4

AGED 54-5

HARROW-ON-THE-HILL — CANONRY OF WESTMINSTER — CONGRATULATIONS — PARTING FROM CHESTER — SERMONS IN WESTMINSTER ABBEY AND AT KING'S COLLEGE — VOYAGE TO AMERICA — EASTERN CITIES AND WESTERN PLAINS — LETTER FROM JOHN G. WHITTIER — NIAGARA — SALT LAKE CITY — YOSEMITE VALLEY AND BIG TREES — SAN FRANCISCO — ILLNESS — ROCKY MOUNTAINS AND COLORADO SPRINGS — LAST POEM — RETURN HOME.

"One of the kind wishes expressed for me is a long life. Let anything be asked for me except that. Let us live hard, work hard, go a good pace, get to our journey's end as soon as possible — then let the post-horse get his shoulder out of the collar. . . . I have lived long enough to feel, like the old post-horse, very thankful as the end draws near. . . . Long life is the last thing that I desire. It may be that, as one grows older, one acquires more and more the painful consciousness of the difference between what *ought* to be done and what *can* be done, and sits down more quietly when one gets the wrong side of fifty, to let others start up to do for us things we cannot do for ourselves. But it is the highest pleasure that a man can have who has (to his own exceeding comfort) turned down the hill at last, to believe that younger spirits will rise up after him, and catch the lamp of Truth, as in the old lamp-bearing race of Greece, out of his hand before it expires, and carry it on to the goal with swifter and more even feet.
"C. K." (Speech at the Lotus Club, New York, February, 1874.)

SOME months of this year were spent at Harrow, where his youngest son was at school; a change to high ground having been recommended for some of his family, for which the

Bishop gave him leave of non-residence; but he went regularly for his Sundays to Eversley, and helped to prepare the candidates for confirmation. While at Harrow, he received this letter from Mr. Gladstone:

"I have to propose to you, with the sanction of her Majesty, that, in lieu of your canonry at Chester, you should accept the vacant stall in Westminster Abbey. I am sorry to injure the people of Chester; but I must sincerely hope your voice will be heard within the Abbey, and in your own right."

"This is good news indeed," writes his friend Dean Stanley, from Westminster. "I had entertained some hope, but it was beginning to fade away. . . . How many waters, as the French say, have run under the bridge since we first met at Exeter College, many years ago. What a meeting of those waters here, and what a world of interest have they now to run through from this happy confluence!"

There was a strong battle in his heart between the grief of giving up Chester and the joy of belonging to the great Abbey, a position which included among many advantages the blessing he had long craved for, of laying down his pen as a compulsory source of income, at once and for all, and devoting his remaining writing powers and strength to sermons alone. He had just written to a member of his scientific class in Chester to say how he longed for May 1, to be back again among them. And a few days later he writes:

"The programme of your Society for the year makes me at once proud and envious. For now I have to tell you that I have just accepted the vacant stall at West-

Canonry of Westminster 343

minster, and shall, in a week or two, be Canon of Chester no more. Had I been an old bachelor, I would never have left Chester. I look back longingly to Chester. Shall we ever go up Hope Mountain, or the Halkin together again, with all those dear, courteous, sensible people? My eyes fill with tears when I think of it. Give them all my love."

"You would have been both glad and sorry," writes a member of the scientific society to Mrs. Kingsley, "if you had been at the cathedral last night, and could have seen the sorrowful little groups all discussing the news that we had heard before, but which I, for one, had steadfastly refused to believe, till the dear Canon's own letter yesterday took away our last little hope. 'What will become of the Natural Science Society? Who will keep up our interest in it? What shall we do now, just as we wanted so much help with the museum?' I heard one group of people saying, 'Look what he has done for us socially!' 'Who will ever be to us what *he* has been in that respect?' said others. 'Well, we have had the honor of his presence among us — no one can take that from us — let us try and remember that.' The Bishop says that the Canon's removal is the greatest blow that the diocese could possibly receive. . . ."

"All Chester mourns. . . ."

The same note is struck in letters, which would fill a small volume, from men and women of all ranks, full of love and loyalty; and to one who had been with him in all his struggles upward, from the days of the earnest unknown curate life, through years of distrust, suspicion, and reproach from men of all parties in the Church, to find the same tone taken by Churchmen, from the Primate downwards, seemed but a just recognition of his character and work. "It is a great sphere," said the Archbishop of Canterbury, "for one who, like you, knows how to use it;" while Bishop Wilberforce wrote of his joy at his having received "so just an acknowledgment of his merits, and so much better a pedestal from which to enlighten many: I am proud to have you in my old Collegiate Church." Mr. Kingsley little thought when he read these words, that his first sermon in the Abbey after his installation would be one among many public lamentations for the sudden death of his diocesan ("The Silence of Faith," Westminster Sermons), and how soon he would follow him into the unseen world. Some of his friends in their congratulations expressed the hope that this distinction might be a stepping-stone to a higher post, but he replied:

"So far from looking on it as an earnest of future preferment, I acquiesce in it as all I want, and more than I deserve. What better fate than to spend one's old age under the shadow of that Abbey, and close to the highest mental activities of England, with leisure to cultivate myself, and write, if I will, deliberately, but not for daily bread? A deanery or bishopric would never give me that power. It cannot be better than it is; and most thankful to God am I for His goodness."

To him in his great humility the outburst of sympathy on all sides was simply a surprise: but to those who knew the history of his life it was a triumph which, while it wiped out many bitter passages in the past, still was tempered by the fear that the ease of circumstances which it seemed to promise came too late to save the over-

Congratulations

strained brain. The candle had already burnt down, and though light and flame still flared up, they flared as from the socket. His eldest son, who had just reached England, to his father's great joy, on his return from a railway survey in Mexico, was so much struck with his broken appearance, that he urged him to take the rest of a long sea voyage before he entered on a position of fresh responsibility. This, however, he refused, on account of the failing state of his mother, then in her 86th year, though it was strongly recommended by medical advisers: but after her death he yielded to the entreaties of his wife and son, who knew there could be no rest for him while within reach of the daily post in England, and decided to cross the Atlantic after Christmas, when the repairs of both homes — at Eversley and Westminster, would enable him to take a holiday.

"When Charles Kingsley was first appointed to the stall in Westminster," says Dean Stanley, "there was a great sense of triumph that a famous name was enrolled in the number of our body. It was felt down to the humblest verger. When he came to live amongst us, this feeling was deepened into a no less universal sentiment of grateful attachment. Every one felt that in him they had gained a friend. Every one was delighted with him, because he was delighted with everything. Much as he loved Eversley — much as he loved Chester, which he was leaving — he enjoyed Westminster as if he had never had anything else to enjoy. 'It was,' he said, 'like coming suddenly into a large inheritance of unknown treasures.' Short as was the time he spent here — but four months divided between the two years of his occupation of the Canonry — the impression which he left on the place was, by the very reason of the brief space in which it was accomplished, a stronger proof perhaps of his power of fascination than the spell which he threw over the spots which were associated with him for longer periods of his life. I was myself absent during the larger portion of his residence — but I could judge of its effects from the glow which it left behind on every heart and face — the glow on the hills after the sun has just set."

He preached in the Abbey for the Temperance Society in April. This sermon was the foundation of an essay, "The Tree of Knowledge," in which, after speaking of Sunday drinking and some of its preventible causes, and of how far behind the Greeks and Romans we are in that education and recreation for the masses which the higher orders derive from works of art and objects of beauty, he says:

"Recollect the — to me — disgraceful fact, that there is not, through the whole of London, a single portico or covered place, in which people can take refuge [on the Sabbath day] during a shower. Where they do take refuge the publican knows but too well. . . . In such a world as this, governed by a Being who has made sunshine and flowers, and green grass, and the song of birds, and happy human smiles; and who would educate by them His human children, from the cradle to the grave ; — will you grudge any particle of that education, even any harmless substitute for it, to those spirits in prison, whose surroundings too often tempt them, from the cradle to the grave, to fancy that the world is composed of bricks and iron, and governed by inspectors and policemen? . . . Preach to those spirits in prison — but let them have, besides, some glimpses of the

Parting from Chester 347

splendid fact that outside their prison-house is a world which God, not man, has made; wherein grows that tree of knowledge which is likewise the tree of life; and that they have a right to some such share of its beauty, and its wonder, and its rest, for their own health of body and soul, and for the health of their children after them."[1]

In July he went to Chester to say good-bye, and to join the Nave Choir and Scientific Society in an excursion into Wales. His kind friends insisted on his still keeping the office of President to the Scientific Society. Professor Hughes, who took his place in 1875, thus speaks of his predecessor in his inaugural lecture:

"Let us then try to carry on our Society in the spirit that pervaded all the work of him to whom this Society owes everything — whose loss we have had so recently to deplore; a spirit of fearless and manly grappling with difficulties — a spirit of vigorous, prompt, and rigorous carrying out of whatever was taken in hand — a spirit of generous and hearty co-operation with fellow-workers — a wide range of interests — not meaning by this, scattered desultory thought — but thought, like Napoleon's, ready to be concentrated at once where the battle must be fought."

[1] "... The deadliest foe of the craving for stimulants is the sanatory reformer; the man who preaches and — as far as ignorance and vested interests will allow him, procures — for the masses, pure air, pure sun-light, pure dwelling-houses, pure food. Not merely each fresh drinking fountain, but every fresh public bath and wash-house, every fresh open space, every fresh growing tree, every fresh open window, every fresh flower in that window — each of these is so much, as the old Persians would have said, conquered for Ormuzd, the god of light and life, out of the dominion of Ahriman, the king of darkness and of death. So much taken from the causes of drunkenness and disease, and added to the causes of sobriety and health. . . ." — *Health and Education.*

The new Canon's first residence at Westminster was during a time in which London was considered "empty," and he preached during September and November to vast congregations twice each Sunday. He preferred these quiet months, as his audience was composed chiefly of men of the middle and lower class, whose ear he wished to gain.

"I got through the sermons without any bodily fatigue, and certainly there were large congregations. But the responsibility is too great for me, and I am glad I have only two months' residence, and that in a quiet time. What must it be in May and June? . . ."

. . . .

"If I find I can get the ear of that congregation, it will be a work to live for, for the rest of my life. What more can a man want? And as for this house, it is most pleasant, and the beauty outside under this delicious gleamy weather, quite lifts my poor heart up awhile. . . . I regret much that I am leaving just as I seemed to be getting hold of the people. But I do not think I could have stood the intense excitement of the Sundays much longer."

In October, Dr. Barry, Principal of King's College, invited him to preach in the college chapel. He had often felt his severance from his old school, and it was with very mixed emotions that he entered that pulpit for the first time. The text was Genesis xlii. 18, "I fear God." As was his wont, he dealt hardly with himself.

"It is, as far as I can recollect, some five-and-thirty years since, I, then a young student, attended service in this chapel. Ah! that I could teach you young men all that I have learnt — often paying a heavy price for bitter experience — during those five-and-thirty years. Ah! still more — that I could teach you all that I ought to have learnt by now, and have not; because laziness, temper, prejudice, conceit, and often mere stupidity, have prevented my interpreting my own experience, and seeing clearly the facts which God had put before me, and to which I was blind. For these and for all other follies, may God forgive me ere I speak to you! And yet — if I could only tell you even all I think I know — to what would it amount? and what would it avail you? Each of you — so I believe and fear — must see with your own eyes, and judge with your own brains, and then act with your own hearts, each of you judge, jury, witness, and alas! barrister at once, in your case. So help you God! and may God help you; for I fear more and more that neither I nor any man can. As you make your bed, so you must lie, in this world and in the next.

"But what is more, no man can make your bed for you, so you must make it for yourself. No man on earth, I believe, can really help you, in the long run. There is but One who can help you or me, or any one man, and that is — God; and He, I think, only helps those who help themselves. Even a Socrates could not train into a hero and a patriot — even an Alcibiades. The grandest of masters tried to save the grandest of pupils — and how that ended we all know. One of the saddest stories, as I think, which has come down to us from the great times of old. And Solomon the wise — he wrote his Proverbs — he wrote his Ecclesiastes — for the main part of both books I believe to be really his — for the sake of Rehoboam, and how that ended we know too well likewise. So, after such examples and such failures, what have I to say to you, save what poor old Solomon said in the weariness of his heart, after all his wasted wisdom, 'Furthermore, my son, by this be admonished: of making many books there is no end and much study is a weariness to the flesh.' Let us hear the conclusion of the whole matter. Fear God and keep His Commandments. For this is the whole duty of man. For God shall bring every work into judgment with every secret thing, whether it be good or whether it be evil."

His last sermon in 1873 in the Abbey was on "The Beatific Vision," and those who heard him were impressed by the deep solemnity of his words and manner as he, in prospect of leaving Europe, bade farewell to a congregation which he had already begun to love. After noble words on God's character, and intense prayer that He, the Glorious, the Just, the Powerful, the Merciful, the One Good, would teach him and his hearers His Name, and "gladden their souls by the beatific vision of Himself till they loved Him, worshipped Him, obeyed Him for His own sake, not for anything which they might obtain from Him, but solely because He is The perfectly Good who inhabits eternity, and yet dwells with him that is of a contrite spirit, and revives the heart of the feeble;" and after an ascription of adoration for "the glory of His justice, and the glory of His love," he closes:

"And now, friends — almost all friends unknown — and, alas! never to be known by me — you who are to me as people floating down a river; while I, the preacher, stand upon the bank, and call, in hope that some of you may catch some word of mine, ere the great stream shall bear you out of sight — oh! catch, at

Voyage to America

least, catch this one word — the last which I shall speak here for many months, and which sums up all which I have been trying to say to you of late.

"Fix in your minds — or rather ask God to fix in your minds — this one idea of an absolutely good God; good with all forms of goodness which you respect and love in man; good as you, and I, and every honest man, understand the plain word good. Slowly you will acquire that grand and all-illuminating idea; slowly and most imperfectly at best: for who is mortal man that he should conceive and comprehend the goodness of the infinitely good God! But see, then, whether, in the light of that one idea, all the old-fashioned Christian ideas about the relation of God to man; whether Providence, Prayer, Inspiration, Revelation, the Incarnation, the Passion, and the final triumph of the Son of God — whether all these, I say, do not seem to you, not merely beautiful, not merely probable, but rational, and logical, and necessary, moral consequences from the one idea of an Absolute and Eternal Goodness, the Living Parent of the universe. And so I leave you to the grace of God." (*Westminster Sermons.*)

In the autumn he wrote three articles, one of them "Nausicaa in London" — all more or less on Sanitary science, to which and to his sermons he proposed to devote the remaining years of his life; and arranged some lectures to take with him to meet the expenses of his American journey, on which his eldest daughter went with him.

". . . We sail on the 29th," he writes to a friend; "we go in April or May (when the prairie is in flower) to San Francisco and then back to Denver and the Rocky Mountains south of Denver, and then straight home. . . ."

Charles Kingsley

"ON BOARD THE 'OCEANIC,' *January* 30, 1874.

"*The* blessed Psalms this morning! Weather bright and warm, like June. No wind or motion, and the Irish coast most lovely. This is the most luxurious ship I ever was in. All as yet has been most prosperous. The good Dean came from Chester to see us off."

Changes of wind and weather had long been a favorite study of his, and on the voyage he kept the following little log of both for his youngest boy:

"Left Queenstown the forenoon of Jan. 30. Had three days of charming warm April, or rather June, weather. . . . Off Cape Clear, ship rolled a good deal from the *calm*. The 3rd and 4th were two short runs, as we were retarded by an unexpected branch of the Gulf-stream, a knot an hour against us, water 53°, which lost us fifty miles in two days. 5th. A good run to the banks of Newfoundland, where the water shoals from 2,000 fathoms to 30–50, the sea becomes green instead of blue, and the water falls from 53° to 32° in a day. Here we met very cold north-west gales. We had had snow showers on the Gulf-stream, and wind veering and backing from N.W. to S.W. But on the banks the gale set in steadily from the N.W.; and has blown till now (Feb. 7, 2 P.M.) for more than seventy-two hours at an average of eight, all the cold air from the Gulf of St. Lawrence, Newfoundland, the Carriboo barrens, and up to Hudson's Bay, rumpling itself into the Atlantic in a steady stream, as a Mistral does into the Mediterranean, or a Norte into the Gulf of Mexico. We are now past the banks; the water has risen to 40°: but the air is 29°, three degrees of frost, and the whole bow and fore-rigging coated with masses of white ice, very beautiful. The captain thinks we have escaped

Voyage to America

some great cyclone jammed up between us and Cape Race, which can't get out into the Atlantic: *I* think this is rushing down to supply the heated air carried up by some cyclone far south, which will come to the Bay of Biscay, and France, and England as a S.W. gale. Please try and remember if you had a gale about now. Let Grenville work out the places on the map, if you have time. 8th, 12 P.M. Run 241 miles. Gale still continuing, but sea less, so that screw acts better. Temperature just freezing. Just passed Sable Island, about seventy miles W. Many Mother Cary's chickens have reappeared to-day — all flying *against* the gale — towards America. 2 P.M., air 31°. Water suddenly risen to 53°, and the sea covered with flying hot steam (called the Barber), which is melting the ice on the rigging and forecastle, now six inches thick and more. A shoot of the Gulf-stream again more northerly than the Admiralty charts. 9th. Touched beginning of Nantucket Shoals about 4 P.M. At 6 P.M. on the 10th captain called me up to see Nantucket light — first point of the United States; at noon on the 10th very hard breeze from N., going 12¼, were off the E. point of Long Island, 102 miles from New York, shall have come in 3,015 miles, the shortest possible great circle being 3,012. So we have steered very straight, though slow. Took in pilot at three. Got to Sandy Hook at about nine. Lay all night off bar, and got to New York at 9 A.M. Cold, bright and calm. *Floe ice* in river."

A few extracts of his letters to his wife will keep up the thread of his American journey. He wrote to no one else, and took no notes, not intending to publish anything on his return. His daughter, having been in America before, arranged all the details of his journeys from the moment they landed.

STATEN ISLAND: *February* 12. — "I have, thank God, nothing to say but what is pleasant and hopeful. We got here yesterday afternoon, and I am now writing in a blazing, sunny, south window, in a luxurious little room, in a luxurious house, redolent of good tobacco and sweet walnut-wood smoke, looking out on a snow-covered lawn, and trees, which, like the people, are all English, *with a difference*. I have met with none but pleasant, clever people as yet, afloat or ashore.

"As for health, this air, as poor Thackeray said of it, is like champagne. Sea-air (there is a mighty salt-water river, Papaio, at the bottom of the garden) and mountain-air combined, days already an hour longer than in England, and a blazing hot sun and blue sky. It is a glorious country, and I don't wonder at the people being proud of it. To-day we go into New York by steamer to see various people and do business. I enclose a log and chart of the voyage which should interest and teach Grenville. I dine with the Lotus Club on Saturday night, and then start for Boston."

CAMBRIDGE, MASS., *February* 19, 1874. "Here is a little haven of rest, where we arrived last night. Longfellow came to dinner, and we dine with him to-night. Yesterday, in Boston, dear old Whittier called on me and we had a most loving and likeminded talk about the other world. He is an old saint. This morning I have spent chiefly with Asa Gray and his plants, so that we are in good company.

"New York was a great rattle, dining, and speechifying, and being received, and so has Boston been; and the courtesy, and generosity, and compliments would really turn any one's head who was not as disgusted with himself as I always (thank God) am. Salem was very interesting, being next to Plymouth, *the* Pilgrim Fathers' town. People most intelligent, gentle, and animated. They gave me a reception supper, with speeches after, and want us to come again in the summer to their Field Naturalists' Club. New England is, in winter at least, the saddest country: all brown grass, ice-polished rocks sticking up through the copses, cedar scrub, low, swampy shores; an iron land which only iron people could have settled in. The people must have been heroes to make what they have of it. Now, under deep snow, it is dreadful. But the summer, they say, is semi-tropic, and that has kept them alive. And, indeed already, though it is hard frost under foot, the sun is bright, and hot, and high, for we are in the latitude of Naples! I cannot tell you a thousandth part of all I've seen, or of all the kindness we have received; and I feel better than I have felt for years; but Mr. Longfellow and others warn me not to let this over-stimulating climate tempt me to over-work. One feels ready to do anything, and then suddenly very tired. But I am at rest now. . . ."

In a letter to Mrs. Kingsley, in 1876, Mr. Whittier the poet beautifully recalls the visit mentioned above:

"I shall never forget my first meeting with him in Boston. I began, naturally enough, to speak of his literary work, when he somewhat abruptly turned the conversation upon the great themes of life and duty. The solemn questions of a future life, and the final destiny of the race, seemed pressing upon him, not so much for an answer (for he had solved them all by simple faith in the Divine Goodness), as for the sympathetic response of one whose views he believed to be, in a great degree, coincident with his own. 'I sometimes doubt and distrust myself,' he said, 'but I see some hope for everybody else. To me the Gospel of Christ seems indeed

Good Tidings of great joy to all people; and I think we may safely trust the mercy which endureth *for ever.*' It impressed me strongly to find the world-known author ignoring his literary fame, unobservant of the strange city whose streets he was treading for the first time, and engaged only with 'thoughts that wander through eternity.' All I saw of him left upon me the feeling that I was in contact with a profoundly earnest and reverent spirit. His heart seemed overcharged with interest in the welfare — physical, moral, and spiritual — of his race. I was conscious in his presence of the bracing atmosphere of a noble nature. He seemed to me one of the manliest of men. In this country his memory is cherished by thousands, who, after long admiring the genius of the successful author, have learned, in his brief visit, to love him as a man.

"I forbear to speak of the high estimate which, in common with all English-speaking people, I place upon his literary life-work. My copy of his 'Hypatia' is worn by frequent perusal, and the echoes of his rare and beautiful lyrics never die out of my memory. But since I have seen *him*, the man seems greater than the author. With profound respect and sympathy,

"I am truly thy friend,   JOHN G. WHITTIER."

NEW YORK: *March* 1. "Here, as at Boston, we have been seeing all the best people. Nothing can exceed the courtesy and hospitality everywhere. . . . On Thursday we are off to Philadelphia, then Washington. Here the streets are full of melting snow. But it is infinitely healthy, and I am suddenly quite well. . . . I never want medicine or tonic, and very little stimulant. But one cannot do as much here as at home. All say so and I find it. One can go faster for a while but gets exhausted sooner. As for the people, they are quite charming, and I long to see the New Englanders again when the humming-birds and mocking-birds get there, and the country is less like *Greenland*. . . . I have been assisting Bishop Potter at an ordination. The old man was very cordial, especially when he found I was of the respectful and orthodox class. So that is well, but I will not preach, at least not yet."

His meeting with William Cullen Bryant, whose poetry he had loved in his boyhood, was a great interest to him. At Philadelphia he gave a lecture on Westminster Abbey in the Opera House to an audience of nearly 4,000 — every seat being occupied, and the aisles and steps crowded with people, who stood the whole time.

" On Monday the 9th, I was asked by the Speaker of the House of Representatives to open the session of the House with prayer,[1] and I simply repeated two collects from the English Prayer-book, mentioning, as is the custom, the President of the United States, the Senate, and the House of Representatives, and ended with the Lord's Prayer. . . . We are housed and feasted everywhere. I do not tire the least. — Sleep at night, and rise in the morning as fresh as a lark. I have not been so well for *years*, and am in high spirits. But I am homesick at times, and would give a finger to be one hour with you, and G., and M. I dream of you all every night. The Americans make themselves ill by hot-air and want of exercise; I, who sleep with my window open and get all the fresh air I can by day, am always well. . . . Sumner's death has been an awful blow here. I do not wonder, for he was a magnificent man. He and I were introduced to each other in the Senate

[1] This was considered a most unusual distinction, and the deep solemnity of manner and simplicity with which it was done struck every one present.

an hour before his attack. He was most cordial, and we had much talk about Gladstone, and the Argylls."

BOSTON.] — "Oh, dear, I wish spring would come, the winter here is awful. The grass as brown with frost as a table. But the blue-bird and the robin, as they call a great parti-colored thrush, are just beginning to come, to my intense delight. However, when we go north to-morrow we shall run into *Arctic* weather again. Don't frighten yourself at our railroads, they seem utterly safe."

MONTREAL: *March* 28. — "Here we are safe, in this magnificent city, in intense frost, snow, and sunshine, on what I hope is our dear Maurice's wedding-day, thank God. We ran through the wonderful tubular St. Lawrence bridge, one-and-a-half mile long, by moonlight, and got here at 10.30. I have been just walking on the St. Lawrence, where ocean steamers will be lying in two months' time. I read a poem just now in Whittier's new volume, which spoke to me so much of you that I must get the book and bring it to you . Tell G. there is a hill 400 feet high, mostly cliff, in front of my window now, (the old Mont Royal of the first settlers,) with a few pines 100 feet high on the top, and though they must be a mile off, they look as if you could touch them, the air is so clear. We came yesterday through grand scenery, though obscured by snow showers in the upper mountains, 5,000 to 6,000 feet high, but got such a crimson sunset behind the Adirondacks, across Lake Champlain, as made me long for you to see it with me. There, this is a disjointed letter: but I wanted you to know we were safe; and my heart is so full of you, and of all at home. . . ."

QUEBEC: *April* 1. — "In a beautiful little old city, with tin roofs and spires, we in the citadel, on the top of a cliff like St. Vincent's Rocks, with the blazing sun above and blazing snow below, and the St. Lawrence, a

Eastern Cities 359

mile wide of snowy ice, at our feet, with sledges crawling over it like flies. We have crossed the river in a tandem sledge and driven out to the Falls of Montmorency, which look two miles off, and are six or seven, and seen the most awful and beautiful thing I ever saw. The fall, 260 feet high, fringed with icicles 50 feet long, roaring into a horrible gulf of ice, under an exquisite white ice cone 100 feet high, formed of its own spray. I looked in silence. One had no more right — when we went to the top and looked *into* the gulf — to talk there than in church. Every one, as usual, is most kind. Dear Col. Strange is most charming. To-morrow we start for Ottawa to stay with Lord and Lady Dufferin, in quiet for Good Friday and Easter. The bishop here is a Hampshire man and a fisherman. All goes well. The cold is less than I expected. Tell G. I have eaten *moose*, but the Indians have only killed one this winter, because the snow is so light, only two feet instead of six! that the moose can get away from them. There was a plague of lynxes round the city last winter, who came to eat the cats, the hares being dead of distemper; and they killed seventeen close round; this year there are none. We saw a wolf track, and I think moose, from the railway."

In speaking of this incident, Colonel Strange wrote:

"You allude to his pleasure in seeing the semi-frozen fall of Montmorency, with its boiling caldron and marvellous cone of frozen foam, and it will seem so like him when I tell you that, as he stood on a little platform over the abyss, I left him to commune with the nature he loved so well. A little time afterwards he said, 'Thank you; *you understand me*. I would as soon a fellow talked and shouted to me in church as in that presence.' I was afraid somebody would shout above the roar of the torrent how many cubic feet of water per second went down it, etc., or something of that sort. He knows many things now; what unconsciously he taught me and others. It may be some little consolation to you to know his kindly large-hearted presence seems to come sometimes in the silent night into my study in the old citadel, where I sit, and remember him pacing the little room with brave kind words to me, upon my dear mother's death, who also loved and reverenced him. He spoke then of his readiness to go to *his own place.* . . . ."

. . . . . .

WASHINGTON: *April* 9. — "Here we are safe and sound, having run 500 miles in thirty hours to Baltimore, from the delightful Dufferins. . . . The long journeys do not in the least tire me, so have no fears for me. We have come out of intense winter into damp spring. The birds (such beauties) are coming fast from the Bahamas and Floridas; the maples are in crimson clouds of little flowers; the flowers are coming out in the gardens. I have seen two wasps like West India ones, an inch and a half long, and heard a tree-toad, and am warm once more. All goes well. We have a dinner-party to-night; we are staying with Senator Potter, and to-morrow a dinner-party with the President. So we shall have seen quasi-royalty, British and American, both in one week. . . . Thank God for our English letters. I cannot but hope that there is a time of rest and refreshing for us after I return. . . . To me the absence of labor and anxiety is most healthy. I am quite idle now for days together, and the rail itself is most pleasant idleness."

NIAGARA: *April* 23. — "At last we are here, safe and well, thank God, in the most glorious air, filled with the soft thunder of this lovely phantom, for such, and not

Niagara 361

stupendous, it seems as yet to me. I know it could and would destroy me pitilessly, like other lovely phantoms, but I do not feel awed by it. After all, it is not a quarter of the size of an average thunderstorm, and the continuous roar, and steady flow, make it less terrible than either a thunderstorm or a real Atlantic surf. But I long for you to sit with me, and simply look on in silence whole days at the exquisite beauty of form and color. . . ."

CLERK'S HILL: " After a delightful time at Hamilton, we are here again, the loveliest house in the loveliest grounds, and as I write the whole rapids of Niagara roaring past 100 yards off, between the huge arbor vitæ, forty feet high, like a tremendous gray Atlantic surf rushing down-hill instead of up. I could not describe the beauty of this place in a week. I can see the smoke of the horse-shoe through a vista on my left, not half a mile off as I sit (sketch enclosed)."

ST. LOUIS, *May* 4. — " Safe and well, thank God, in the capitol of the West, and across the huge rushing muddy ditch, the Mississippi. Having come here over vast prairies, mostly tilled, hundreds of miles like the Norfolk fens, without the ditches, a fat, dreary, aguish, brutalizing land, but with a fine strong people in it, and here is a city of 470,000 souls growing rapidly. It is all very wonderful, and like a dream. But there is material civilization and comfort everywhere (except at the stations where the food is bad), and all goes well. Only I wish already that our heads were homeward, and that we had done the great tour, and had it not to do. However, we shall go West in comfort. And I cannot but feel that I have gained much if only in the vast experience of new people and new facts. I shall come home, I hope, a wider-hearted and wider-headed man; and have time, I trust, to read and think as I have not done for many years. At least, so runs my dream. We are going out to see the Botanic Garden this afternoon, and there is plenty to interest us before we start for Omaha, where we pick up our party, and then away to Denver and Salt Lake, etc. Ah, that you were here! . . ."

"On the 15th," says his daughter, "we left Omaha in the magnificent Pullman car which was our home for the next fortnight, with a party of eleven American and five English for our Californian journey. Mr. Cyrus Field and Mr. J. A. C. Gray, of New York, organized the expedition. Our first halt was at Salt Lake City, where we arrived one day too late, unfortunately, for my father to take part in the consecration of St. Mark's, the first Episcopal church which has been built in Utah. On Sunday, the 17th, however, he preached the evening sermon at the church, to such a crowded congregation that there was not standing room in the little building, and numbers had to go away, the steps outside, and even the pavement, being crowded with listeners, among whom were many Mormons as well as 'Gentiles.' Brigham Young sent to offer my father the tabernacle to lecture or preach in, but of this offer he of course took no notice whatever."

To HIS WIFE] : *May* 16. — "After such a journey of luxury — through a thousand miles of desert, plain, and mountain, treeless, waterless almost, sage brush and alkali. Then cañons and gorges, the last just like Llanberris Pass, into this enormous green plain, with its great salt lake ; and such a mountain ring, 300 to 400 miles in circumference ! The loveliest scene I ever saw. As I sit, the snow-peaks of the Wasatch tower above the opposite houses five miles off, while the heat is utterly tropical in the streets. Yesterday we were running through great snowdrifts, at from 5,000 to 7,000 feet above the sea (we are 5,000 here), and all along by our side the old trail, where every mile is fat with Mormon bones. Sadness and astonishment overpower me at it all. The 'city' is thriving enough, putting one in mind, with its swift streams in all streets, and mountain background, of Tarbes, or some other Pyrenean town. But, ah! what horrors this place has seen. Thank God, it is all breaking up fast. The tyrant is 70, and must soon go to his account, and what an awful one! I am deeply interested in the good bishop here, and his mission among the poor little children, whose parents are principally Cornish, Worcestershire, and South Welsh; and if I can do aught for him when I come home, I will do it with a will. Meanwhile our kind hosts insist on our being their guests right through, and let us pay for nothing. It is an enormous help, for they control both railways and telegraphs, and do and go exactly as they like. The flowers are exquisite, yellow ribes all over the cliffs, etc., and make one long to jump off the train every five minutes; while the geology makes me stand aghast; geologizing in England is child's play to this. R. is quite well, and the life of everything, and I am all right, but don't like a *dry* air at 95°, with a sirocco. Interrupted by a most interesting and painful talk with a man who has been United States Governor here. It is all very dreadful. Thank God we in England know what love and purity is. I preach to-morrow evening, and the Bishop of Colorado in the morning."

"On the 20th," his daughter writes, "our car was slipped during the night at Reno, and when we awoke at 5 A.M., we found ourselves on a branch line at Carson city. After breakfast, we went up to Virginia city, and spent the day among silver mines and stamp mills, and dust, and drought, my dear father finding, even in the out-of-the-way spot, a warm and hearty welcome from many. We breakfasted at Summit, on the top of the Sierra Nevada next morning, and arrived at Sacramento at midday on the 21st. My father was delighted at finding himself once more in almost tropical heat, and spent all the afternoon driving about the city, and revelling in the gorgeous sub-tropical flowers which hung over every garden fence; that night we left Sacramento in our car, with a special engine, for Merced, which we reached before dawn. Next morning, the 22nd, we were all up about four, and before starting on our Yosemite trip, Mr. Cyrus Field sent off a telegram to the Dean of Westminster, to my mother, and various friends in England:— 'We are, with Canon Kingsley and his daughter and other friends, just entering Yosemite Valley, all in excellent health and spirits. Mr. Kingsley is to preach for us in Yosemite on Sunday.' We started at 6 A. M. in two open stages with five horses, and drove 54 miles that day through exquisite country, botanizing all the way to Skeltons, a ranch in the forest. On the 23rd we were all up betimes, my father, the earliest of all, came up with his hands full of new and beautiful flowers, after a chat with the guides, who had driven the mules and ponies in from their grazing ground, and were beginning to saddle them for our day's ride. At 6 we started, and my father said he felt a boy again, and thoroughly enjoyed the long day in

Yosemite Valley

the saddle, which many of our friends found so tiring. We chose a new and unfrequented route, and having to climb two mountains and ride along precipices, and ford four rivers in flood in 29 miles, we were not sorry to reach the Valley at sunset. But rough as the ride was, it surpassed in beauty anything we had ever seen before, as we followed the windings of the Merced river between pine-clad mountains, still white with snow on their highest points, till we reached the mouth of the valley itself, and, emerging from a thicket of dogwood, pines, and azaleas, 'El Capitan,' just tipped with the rosy setting sun on one side, and the Bridal Veil Fall rushing in a white torrent, 900 feet high, over the gloomy rocks, on the other side, revealed themselves to us in a glow of golden rosy light. The next day (Whit-Sunday), we feasted our eyes on the almost overpowering scene around us, which seemed, if possible, to increase in beauty in every fresh phase of light or shade, sunlight or moonlight. At 5 P. M. the visitors at both hotels assembled, and my father gave a short service, after which we sang the 100th Psalm, and he preached a short sermon on verses 10–14, 16–18 of the 104th Psalm, the Psalm for the day.[1] We spent the 25th in riding all over the

[1] In Westminster Abbey, on Whit-Sunday, the Dean preached on Psalm civ., 2, 14, 15, 24: "On this very day," he says "(so I learnt yesterday by that electric flash which unites the old and new worlds together), a gifted member of this Collegiate Church, whose discourses on this and like Psalms have riveted the attention of vast congregations in this Abbey, and who is able to combine the religious and scientific aspects of Nature better than any man living — on this very day, and perhaps at this very hour, is preaching in the most beautiful spot on the face of the earth, where the glories of Nature are revealed on the most gigantic

Valley, and on Tuesday, 26th, we left it at 6 A. M., and rode 24 miles to Clarks Ranch, near the Mariposa Grove. It was bitterly cold, for the snow had not melted on some of the high passes, which were 7,000 feet above the sea; but we found blazing fires and a good supper, and rode out the next day to the Mariposa Grove of Sequoias (Wellingtonias). My father and I agreed to see the first one together, and riding on ahead of our party a little, we suddenly came upon its huge cinnamon-red stem standing up pillar-like, with its head of delicate green foliage among the black sugar pines and Douglas spruce, and I shall never forget the emotion with which he gazed silently — and as he said ' awe-struck ' — on this glorious work of God. It was very cold, and we rode over snow for some two miles under the ' big trees,' and were glad to camp in a little empty shanty under a group of some of the largest of the sequoias. A roaring fire was soon lighted, and, seated on a bed of fragrant hemlock twigs, we warmed ourselves and ate our luncheon, and then rode back, with a collection of flowers that took our whole evening to dry. Next day,

scale — in that wonderful Californian Valley, to whose trees the cedars of Lebanon are but as the hyssop that groweth out of the wall — where water and forest and sky conjoin to make up, if anywhere on this globe, an earthly paradise. Let me, from this pulpit, faintly echo the enthusiasm which I doubt not inspires his burning words. Let us feel that in this splendid Psalm and this splendid festival, the old and the new, the east and the west, are indeed united in one."

On Whit-Tuesday, Mrs. Kingsley received the following telegraphic message from Mr. Cyrus Field: "Yosemite Valley, California, May 24th. — We arrived here safely Saturday evening, all delighted with the magnificent scenery. Canon Kingsley preached in the Valley this Sunday afternoon. We leave here Tuesday for the Big Trees. Arrive in San Francisco, Friday."

the 28th, we drove down to Merced, 65 miles, and there joined the railroad, arriving on the 29th in San Francisco. While at San Francisco my father was invited to see Berkeley University, where he made an address to the students on Culture."

"His speech," said the President, "so invigorating, and yet so simple, will long be remembered — like a draught of pure water in a thirsty clime. The man was inspired, and felt every word that he spoke. Though the tone of his voice was low, and his manner of delivery slow and quiet, there was a magnetism in his presence that held the attention of his hearers. They saw a new world beyond the new world, containing much that tends to make a world great and good. But behind this fact was one equally potent: the old world was the seat of culture and learning, and to her the young men could look for many useful lessons. He drew a line of demarcation between culture and learning. He pressed upon them not only technical knowledge, and moral as well as intellectual education, but the culture so highly appreciated by the ancient Greeks and Romans and the Japanese of to-day. Such an education would humble them in the present, and render them hopeful of the future. . . . The culture and knowledge of the old world must tell the student when, where, and how to rise. This University, he said, ought to be the glory of California and the coast, as a common civilizer of the Pacific. It should represent civilization itself in the highest sense. Mr. Kingsley was impressed with the fact that the University bore the name of the man who, next to Plato, had taught him himself the most instructive lessons in philosophy — Berkeley. The Bishop, he said, was one of the noblest, calmest, and kindest of all philosophers. No one can read his works too often. He read them himself when he desired relaxation. If he could see a school of Berkeleyan philosophy founded on this side of the continent, he should think that California had done a great deal for the human race — a great deal for America, and for Europe likewise. He urged the students also to cultivate the æsthetic faculty — a taste for music and the fine arts; to learn to appreciate grace and manners, and beauty of form as studied by the Greeks, who produced the sculptors, painters, and musicians of old. He paid a special tribute to music. He trusted that music would reach the dignity of a science in this University. Not one student in one hundred might continue to give attention to music in after life, and yet the beneficial influence of the study would still be manifest. Music was necessary to the rounding and finishing of the perfect character. With the high regard for the eternal fitness of things that is peculiar to him, the Canon did not indulge in fulsome eulogies of the people and institutions of California, but talked of the future rather than of the present."

To HIS WIFE: *May* 31. — "Safe at San Francisco after such adventures and such wonders in the Yosemite and the Big Trees, and found the dear English letters waiting for us. . . . Tell G. I will write to him all about the sea lions, which I saw this morning. All is more beautiful and wonderful than I expected — and oh! the flowers."

June 9. — "We start east to-morrow, thank God, and run the Sierras, and the desert back again, and beautiful as California is, (I think it destined to be the finest country in the world), I want to be nearer and nearer home. We have been so heaped with kindness that this trip will cost us almost nothing. I have got cones from

Illness

the big trees, with seeds in them; and we have collected heaps of most exquisite plants. The letters are delectable. Tell all the servants that I wish heartily I was through and safe home again, for there is no place like England."

"During the last few days of his stay in San Francisco, he caught a severe cold, which turning to pleurisy, the doctors ordered him to leave the city as quickly as possible; and after reaching Denver, he went south to Colorado Springs, by the narrow gauge railway, which his son had helped to build four years before. Here Dr. and Mrs. Bell received him and helped his daughter nurse him with the most devoted care, in their English home at the foot of Pike's Peak, and when he was equal to the move took him up to a mountain ranch for change. His chief amusement during these weeks of illness was botany, and though he was not able to get many specimens himself, he took a keen delight in naming those brought in to him every day. On Sunday, the 5th July, he had recovered enough to be able to read a short service in the large dining-room of the ranch, a service to which he often reverted with pleasure and emotion. He then moved down to Glen Eyrie to stay with his kind friends General and Mrs. Palmer, and on July 12 preached in the Episcopal Church at Colorado Springs, in which only one service had as yet been held. The church was crowded, many young Englishmen riding in, twenty miles and more, from distant ranches to hear him. He gave a lecture also in Colorado Springs for the benefit of the church, to a large audience. The place was very dear to him from the fact of his eldest son having been one of the first pioneers there. From Manitou, June 18, he had written to his wife, from whom he desired that his illness might be carefully concealed:

"We are here in perfect peace, at last, after the running and raging of the last three weeks, and safe back over those horrid deserts, in a lovely glen, with red rocks, running and tinkling burn, whispering cotton woods, and all that is delicious, with Pike's Peak and his snow seemingly in the back garden, but 8000 feet over our heads. Oh, it is a delicious place, and the more so, because we have just got a telegram from M. Thank God ! . . . The heat is tremendous, but not unwholesome. God's goodness since I have been out no tongue can tell. . . . Please God I shall get safe home, and never leave you again, but settle down into the quietest old theologian, serving God, I hope, and doing nothing else, in humility and peace."

June 29. — " A delightful party has clustered here; and we all go up to Bell's Ranch in Bergun's Park tomorrow, for a few days, to get *cool*, for the heat here is tropic, and we cannot move by day. That has given me rest, though, and a time for reading. God has been so gracious that I cannot think that He means to send my gray hairs down in sorrow to the grave, but will, perhaps, give me time to reconsider myself, and sit quietly with you, preaching and working, and writing no more. Oh ! how I pray for that ! Tell the Dean I have been thinking much of him as I read Arnold's life and letters. Ah, happy and noble man ; happy life, and happy death ! But I must live, please God, a little longer, for all your sakes."

BERGUN'S PARK : *July* 2. — " Oh, my Love, your birthday-letter was such a comfort to me, for I am very

Colorado Springs

home-sick, and counting the days till I can get back to you. Ah, few and evil would have been the days of my pilgrimage had I not met you; and now I do look forward to something like a peaceful old age with you. . . . This place is like an ugly Highland strath, bordered with pine woods. Air almost too fine to breathe, 7,200 feet high. Pike's Peak 7,000 feet more at one end, fifteen miles off; and, alas! a great forest-fire burning for three days between us and it; and at the other end wonderful ragged peaks, ten to twenty miles off. Flowers most lovely and wonderful. Plenty of the dear common harebell, and several Scotch and English plants, mixed with the strangest forms. We are (or rather Rose is) making a splendid collection. She and the local botanist got more than fifty new sorts one morning. Her strength and activity and happiness are wonderful; and M.'s letters make me very happy. Yes; I have much to thank God for, and will try and show my thankfulness by deeds. Love to G. Tell him there are lots of trout here; but it is too hot to catch them."

GLEN EYRIE: *July* 11. — "Thank God our time draws nigh. I preach at Colorado Springs to-morrow, and lecture for the church on Wednesday; Denver Friday, and then right away to New York, and embark on the 25th. . . . This is a wonderful spot; such crags, pillars, caves — red and gray — a perfect thing in a stage scene; and the flora, such a jumble — cactus, yucca, poison sumach, and lovely strange flowers, mixed with Douglas's and Menzies' pine, and *eatable* piñon, and those again with our own harebells and roses, and all sorts of English flowers. Tell Grenville I have seen no rattlesnakes; but they killed twenty-five here a year or two ago. Tell him that there are painted-lady butterflies here, just like our English, and a locust, which, when he opens his wings, is exactly like a white admiral butterfly; and with them enormous tropic butterflies, all colors, and as big as bats. We are trying to get a horned toad to bring home alive. There is a cave opposite my window which must have been full of bears once, and a real eagle's nest close by, full of real young eagles. It is as big as a cartload of bavins. I will write again before we start over the plains. Oh! happy day!"

GLEN EYRIE: *July* 14.—"I cannot believe that I shall see you within twenty-one days; and never longed so for home. I count the hours till I can cross the Great Valley, on this side of which God has been so good to me. But, oh! for the first rise of the eastern hills, to make me sure that the Mississippi is not still between me and beloved Eversley. I am so glad you like Westminster. Yes! we shall rest our weary bones there for awhile before kind death comes, and, perhaps, see our grandchildren round us there.[1] Ah! please God, *that!* I look forward to a blessed quiet autumn, if God so will, having had a change of scene which will last me my whole life, and has taught me many things. The collection of plants grows magnificent. . . . Give my love to W. Harrison. I long to hear him preach in the Abbey, and to preach there myself likewise."

On July 25 he embarked on the *Adriatic* for England, and was so far recovered that he was said to be the life and soul of all on board on the homeward voyage; but the beginning of the end had come.

During his severe illness in Colorado, he composed these lines; they were the last he ever wrote:

[1] His first grandchild passed away at its birth just before he himself went into the unseen world. Happily he was spared the news.

Last Poem

1.

"'Are you ready for your steeple-chase, Lorraine, Lorraine, Lorrèe?
   Barum, Barum, Barum, Barum, Barum, Barum, Baree.
You're booked to ride your capping race to-day at Coulterlee,
You're booked to ride Vindictive, for all the world to see.
To keep him straight, and keep him first, and win the run for me.
   Barum, Barum, &c.'

2.

"She clasped her new-born baby, poor Lorraine, Lorraine, Lorrèe,
   Barum, Barum, &c.
'I cannot ride Vindictive, as any man might see,
And I will not ride Vindictive, with this baby on my knee;
He's killed a boy, he's killed a man, and why must he kill me?'

3.

"'Unless you ride Vindictive, Lorraine, Lorraine, Lorrèe,
Unless you ride Vindictive to-day at Coulterlee,
And land him safe across the brook, and win the blank for me,
It's you may keep your baby, for you'll get no keep from me.'

4.

"'That husbands could be cruel,' said Lorraine, Loraine, Lorèe,
'That husbands could be cruel, I have known for seasons three;
But oh! to ride Vindictive while a baby cries for me,
And be killed across a fence at last for all the world to see!'

5.

"She mastered young Vindictive — Oh! the gallant lass was she,
And kept him straight and won the race as near as near could be;
But he killed her at the brook against a pollard willow tree;
Oh! he killed her at the brook, the brute, for all the world to see.
And no one but the baby cried for poor Lorraine, Lorrèe."

CHAPTER XXVIII

1874-5.

AGED 55

RETURN FROM AMERICA — WORK AT EVERSLEY — ILLNESS AT WESTMINSTER — NEW ANXIETY — LAST SERMONS IN THE ABBEY — LEAVES THE CLOISTERS FOR EVER — LAST RETURN TO EVERSLEY — THE VALLEY OF THE SHADOW OF DEATH — LAST ILLNESS AND DEPARTURE — ANSWERED PRAYER — HIS BURIAL — FUNERAL SERMONS — LETTERS OF SYMPATHY — THE TRUE AND PERFECT KNIGHT — AT HIS GRAVE — THE VICTORY OF LIFE OVER DEATH AND TIME.

"Death, beautiful, wise, kind Death, when will you come and tell me what I want to know?" C. K.

"Out of God's boundless bosom, the fount of life, we came; through selfish stormy youth, and contrite tears — just not too late; through manhood not altogether useless; through slow and chill old age, we return Whence we came, to the Bosom of God once more — to go forth again with fresh knowledge and fresh powers, to nobler work. Amen." C. K.

IT was sultry August weather when he returned to Eversley from America, and his great joy at being at home again made him plunge too eagerly and suddenly into work and Sunday services, before he had regained his full strength after his illness in Colorado. There was much sickness and a great mortality in the parish; and he was out among his poor people twice and three times a day in the burning sun and dry easterly wind. When he went up to Westminster in September, a severe attack of congestion of the liver came on, which alarmed his friends, and prevented his preaching in the Abbey on the first Sunday of his residence. This attack shook him terribly, and from that time he was unable to preach more than once a week during his residence; but, though altered and emaciated, he seemed recovering strength, when, early in October, a shadow came over his home, in the dangerous illness of his wife, touching him in his tenderest point, and filling him with fears for the future. When all immediate danger for her was over, it was with difficulty he was persuaded to leave her and take a few days' change of air and scene, at Lord John Thynne's, in Bedfordshire, and with his friend Mr. Fuller Maitland, in Essex. From these visits he returned invigorated in health and spirits for his November work, and got through his sermons in the Abbey with less fatigue. The congregations were enormous — the sermons powerful as ever, though their preparation was an increasing labor: but the change in his appearance was observed by many. "I went back," said an old correspondent, "from the Abbey service, sad at the remembrance of the bent back and shrunken figure, and while hoping the weakness was but temporary, I grieved to see one who had carried himself so nobly, broken down by illness."

His All Saints' Day sermon will never be forgotten by those who heard it. It was like a note of preparation for the life of eternal blessedness in the vision of God upon which he himself was so soon to enter. It was a revealing too of his own deepest belief as to what that blessedness

At Eversley

meant, with back glances into the darker passages and bitter struggles of his own earthly life and warfare with evil. In it he speaks of the mystery of evil, and of the soul puzzled, crushed, and "sickened by the thought of the sins of the unholy many — sickened, alas! by the imperfections of the holiest few."

"And have you never cried in your hearts with longing, almost with impatience, 'Surely, surely, there is an ideal Holy One somewhere — or else, how could have arisen in my mind the conception, however faint, of an ideal holiness? But where? oh where? Not in the world around strewn with unholiness. Not in myself, unholy too, without and within — and calling myself sometimes the very worst company of all the bad company I meet, because that company is the only company from which I cannot escape. Oh! is there a Holy One, whom I may contemplate with utter delight? and if so, where is He? Oh that I might behold, if but for a moment, His perfect beauty, even though, as in the fable of Semele of old, the lightning of His glance were death. . . .'

"And then, oh, then — has there not come to such a one — *I know that it has come* — that for which his spirit was athirst — the very breath of pure air, the very gleam of pure light, the very strain of pure music — for it is the very music of the spheres — in those same words, 'Holy, holy, holy, Lord God Almighty, which was, and is, and is to come;' and he has answered with a flush of keenest joy — 'Yes, whatever else is unholy, there is a Holy One — spotless and undefiled, serene and self-contained. Whatever else I cannot trust, there is One whom I can trust utterly. Whatever else I am dissatisfied with, there is One whom I can contemplate with utter satisfaction, and bathe my stained soul in that eternal fount of purity.

And who is He? Who, save the Cause and Maker, and Ruler of all things, past, present, and to come? Ah, gospel of all gospels — that God Himself, the Almighty God, is the eternal realization of all that I and all mankind, in our purest and our noblest moments, have ever dreamed concerning the true, the beautiful, and the good.' . . . Whosoever has entered, though but for a moment, however faintly, partially, stupidly, into that thought of thoughts, has entered in so far into the communion of the elect, and has had his share in the Everlasting All Saints' Day which is in heaven."[1]

He little thought when preaching this sermon that in less than three months' time he too should himself be entering the Holy of Holies. Of that very beatific vision he spoke once more shortly before his death; when, conscious of no human presence, he was heard in the night by his daughter to cry out, in a clear voice, "How beautiful God is!"

One of the last letters he ever wrote was on November 22nd, to Mr. Shone, of Chester, to thank him for an "Address on the Tendency of Modern Thought."

"My young friend," he says, "You see the broad truth, and you have put it in very manly words. . . . Only — don't lose hold of that belief in the old faith, which is more precious to my *reason*, as well as to my moral sense, the older I grow, and have to do with sorrows and difficulties which you, in your youth and strength, do not know yet — and God grant you never may know. Be true to your own manly words: and in due time God will pay you all, for He is very just and very merciful. Give my love to all the dear Chester people."

[1] All Saints' Day and other Sermons.

Last Sermons

To this "old faith" he clung more and more strongly; and a friend about this time with whom he was speaking of the deep things of God, said she could never forget his look and voice, as folding his arms he bowed his head and said, "I cannot — cannot *live* without the Man Christ Jesus."

On Advent Sunday, November 29, he preached his last sermon in Westminster, with intense fervor. It was the winding-up of his year's work in the Abbey, but neither he nor those who hung upon his words thought that it was the winding-up of his public ministrations and the last time he would ever enter the pulpit. The text was Luke xix. 41, Christ weeping over Jerusalem. A great storm was raging over London that afternoon, and the gale seemed almost to shake the Abbey, which made the service to one who was keenly sensitive, as he was, to all changes of weather, especially those which would affect the fate of ships at sea, most exciting.

The sermon was a characteristic one. "Advent," he said, "should be a season not merely of warning, awe, repentance, but a season of trust and hope and content." He sketched the leading features of his past teaching in the Abbey — dwelling on the Kingship and Divine Government of Christ over races, nations, individuals — His infinite rigor and yet infinite tenderness of pity — the divine humanity which possessed Him as He wept over the doomed city, and cried out, "How often would I have gathered thee as a hen gathereth her chickens under her wings." He closed with these words:

Charles Kingsley

"And what is true of nations and of institutions — is it not true of individuals, of each separate human brother of the Son of Man? . . .

"Ah — and is there a young life ruined by its own folly — a young heart broken by its own wilfulness — an elder man or woman too, who is fast losing the finer instincts, the nobler aims, of youth in the restlessness of covetousness, of fashion, of ambition? Is there one such poor soul over whom Christ does not grieve? To whom, at some supreme crisis of their lives, He does not whisper — 'Ah, beautiful organism — thou, too, art a thought of God — thou, too, if thou wert but in harmony with thyself and God, a microcosmic *City of God!* Ah! that thou hadst known — even thou — at least in this thy day — the things which belong to thy peace!"

"Shall I go on? shall I add to the words of doom? 'But now they are hid from thine eyes.' Thou hast gambled with thine own destiny too long. Thou hast fixed thy habits. Thou hast formed thy character. It is too late to mend. Thou art left henceforth to the perpetual unrest which thou hast chosen — to thine own lusts and passions; and the angels of peace depart from thy doomed heart, as they did in the old legend, from the doomed Temple of Jerusalem — sighing — 'Let us go hence.' Shall I say that? God forbid — it is not for me to finish the sentence — or to pronounce the doom of any soul.

"But it is for me to say — as I say now to each of you — Oh that you each may know the time of your visitation — and may listen to the voice of Christ, *whenever* and *however* He may whisper to you, 'Come unto Me, thou weary and heavy-laden heart, and I will give thee *Rest.*'

"He may come to you in many ways. In ways in which the world would never recognize Him — in which

Last Sermons

perhaps neither you nor I shall recognize *Him*; but it will be enough, I hope, if we but hear His message, and obey His gracious inspiration, let Him speak through whatever means He will. He may come to us, by some crisis in our life, either for sorrow or for bliss. He may come to us by a great failure; by a great disappointment — to teach the wilful and ambitious soul, that not in *that* direction lies the path of peace. He may come in some unexpected happiness to teach that same soul that He is able and willing to give abundantly beyond all that we can ask or think. He may come to us, when our thoughts are cleaving to the ground, and ready to grow earthy of the earth — through noble poetry, noble music, noble art — through aught which awakens once more in us the instinct of the true, the beautiful, and the good. He may come to us when our souls are restless and weary, through the repose of Nature — the repose of the lonely snow-peak, and of the sleeping forest, of the clouds of sunset and of the summer sea, and whisper Peace. Or He may come, as He may come this very night to many a gallant soul — not in the repose of Nature, but in her rage — in howling storm, and blinding foam, and ruthless rocks, and whelming surge — and whisper to them even so — as the sea swallows all of them which *it* can take — of calm beyond, which this world cannot give and cannot take away. He may come to us, when we are fierce and prejudiced, with that still small voice — so sweet and yet so keen. 'Understand those who misunderstand thee. Be fair to those who are unfair to thee. Be just and merciful to those whom thou wouldst like to hate. Forgive, and thou shall be forgiven.' He comes to us surely, when we are selfish and luxurious, in every sufferer who needs our help, and says, 'If you do good to one of these, My brethren, you do it unto Me.' But most surely does Christ come to us, and often most happily, and most clearly does He speak to us — in the face of a little child, fresh out of heaven. Ah, let us take heed that we despise not one of these little ones, lest we despise our Lord Himself. For as often as we enter into communion with little children, so often does Christ come to us. So often, as in Judæa of old, does He take a little child and set it in the midst of us, that from its simplicity, docility, and trust — the restless, the mutinous, and the ambitious may learn the things which belong to their peace — so often does He say to us, 'Except ye be changed and become as this little child, ye shall in no wise enter into the Kingdom of Heaven. Take my yoke upon you and learn of Me, for I am meek and lowly of heart: and ye shall find rest unto your souls.'

"AND THEREFORE LET US SAY, IN UTTER FAITH, 'COME AS THOU SEEST BEST — BUT IN WHATSOEVER WAY THOU COMEST — EVEN SO COME, LORD JESUS.'"

As soon as the Abbey service was over, he came home much exhausted, and went straight up to his wife's room. "And now my work here is done, thank God! and . . . I finished with your favorite text."

The next day he dined at the Deanery to meet Dr. Caird, before attending his lecture in the Abbey at the special evening service. The air was damp, and coming out into the cold cloister he caught a fresh cold, and coughed all through the night; but he made light of it, for he could think of nothing but the happiness of returning with his wife to Eversley for Christmas and the quiet winter's work. And on the 3rd of December he left the cloisters forever, full of joy and thankfulness, and took her with tenderest care to

The Shadow of Death

Eversley. But his happiness was short lived; the journey down had had serious consequences for her, and that night the Angel of Death for the first time for thirty-one years seemed hovering over the little rectory. He had been engaged by the Queen's command to go to Windsor Castle the following Saturday for two days. Telegrams were sent there, and to his absent children. Still he could not believe the threatened danger, till he was told that it was a hopeless case; and then — "My own death-warrant was signed," he said, "with those words."

Children and friends collected round him, while he gathered himself up with a noble self-repression to give comfort where it was needed. His ministrations in the sick room showed the intensity of his own faith, as he strengthened the weak, encouraged the fearful, and in the light of the Cross of Christ and the love of God, spoke of an eternal reunion and the indestructibility of that married love which, if genuine, can only seem to be severed for a brief moment. When asked if he thought it cowardly for a poor soul, who had been encompassed with such protecting love as his, to tremble on the brink of the dark river which all must cross alone — to shrink from leaving husband, children — the love that had made life blessed and real and full for so many years — and to go alone into the unknown: "Cowardly!" he said, "don't you think I would rather some one put a pistol to my head than lie on that bed there waiting? *But*, — " he added, "it is not darkness you are going to, for God is light. It is not lonely, for Christ is with you. It is not an unknown country, for Christ is there."

And when the dreary interval before reunion was mentioned, he spoke of the possibility of all consciousness of Time being so destroyed that what would be long years to the survivor might be only a moment to the separated soul that had passed over the river of death. And so, with words of strong consolation and hope, with daily prayer, and reading from the Psalms and the Gospel and Epistles of St. John he preached peace and forgiveness till all was calm; and dwelling on the borderland together for weeks of deep communion, every chapter of the past was gone over once more, and "life was all retouched again," — favorite poetry was read for the last time, Wordsworth's "Intimations of Immortality," Milton's magnificent Ode to "Time" again and again, Matthew Arnold's "Buried Life," and certain passages from Shakespeare. Once more he administered the Holy Communion to his wife, children, and servants; and once again, before he himself lay down to die, he received it with them from the hands of Mr. Harrison. But though his own iron will and utter submission to the will of God enabled him to appear outwardly calm in the sick room, and even to speak of the lonely years which he feared were before him, to the grave where, he said, he would allow no one but himself to do the last office, where he would place the three Latin words in which the life of his life, past, present, and future, are gathered up, — the charm of this world for him was over, and he spoke simple truth when he said his "heart was broken," for so it was. Though ill himself, he was reckless of his own state, careless of cold and snow; and soon his cough became

Last Illness

bronchitic. On the 28th of December he took to his bed, and pneumonia, with its terrible symptoms, came on rapidly. He had promised his wife to "fight for life" for his children's sake, and he did so for a time; but the enemy, or, as he would have said himself, "kindly Death," was too strong for him, and in a few weeks the battle was over and he was at rest. The weather was bitter, and he had been warned that his recovery depended on the same temperature being kept up in his room, and on his never leaving it; but one day he leaped out of bed, came into his wife's room for a few moments, and taking her hand in his, he said, "This is heaven, don't speak;" but, after a short silence, a severe fit of coughing came on, he could say no more, and they never met again. When told that another such effort might be fatal to both, he replied, "Well, we have said all to each other, we have made up our accounts. It is all right, all *as it should be.*" For a few days a correspondence was kept up in pencil; and on December 30 he wrote of this "terrible trial," the fiery trial of separation, to both so bitter at such a moment. "But," he adds, "I am somewhat past fretting — almost past feeling. . . . I know it *must* be right, because it is so strange and painful." Again, on New Year's Eve, "I am much better in all ways. Thank God for the gleam of sun and the frost on the window-pane. . . ." And again, in the last letter he ever wrote, on January 3rd, a bright morning, the first Sunday in the year: "Ah! what a good omen for the coming year — this lovely Sunday morning. May it mean light and peace and blessing in both worlds for us all! . . . ." But, to use his own words, the letters then became "too painful, too tantalizing" for both, and they ceased.

He was now kept constantly under the influence of opiates to quiet the cough and keep off hemorrhage, and his dreams were always of his travels in the West Indies, the Rocky Mountains, and California. These scenes he would describe night after night to the trained nurse from Westminster Hospital who sat up with him; and he would tell her, too, of the travels of his eldest son in America, of whom he continually spoke with love and pride, and to whose success in life he so eagerly looked. Though he did not care to recover, he watched his own symptoms as a scientific spectator might have done, saying that his physical experiences were so singular that if he got well he would write a book about them, and describing them brilliantly to Dr. Hawkesley, who twice came down from London. Dr. Hawkesley said he had never seen a more splendid fight for life.

He spoke but little latterly, and the fear of exciting him made those around afraid of telling him anything that would rouse him to the sense of his great loneliness. But one morning before his condition became hopeless, when some little letters, enclosing some drawings to amuse him, had come from the young Princes at Sandringham, who loved him well and were sorry for his illness and his grief, his doctor said they might be shown him. They touched him deeply; and his messages in answer were among the last he sent. On Sunday, the 17th, he sat up for a few moments, where he could see from the bedroom window which looked into the churchyard his dear people go into church, and spoke of their "goodness" to him and how he loved them. He reiterated the words, "It is all right." "All *under rule*." One morning early he asked the nurse, if it was light, to open the shutters, for he loved light. It was still dark. "Ah! well," he said, "the light is good and the darkness is good — it is all good." From sleeping so much he was unconscious of the lapse of time. Since his boyhood he had never till now been confined to his bed for more than a day. "How long have I been in bed?" he asked one day, and on being told three weeks, he said, "It does not seem three days. Does F. know how ill I have been? Ah, I live in fairyland, or I should go mad!"

On the 20th of January the Prince of Wales, whose regard and affection for fourteen years had never failed, requested Sir William Gull to go down to Eversley. Dr. Gull thought recovery possible; but immediately after his visit the hemorrhage returned — the end seemed near, and then the full truth — and not a painful one — burst upon him. "Heynes," he said to his own devoted medical man, who was with him day and night, "I am hit; this last shot has told — did F. tell you about the funeral? We settled it all;" and then he went over every arrangement that had been agreed upon a few weeks before in view of the event he had so dreaded, and which God so mercifully spared him; even to the names of the bearers selected by his wife (laboring men endeared by old parish memories), adding, "Let there be no paraphernalia, no hatbands, no carriages. . . ." He was calm and content. He had no need to put his mind into a fresh attitude, for his life had long been "hid with Christ in God." Many years before, in speaking of a friend who rejected Christianity, he had said, "The more I see of him, the more I learn to love the true doctrines of the Gospel, because I see more and more that only in faith and love to the Incarnate God, our Saviour, can the cleverest, as well as the simplest, find the Peace of God which passes understanding." In this faith he had lived — and as he had lived, so he died — humble, confident, unbewildered. That night he was heard murmuring, "No more fighting — no more fighting;" and then followed intense, earnest prayers, uttered in a low voice, as was his habit when alone, — too sacred for any listener. Yes, his warfare was accomplished, he had fought the good fight, and never grounded his arms till God took them mercifully out of his brave hands and gave him rest.

It was on one of those, his last nights on earth, his daughter heard him exclaim, "How beautiful God is!" true to his own words written long before, "Self should be forgotten most of all in the hour of death." For the last two days before he departed, he asked no questions, and sent no messages to his wife, thinking all was over, and hoping that at last the dream of his life was fulfilled of their dying together; and under this impression, it is thought, when the faithful nurse who had been with his children since their birth, left his wife for a moment to come to her dying master the day before he went, he said, "Ah, dear nurse, *and I, too*, am come to an end; it is

Departure

all right — all as it *should be*," and closed his eyes again. On that same morning from his bed he had looked out over the beloved glebe once more. The snow, which had been deep for weeks, had cleared a little, the grass of the pasture was green, and he said, "Tell Grenville (his youngest son, who had just left him after helping to arrange his bed) I am looking at the most beautiful scene I ever saw," adding some words of love and approval of his boy, that were scarcely audible.

The last morning, at five o'clock, just after his eldest daughter, who, with his medical man and Mr. Harrison, had sat up all night, had left him, and he thought himself alone, he was heard, in a clear voice, repeating the words of the Burial Service:

"Thou knowest, O Lord, the secrets of our hearts; shut not Thy merciful ears to our prayer, but spare us, O Lord most holy, O God most mighty, O holy and merciful Saviour, Thou most worthy Judge Eternal, suffer us not, at our last hour, for any pains of death, to fall from Thee."

He turned on his side after this, and never spoke again, and before midday, on the 23rd of January — without sigh or struggle — breathed his last breath, so gently that his eldest daughter and the family nurse, who were watching him, could scarcely tell that all was over. Twenty years before, and how often since, he had thus expressed his longing for that moment: "God forgive me if I am wrong, but I look forward to it with an intense and reverent curiosity." And now the great secret that he had craved to know was revealed to him, and he was satisfied.

"Never shall I forget," said Max Müller, "the moment when for the last time I gazed upon the manly features of Charles Kingsley, features which death had rendered calm, grand, sublime. The constant struggle that in life seemed to allow no rest to his expression, the spirit, like a caged lion, shaking the bars of his prison, the mind striving for utterance, the soul wearying for loving response — all that was over. There remained only the satisfied expression of triumph and peace, as of a soldier who had fought a good fight, and who, while sinking into the stillness of the slumber of death, listens to the distant sounds of music and to the shouts of victory. One saw the ideal man, as Nature had meant him to be, and one felt that there is no greater sculptor than Death.

"As one looked on that marble statue which only some weeks ago had so warmly pressed one's hand, his whole life flashed through one's thoughts. One remembered the young Curate and the 'Saint's Tragedy'; the Chartist parson and 'Alton Locke'; the happy poet and the 'Sands of Dee'; the brilliant novel-writer and 'Hypatia' and 'Westward Ho!'; the Rector of Eversley and his 'Village Sermons'; the beloved professor at Cambridge, the busy Canon at Chester, the powerful preacher at Westminster Abbey. One thought of him by the Berkshire chalk streams, and on the Devonshire coast, watching the beauty and wisdom of Nature, reading her solemn lessons, chuckling too over her inimitable fun. One saw him in town-alleys, preaching the Gospel of godliness and cleanliness, while smoking his pipe with soldiers and navvies. One heard him in drawing-rooms, listened to with patient silence, till one of his vigorous or quaint speeches bounded forth, never to be

Answered Prayer

forgotten. How children delighted in him! How young wild men believed in him, and obeyed him too! How women were captivated by his chivalry, older men by his genuine humility and sympathy! All that was now passing away — was gone. But as one looked at him for the last time on earth, one felt that greater than the curate, the poet, the professor, the canon, had been the man himself, with his warm heart, his honest purposes, his trust in his friends, his readiness to spend himself, his chivalry and humility, worthy of a better age. Of all this the world knew little; — yet few men excited wider and stronger sympathies."[1]

"As he lay," said Dean Stanley, "the other day, cold in death, like the stone effigy of an ancient warrior, the 'fitful fever' of life gone, the strength of immortality left, resting as if after the toil of a hundred battles, this was himself idealized. From those mute lips there seemed to issue once more the living words with which he spoke ten years ago, before one who honored him with an unswerving faithfulness to the end. 'Some say' — thus he spoke in the Chapel of Windsor Castle — 'some say that the age of chivalry is past, that the spirit of romance is dead. The age of chivalry is never past, so long as there is a wrong left unredressed on earth, or a man or a woman left to say, I will redress that wrong, or spend my life in the attempt. The age of chivalry is never past so long as we have faith enough to say, God will help me to redress that wrong, or if not me, He will help those that come after me, for His eternal will is to overcome evil with good.' . . ."[2]

On the afternoon of his departure a telegram was sent to Chester, where the daily bulletins had been watched for so eagerly, "Canon Kingsley peacefully expired;" and on the Sunday

---

[1] Max Müller — Preface to "The Roman and the Teuton."
[2] Dean Stanley. — Sermon in Westminster Abbey.

morning the tolling of the Cathedral bell, and the omission of his name in the daily prayers for the sick, confirmed the worst fears of many loving hearts. For many weeks the prayers of the congregation had been asked for "Charles and Fanny Kingsley." Not only in Chester Cathedral and Westminster Abbey, but in other churches and in Nonconformist chapels; at prayer-meetings, too, in London, Sheffield, and elsewhere, his life was prayed for, and God in His great mercy had answered all by giving him immortal life.

As soon as the news reached Westminster, a telegram from the Dean brought these words to his children: "Bear up under the blow. You will perhaps choose Eversley, but the Abbey is open to the Canon and the Poet." The telegram was followed by this letter.

DEANERY, WESTMINSTER: *January* 24, 1875.—"I cannot let the day pass without a word in addition to the brief telegram I sent last night. It seems but a few years, though it is many, since I first saw your dear father at Oxford, and again still fewer, though that is also long ago, since I for the first time was at Eversley — and our meetings have been but few and far between — but I always felt that he was a faithful friend, and a brave champion for much and many that I loved: and when he was transplanted among us, my dear wife and I both looked forward to the multiplication of these meetings — to long years of labor together. God has ordered it otherwise. He had done his work. He had earned his rest. You had seen all that was highest and best in him. The short stay amongst us here had given him a new life, and had endeared him to a new world. He has gone in the fulness of his strength, like one of his

His Burial

own tropical suns — no twilight — no fading. Be of good heart, for you have much for which to be thankful. I ventured to say something about the place of burial. It is far the most probable (from what I have heard that he had said) that Eversley will have been the place chosen by him and by you — most natural that it should be so. Had his days ended here, then I should have pressed that the right which we have acquired in him should have the chief claim, and you know that should the other not be paramount, here we should be too glad to lay him, not by that official right which I try to discourage, but by the natural inheritance of genius and character. Any way, let me know the day and hour of the funeral. If none nearer or more suitable should be thought of, I, as the chief of his last earthly sphere, would ask to render the last honors.

There was no hesitation with those who knew his own feelings, and at Eversley he was buried on the 28th of January; no one was invited to attend, but early in the day the churchyard was full. There had been deep snow and bitter cold for many weeks. But that day was kindly, soft and mild, with now and then gleams of sunshine, and at two o'clock in the afternoon the coffin, covered with flowers, was met at the garden-gate by the Bishop of Winchester, the Dean of Westminster, his oldest friend, Mr. Powles, his two last curates, Mr. Harrison and Mr. Elis Price, and his churchwarden Sir William Cope, and was laid before the altar in the church, where for thirty-two years he had ministered so faithfully. He was carried to the grave by villagers who had known, loved, and trusted him for years. Roman Catholic and Protestant, Churchman and Dissenter, American and English, working-men and gipsies, met at that grave; every profession, every rank, every school of thought was represented there. Soldiers[1] and sailors were there; among them three Victoria Cross officers, men whom he had loved, and who honored him. The Master of Fox Hounds, with the huntsman and the whip, were there also, and from his beloved Chester came the Dean and a deputation from the Natural Science Society he had founded. "I have been at many State funerals," said a naval officer who was present, "but never did I see such a sight as Charles Kingsley's."

"Who," says Max Müller, "can forget that funeral on the 28th of January, 1875, and the large and sad throng that gathered round his grave? There was the representative of the Prince of Wales, and, close by, the gipsies of Eversley Common, who used to call him their 'Patrico-rai' (their Priest King). There was the squire of his village, and the laborers young and old, to whom he had been a friend and a father. There were governors of distant colonies,[2] officers, and sailors, the bishop of his diocese, and the dean of his abbey; there were the leading Nonconformists of the neighborhood, and his own devoted curates, peers and members of the House of Commons, authors and publishers, and the huntsmen in pink; for though as good a clergyman as any, Charles Kingsley had been a good sportsman, and had taken in his life many a fence as bravely as he took the last fence of all, without fear or trembling. All that he had loved and all that had loved him was there, and few eyes were dry when he was laid in his own gravel bed, the old trees, which he had planted and

[1] Gen. Sir William Codrington; Col. Sir Charles Russell, V. C.; Col. Alfred Jones, V. C.; Col. Evelyn Wood, V. C., &c.
[2] Sir Arthur Gordon; Col. Sir Thomas Gore Browne.

Funeral Sermons

cared for, waving their branches to him for the last time, and the gray sunny sky looking down with calm pity on the deserted rectory, and on the short joys and the shorter sufferings of mortal man. All went home feeling that life was poorer, and every one knew that he had lost a friend who had been, in some peculiar sense, his own. Charles Kingsley will be missed in England, in the English colonies, in America, where he spent his last happy year; aye, wherever Saxon speech and Saxon thought is understood. He will be mourned for, yearned for, in every place in which he passed some days of his busy life. As to myself, I feel as if another cable had snapped that tied me to this hospitable shore."

Such was the scene at Eversley, while at Chester and at Westminster the cathedral bell tolled for the well-beloved Canon, whom they should see no more.

. . . .

The Sunday following his funeral, sermons on his life and death were numerous, by Churchmen, Baptists and other Nonconformists, both in London, Chester, and elsewhere — from Dean Stanley in London, Dean Howson at Chester — while his own pulpit at Eversley Church was occupied by Sir William Cope in the morning, and by his last attached curate, the Rev. Elis Price, in the afternoon. At Westminster Abbey Dean Stanley spoke of that —

"One brilliant light which shone in our dim atmosphere, and has been suddenly extinguished, and which cannot be allowed thus to pass away without asking ourselves what we have gained by its brief presence amongst us — what we have lost by its disappearance.

Others have spoken and will long speak on both sides of the Atlantic of the gifted poet whose dust might well have mingled with the dust of his brother poets in these walls. Others will speak, in nearer circles, of the close affection which bound the pastor to his flock, and the friend to his friend, and the father to his children, and the husband to the wife, in that romantic home which is now for ever identified with his name, and beside which he rests, beneath the yews which he planted with his own hands, and the great fir-trees that fold their protecting arms above. But that alone which is fitting to urge from this place is the moral and religious significance of the remarkable career which has left a spot void, as if where a rare plant has grown, which no art can reproduce, but of which the peculiar fragrance still lingers with those who have ever come within its reach. To the vast congregations which hung upon his lips in this church — to the wide world which looked eagerly for the utterances that no more will come from that burning spirit — to the loving friends who mourn for the extinction of a heart of fire, for the sudden relaxation of the grasp of a hand of iron — I would fain recall some of those higher strains which amid manifold imperfections, acknowledged by none more freely than himself, placed him unquestionably amongst the conspicuous teachers of his age, and gave to his voice the power of reaching souls to which other preachers and teachers addressed themselves in vain. It has seemed to me that there were three main lessons of his character and career which may be summed up in the three parts of the apostolic farewell 'Watch ye: quit you like men and be strong ; stand fast in the faith.' . . ."

After a masterly enumeration of his works, and the principle which was the keynote to each, the Dean says:

Funeral Sermons

"And this leads me to that clause in the apostle's warning, which I have kept for last, 'Stand fast in the faith.' I have hitherto spoken of our lost friend in his natural God-given genius, not in his professional or pastoral functions. He was what he was, not by virtue of his office, but by virtue of what God made him in himself. He was, we might almost say, a layman in the guise or disguise, and sometimes hardly in the guise, of a clergyman — fishing with the fisherman, hunting with the huntsman, able to hold his own in tent and camp, with courtier or with soldier; an example that a genial companion may be a Christian gentleman — that a Christian clergyman need not be a member of a separate caste, and a stranger to the common interests of his countrymen. Yet human, genial layman as he was, he still was not the less — nay, he was ten times more — a pastor than he would have been had he shut himself out from the haunts and walks of man. He was sent by Providence as it were, 'far off to the Gentiles,' — far off, not to other lands, or other races of mankind, but far off from the usual sphere of minister or priest, to 'fresh woods and pastures new,' to find fresh worlds of thought, and wild tracts of character, in which he found a response for himself, because he gave a response to them. Witness the unknown friends that from far or near sought the wise guidance of the unknown counsellor, who declared to them the unknown God after whom they were seeking if haply they might find Him. Witness the tears of the rough peasants of Hampshire, as they crowded round the open grave, to look for the last time on the friend of thirty years, with whom were mingled the hunter in his red coat and the wild gypsy wanderers, mourning for the face that they should no more see in forest or on heath. Witness the grief which fills the old cathedral town of the native county of his ancestors, beside the sands of his own Dee, for the recollection of the energy with which he gathered the youth of Chester round him for teachings of science and religion. Witness the grief which has overcast this venerable church, which in two short years he had made his own, and in which all felt that he had found a place worthy of himself, and that in him the place had found an occupant worthy to fill it. In these days of rebuke and faintheartedness, when so many gifted spirits shrink from embarking on one of the noblest, because the most sacred of all professions, it ought to be an encouragement to be reminded that this fierce poet and masculine reformer deemed his energies not misspent in the high yet humble vocation of an English clergyman — that, however much at times suspected, avoided, rebuffed, he yet, like others who have gone before him, at last won from his brethren the willing tribute of honor and love, which once had been sturdily refused or grudgingly granted. Scholar, poet, novelist, he yet felt himself to be, with all and before all, a spiritual teacher and guide. . . . Amidst all the wavering inconstancy of our time, he called upon the men of his generation with a steadfastness and assured conviction that of itself steadied and reassured the minds of those for whom he spoke, 'to stand fast in the faith.' . . ."[1]

Telegrams and letters, full of reverent love for him and of sympathy for those whom he had left — many of which will be heirlooms to his children, too private, too sacred, to meet the public eye, — all poured in from the highest to the lowest in this land, and from many in other lands, where his words had brought light in darkness, comfort in sorrow, hope in despair — from the heart of Africa, from Australia, from Cali-

[1] "Charles Kingsley." Sermon preached on Jan. 31, 1875, in Westminster Abbey, by Arthur Penrhyn Stanley.

Letters of Sympathy

fornia, as well as from America, where thousands had loved him before they had seen him face to face so recently.

Never had mourners over an unspeakable loss more exultant consolation, lifting them above their own selfish sorrow, to the thought of what they *had* possessed in him, and that if misunderstood by many in his lifetime, he was honored by all in his death — that among men of all parties, there was the unanimous feeling that the great presence which had passed away had left a blank which no other could exactly fill. But to those who knew what the life of his spirit had been, and how his soul had been athirst for God, even the living God, there was higher consolation still, in the thought that that thirst was slaked — that his own prayer offered up years ago before Holy Communion in Eversley church, was answered, — when, after speaking of the "intolerable burden of sin," he cried:

"O Lamb Eternal, beyond all place and time! O Lamb of God, slain eternally before the foundation of the world! O Lamb which liest slain eternally in the midst of the throne of God! Let the blood of life which flows from Thee, procure me pardon for the past; let the water of life, which flows from Thee, give me strength for the future. I come to cast away my own life, my life of self and selfishness, which is corrupt according to the deceitful lusts, that I may live it no more, and to receive Thy life, which is created after the likeness of God, in righteousness and true holiness, that I may live it for ever and ever, and find it a well of life springing up in me to everlasting life. Eternal Goodness, make me good like Thee. Eternal Wisdom, make me wise like Thee. Eternal Justice, make me just like

Thee. Eternal Love, make me loving like Thee. Then shall I hunger no more, and thirst no more; for

> " ' Thou, O Christ, art all I want;
> More than all in Thee I find;
> Raise me, fallen; cheer me, faint;
> Heal me, sick; and lead me, blind.
> Thou of life the fountain art;
> Freely let me take of Thee;
> Spring Thou up within my heart;
> Rise to all eternity.' "[1]

His bust, by Woolner, stands in the new Poet's Corner of Westminster Abbey — a National Memorial.[2]

In Eversley churchyard his wife has placed a white marble cross, on which, under a spray of his favorite passion-flower, are the words of his choice, the story of his life:

"AMAVIMUS, AMAMUS, AMABIMUS."

And above them, circling round the cross, "God is Love," the keynote of his faith.

The green turf round his grave was soon worn by the tread of many footsteps; for months a day seldom passed without strangers being seen in the churchyard. On bank holidays numbers would come to see his last resting-place — little children, who had loved the "Water Babies," and the "Heroes," would kneel down reverently and

[1] The Rock of Ages. Sermon XIV., Town and Country Sermons.
[2] The bust in the Baptistery of the Abbey was unveiled in 1876 by his eldest son. At Eversley the church has been restored; and at Chester a marble bust has been placed in the Chapter House; a medal struck for successful students in the Natural Science Society; and the ladies of Chester undertook to restore one of the Cathedral stalls in memory of the Canon. There is a memorial cot in the Hospital for Incurable Children at Cheyne Walk, Chelsea, the endowment of which is nearly completed.

At his Grave

look at the beautiful wreaths of flowers, which kind hands had placed there, while the gipsies never passed the gate without turning in to stand over the grave in silence, sometimes scattering wild flowers there, believing, as they do, to use their own strange words, that "he went to heaven on the prayers of the gipsies."

. . . .

And now these scattered memories, connected by a feeble thread all unworthy of its great subject, draw to a close. To some it may have seemed a treachery to lift the veil from the inner life of a man, who while here hated the notoriety which he could not escape, and shrunk from every approach to egotism; but his private letters, showing, as they do, the steps by which he arrived at many of his most startling conclusions through years of troubled thought, are a commentary on much that seemed contradictory in his teaching, and justify him, while they teach and strengthen others. Those alone who knew him intimately — and they not wholly — best understood his many-sided mind, and could interpret the apparent contradictions which puzzled others. Those who knew him little, but loved him much, could trust where they could not interpret. But to the public, such explanation, if not due may yet be welcome; and in that invisible state where perhaps he now watches with intensest interest the education of the human race, he would not shrink, as he would have shrunk here, from a publicity which, in revealing the workings of his own mind, may make his teaching of the truths which were most precious to him on earth more intelligible, if such a revelation should only help one poor struggling soul to light, and strength, and comfort, in the sore dark battle of life.

Some, again, may be inclined to say that this character is drawn in too fair colors to be absolutely truthful. But "we speak that we do know, and testify that we have seen." The outside world must judge him as an author, a preacher, a member of society; but those only who lived with him in the intimacy of everyday life at home can tell what he was as a *man*. Over the real romance of his life, and over the tenderest, loveliest passages in his private letters, a veil must be thrown; but it may not be lifting it too far to say, that if in the highest, closest of earthly relationships, a love that never failed for six-and-thirty years — pure, patient, passionate — a love which never stooped from its own lofty level to a hasty word, an impatient gesture, or a selfish act, in sickness or in health, in sunshine or in storm, by day or by night, could prove that the age of chivalry has not passed away forever, then Charles Kingsley fulfilled the ideal of a "most true and perfect knight" to the one woman blest with that love in time and to eternity. To eternity — for such love is eternal; and he is not dead. He himself, the man — lover, husband, father, friend — *he* still lives — in God — who is not the God of the dead but of the living. *He* is not dead; for to use his own inspiring words [1] —

"Those who die in the fear of God and in the faith of Christ do not really taste death; to them there is no

[1] "The Victory of Life," preached at the Chapel Royal in 1862. Milton's "Ode to Time" was the last poem he read to his wife before his death.

The Victory of Life

death, but only a change of place, a change of state; they pass at once into some new life, with all their powers, all their feelings, unchanged; still the same living, thinking, active beings, which they were here on earth. I say active. . . . Rest they may: rest they will, if they need rest. But what is the true rest? Not idleness, but peace of mind. To rest from sin, from sorrow, from fear, from doubt, from care; this is true rest. Above all, to rest from the worst weariness of all — knowing one's duty, and yet not being able to do it. That is true rest; the rest of God, who works forever, and yet is at rest forever; as the stars over our heads move forever, thousands of miles a day, and yet are at perfect rest, because they move orderly, harmoniously, fulfilling the law which God has given them. Perfect rest, in perfect work; that surely is the rest of blessed spirits, till the final consummation of all things, when Christ shall have made up the number of His elect. I hope that this is so. I trust that this is so. I think Our Lord's great words can mean nothing less than this. And if it be so, what comfort for us who must die! What comfort for us who have seen others die, if death be but a new birth into some higher life; if all that it changes in us is our body — the mere shell and husk of us — such a change as comes over the snake when he casts his old skin, and comes out fresh and gay, or even the crawling caterpillar, which breaks its prison, and spreads its wings to the sun as a fair butterfly. Where is the sting of death, then, if death can sting and poison and corrupt nothing of us, for which our friends have loved us; nothing of us with which we could do service to men or God? Where is the victory of the grave, if, so far from the grave holding us down, it frees us from the very thing which holds us down — the mortal body?

"Death is not death, then, if it kills no part of us save

that which hindered us from perfect life. Death is not death, if it raises us from darkness into light, from weakness into strength, from sinfulness into holiness. Death is not death, if it brings us nearer to Christ, who is the fount of life. Death is not death if it perfects our faith by sight, and lets us behold Him in whom we have believed. Death is not death, if it gives to us those whom we have loved and lost, for whom we have lived, for whom we long to live again. Death is not death, if it rids us of doubt and fear, of chance and change, of space and time, and all which space and time bring forth, and then destroy. Death is not death; for Christ has conquered death, for Himself, and for those who trust in Him. And to those who say, 'You were born in Time, and in Time you must die, as all other creatures do: Time is your king and lord, as he has been of all the old worlds before this, and of all the races of beasts, whose bones and shells lie fossil in the rocks of a thousand generations;' then we can answer them in the words of the wise Poet, and in the name of Christ, who conquered death:

"'Fly, envious Time, till thou run out thy race,
Call on the lazy leaden-stepping hours
Whose speed is but the heavy plummet's pace;
And glut thyself with what thy womb devours,
Which is no more than what is false and vain,
And merely mortal dross;
So little is our loss,
So little is thy gain.
For whenas each thing bad thou hast entombed,
And, last of all, thy greedy self consumed,
Then long Eternity shall greet our bliss
With an individual kiss,
And Joy shall overtake us as a flood;
When everything that is sincerely good
And perfectly divine,
With Truth, and Peace, and Love shall ever shine

The Victory of Life

About the supreme throne
Of Him, to whose happy-making sight alone
When once our heavenly-guided soul shall climb,
Then, all this earthly grossness quit,
Attired with stars, we shall for ever sit,
Triumphing over Death, and Chance, and thee, O Time!"

AMEN.

www.ingramcontent.com/pod-product-compliance
Lightning Source LLC
Chambersburg PA
CBHW032143010526
44111CB00035B/989